Activating th
(Training M

Mike Connell

Training Manual
1. Apostolic Reformation 5
2. The Gifts of the Spirit 11
3. How the Gifts Work Together 14
4. Believers Can Operate in all the Gifts 16
5. Believers' Responsibilities concerning the Gifts 18
6. Three Ways of Supernatural Operation 21
7. How Miracles are Released 27
8. How to Hear the Voice of God 30
9. Why Some People Struggle to Receive 37
10. How to Activate the Gifts of the Spirit 40
11. How to Test Revelation 44
12. Gift of Prophecy 47
13. Diverse Kinds of Tongues 52
14. Interpretation of Tongues 58
15. Word of Wisdom 60
16. Word of Knowledge 62
17. Discerning of Spirits 65
18. Gift of Faith 70
19. Gifts of Healings 73
20. The Working of Miracles 78
21. Keys to Ministering in the Spirit 80
22. Practical Guidelines for Ministering to People 82

Audio Transcripts
Introduction 85
1. Hearing from God (1 of 5) 87
2. Prophesy (2 of 5) 140
3. Tongues, Interpretation of Tongues (3 of 5) 167
4. Discerning of Sprits (4 of 5) 206
5. Faith, Miracles, and Healing (5 of 5) 243

Five Supplementary Videos:
(Transcripts included)

Vimeo:
https://vimeo.com/channels/activatingthegifts
Video (1 of 5): http://vimeo.com/47753518
Video (2 of 5): http://vimeo.com/45802644
Video (3 of 5): http://vimeo.com/45874811
Video (4 of 5): http://vimeo.com/45951460
Video (5 of 5): http://vimeo.com/45886661

YouTube:
http://www.youtube.com/playlist?list=PLrhZUkV364KPllr1ciOV7jdIPAL0LdLGM
Video (1 of 5): http://youtu.be/E4eGBHCx1LI
Video (2 of 5): http://youtu.be/62htQXLY42U
Video (3 of 5): http://youtu.be/loLZXw9Fbkc
Video (4 of 5): http://youtu.be/1iuOs5Q9sh4
Video (5 of 5): http://youtu.be/pcCg6HFjdWQ

Ordering/Printing
Copies can be ordered directly from
https://www.createspace.com/4100936
https://www.createspace.com/4199816

More printed materials available here
http://mikeconnellministries.com/books

ISBN-13: 978-1481278867

ISBN-10: 148127886X

Introduction

God has created every person to be a supernatural spiritual being, with the capacity to function not only in a natural world, but also to access the realm of the spirit, access where God is, and to bring heaven to earth.

God's desire is that you be a channel for heaven coming to earth, for His presence and goodness and healing and love and peace and prosperity to flow through you, and to manifest in the world around you.

So in the course we'll be teaching about that supernatural dimension. We'll teach about how miracles are activated, what the keys are around that. We'll teach you what the foundational key is, is out of intimacy with God and hearing the voice of God, and we'll give you practical steps, practical keys, how to start from wherever you are right now, and step by step grow your faith, so you can be starting to operate successfully, and regularly and confidently in the gifts of the spirit.

So in the course we'll teach on the gifts of the spirit, we'll give you a little bit about each. We'll also give you some foundational understanding about the spirit man, and how God works in and through us. Also if you're watching this by DVD you'll see demonstrations of the power of God touching people, you'll see demonstrations of how to move in words of knowledge, hearing the voice of God, minister to people. You'll see all of that in this course, and it will inspire you and help you. God's given me ability to make it extremely clear, and I know that you're going to really enjoy this.

Put in the effort. Invest in yourself. Do the course, and put into practice the things you learn, and you'll just be overjoyed when you see God is far more willing to work through you than you really realize. His plan is that the kingdom comes into the earth through you. All you've got to do is learn how to do it.

In 1 Corinthians, Chapter 12, Verse 1, Paul says I don't want you to be ignorant of spiritual gifts, and this course is to help solve that problem. God bless you. Have a great time on the course and may you extend the kingdom of God boldly.

Activating the Gifts of the Holy Spirit

NB. All scripture quotes are taken from the New King James Version (NKJV) unless otherwise indicated

1. Apostolic Reformation

1.1 The Present Reformation

Key Verse: Acts 3:19-21

"Repent therefore and be converted, that your sins may be blotted out, so that times of refreshing may come from the presence of the Lord, 20 and that He may send Jesus Christ, who was preached to you before, 21 whom <u>heaven must receive until the times of restoration of all things</u>, which God has spoken by the mouth of all His holy prophets since the world began"

Insights:

- **'Restoration'** – NT:605 - *to set back in order, return to its original state*
- **'Reformation'** – NT:1357 - *to set right, to make straight, to restore to original condition something that has got out of line or broken or misaligned, to make a structural adjustment*
- Reformation is a deep inner change of mentality, understanding, behaviors, attitudes, and world views that totally shifts the way the church operates outwardly
- It is not just a 'manifestation' move of God, in which something unexpected happens and people are **blessed**. - It is received as revelation from heaven and **progressively built** by people who are willing to change - Reformation challenges us to become co-workers with God (1Cor.3:9)

1.2 The Church Jesus is Building

Key Verse: Matt 16:17-19

Jesus answered and said to him, "Blessed are you, Simon Bar-Jonah, for flesh and blood has not revealed this to you, but My Father who is in heaven. 18 And I also say to you that you are Peter, and on this rock I will build My church, and <u>the gates of Hades shall not prevail against it.</u> 19 And I will give you the keys of the kingdom of heaven, and whatever you bind on earth will be bound in heaven, and whatever you loose on earth will be loosed in heaven."

Insights:

- The Church Jesus is building is a centre of spiritual government
- An Apostolic Church exercises dominion over the spirit realm, keeping the heavens open for moves of the Holy Spirit into the region and beyond
- **'Prevail'** - NT:2729 - to be superior in strength, to overpower
- An Apostolic Church prevails over the gates of hell ie exercises spiritual authority that restricts and shuts down demonic activity
- **'Authority'** - NT:1849 - the power and right to command

1.3 Apostolic Ministry

a) The Church is built upon Apostolic foundations

Key Verse: Eph 2:20-22

"having been <u>built on the foundation of the apostles and prophets,</u> Jesus Christ Himself being the chief cornerstone, 21 in whom the whole building, being fitted together, grows into a holy temple in the Lord, 22 in whom you also are being built together for a dwelling place of God in the Spirit."

Insights:

- **'Build'** - NT:2026 - *to construct, assemble, create by following a design or blueprint*
- *The foundation that supports any building must be stable and able to support the total weight of the building or it will collapse*
- **'Foundation'** - NT:2310 - *the beginnings, the first principles, the sub-structure*
- *Apostles break open spiritual atmospheres and impart principles and patterns of the church God is wanting to build*

b) The Apostle is first in rank

Key Verse: 1 Cor 12:28

"And God has appointed these in the church: <u>first apostles</u>, second prophets, third teachers, after that miracles, then gifts of healings, helps, administrations, varieties of tongues"

Insights:

- **'First'** - NT:4412 - *first in time, place, order, importance, or rank, chief component*
- *First does not indicate that apostles are better than any other Ministry*
- *First does indicate a particular quality of the apostolic gift. It has a breakthrough capability other ministries do not have*

c) Apostles are builders

Key Verse: Eph 4:11-13

"And He Himself gave some to be apostles, some prophets, some evangelists, and some pastors and teachers, 12 for <u>the equipping of the saints</u> for the work of ministry, for the edifying of the body of Christ, 13 till we all come to the unity of the faith and of the knowledge of the Son of God, to a perfect man, to the measure of the stature of the fullness of Christ"

Insights:

- **'Apostle'** NT:652 - to send forth, to send on a military campaign
- An apostle is an ambassador, a delegate, a sent one
- An apostle is sent out from the local church, commissioned by the Holy Spirit to pioneer breakthroughs and advances of the kingdom of God
- Apostles equip believers and impart an apostolic spirit upon their lives so they can be effective in breaking through into the community

1.4 Characteristics of an Apostolic Church

Key Verse: Luke 10:1-2

"After these things the Lord <u>appointed seventy others also</u>, and sent them two by two before His face into every city and place where He Himself was about to go. 2 Then He said to them, The harvest truly is great, but the laborers are few; therefore pray the Lord of the harvest to send out laborers into His harvest."

Insights:

- **'Appoint'** - NT:322 - to lift up to another level, to put on display for all to see
- The seventy disciples received the same mandate as the twelve apostles who went before them
- They carried an apostolic spirit and broke through demonic positions all across the territory

Some Characteristics of the Apostolic Church

- It keeps the heavens open so that people can experience the presence and power of God and be changed
- It has a governing mentality that confronts spirit powers
- It has strong praise and worship that releases flows of the Spirit of God
- It has militant prayer and fasting that releases apostolic strength and authority
- It raises up and equips believers to become effective ministers of the Spirit
- It commissions and sends believers into the community to overcome entrenched spiritual forces, release the presence of God, win souls, and transform the community
- It focuses on advancing the kingdom of God locally and globally
- It releases finances and resources for advancing the Kingdom of God

1.5 Breakthrough Believers

Key Verse: Acts 6:8

"And Stephen, full of faith and power, did great wonders and signs among the people"

Insights:

- Stephen was a deacon in the church responsible for distributing food
- Stephen was full of faith and power and worked miracles that impacted the lives of many
- Stephen was a breakthrough believer flowing in apostolic anointing

2. The Gifts of the Spirit

2.1 God Wants You to Move in the Supernatural

Key Verse: 1Cor. 12:1

"Now concerning spiritual gifts, brethren, I would not have you to be ignorant"

Insights:

- Believers must not remain ignorant of the Gifts of the Spirit, their proper use, and their purpose
- **'Ignorant'** - NT:50 - to lack experience and practical understanding; to ignore through lack of desire or interest
- God wants us to be informed about, and operate effectively in, the Gifts of the Spirit

2.2 The Gifts of the Spirit are Supernatural

Key Verse: 1Cor 12:7
"But the manifestation of the Spirit is given to each one for the profit of all"

Insights:

- You are a spirit being living in a body uniquely designed to express the presence and life of God on the earth
- God clearly desires each believer to manifest the life and power of the Holy Spirit
- **'Manifestation'** - NT:5321 - clearly visible supernatural activity of the Holy Spirit
- **'Each one'** - NT:1538 - every believer has this privilege to express the Gifts of the Spirit
- **'Gifts'** - NT:5486 – grace; benefit one receives without any merit of one's own
- **'Profit'** - NT:4851 - to benefit people, and advance the Kingdom of God
- The Holy Spirit distributes the Gifts to each believer as He wills, and energizes them to make the believer fruitful in manifesting the presence of God
- Gifts are:
- not an indicator of personal maturity
- not a sign that one's life is completely right with God
- given, not earned
- received by active faith

2.3 Different Categories of the Gifts

Key Verse: 1Cor.12:7-11

"But the manifestation of the Spirit is given to each one for the profit of all: 8 for to one is given the word of wisdom through the Spirit, to another the word of knowledge through the same Spirit, 9 to another faith by the same Spirit, to another gifts of healings by the same Spirit, 10 to another the working of miracles, to another prophecy, to another discerning of spirits, to another different kinds of tongues, to another the interpretation of tongues. 11 But one and the same Spirit works all these things, distributing to each one individually as He wills."

- Although each gift has its own unique function, it is helpful to consider them in three different categories of operation.

i) Gifts of Revelation - information previously hidden is made known

- Word of Knowledge
- Word of Wisdom
- Discerning of Spirits

ii) Gifts of Utterance - something is spoken

- Prophecy
- Diverse Tongues
- Interpretation of Tongues

iii) Gifts of Power - something supernatural is done; power is imparted

- Faith
- Gifts of Healing
- Working of Miracles

3. How the Gifts Work Together

3.1 The Gifts Work Together
Key Principle:

- *Gifts of the Spirit operate together to produce a tangible manifestation of the presence the Holy Spirit.*
  Pattern: Revelation + Words Spoken + Active Faith = Manifestation of Holy Spirit

3.2 Bible Examples of Gifts Working Together
a) Joshua and the Sun and Moon - Josh 10:13

- *Joshua commanded the sun and moon to stay, and they did not move for a day*
  Revelation + Words Spoken + Active Faith = Manifestation of Holy Spirit

b) The Fig Tree Cursed - Mark 11:12-13;20-21

- *Jesus cursed the fig tree by speaking to it, and it subsequently withered and died*
  Revelation + Words Spoken + Active Faith = Manifestation of Holy Spirit

c) The Man Healed at the Pool at Bethesda - John 5:1-15

- *Jesus selected one man, spoke to him, and he arose and walked*
  Revelation + Words Spoken + Active Faith = Manifestation of Holy Spirit

d) The Man Healed at the Temple Gate - Acts 3:1-6;15

- *Peter selected a man Jesus had previously passed by, spoke a word of command to him, and the man received a gift of healing and walked*
  <u>Revelation + Words Spoken + Active Faith = Manifestation of Holy Spirit</u>

e) Ananias Heals Paul - Acts 9:10-18

- *Ananias received revelation to go to Paul. He spoke to him and released a gift of healing to him*
  <u>Revelation + Words Spoken + Active Faith = Manifestation of Holy Spirit</u>

f) Paul Heals the Lame Man - Acts 14:8-10

- *Paul perceived that the man had faith to be healed, and spoke a command to him and a miracle of healing manifested*
  <u>Revelation + Words Spoken + Active Faith = Manifestation of Holy Spirit</u>

4. Believers Can Operate in all the Gifts

4.1 The Great Commission

Key Verse: Mark 16: 17-18
"And these signs will follow those who believe: In My name they will cast out demons; they will speak with new tongues; 18 they will take up serpents; and if they drink anything deadly, it will by no means hurt them; they will lay hands on the sick, and they will recover."

Gifts of the Spirit

- Cast out demons…discerning of spirits, working of miracles, faith
- Speak in new tongues…tongues, and maybe interpretations
- Take up serpents (wrestle with spirit powers)…revelation gifts and prophecy
- Drink any deadly thing (by accident)it will not harm them…miracles
- Lay hands on the sick….Gifts of faith and healings

4.2 Paul's Instruction

Key Verses: 1 Cor 12:7-11

"But the manifestation of the Spirit is <u>given to each one</u> for the profit of all: 8 for to one is given the word of wisdom through the Spirit, to another the word of knowledge through the same Spirit, 9 to another faith by the same Spirit, to another gifts of healings by the same Spirit, 10 to another the working of miracles, to another prophecy, to another discerning of spirits, to another different kinds of tongues, to another the interpretation of tongues. 11 But one and the same Spirit works all these things, <u>distributing to each one</u> individually as He wills."

1Cor. 1:5

"so that you come <u>short in no gift,</u> eagerly waiting for the revelation of our Lord Jesus Christ,"

Insight:

- The Holy Spirit is present in every believer to help them produce the maximum they can for the Kingdom of God

4.3 Example of Ananaias - Acts 9:10-18

- *Ananaias was an ordinary disciple. God used him to minister healing and baptism in the Spirit to Paul*
- *He operated in five Gifts:*
    - *word of knowledge*
    - *wisdom*
    - *prophetic utterance*
    - *faith*
    - *healing*
- *Note how the miracle happened: Revelation + Words Spoken + Active Faith = Manifestation of Holy Spirit*

5. Believers' Responsibilities concerning the Gifts

5.1 God Expects Something of Us

Key Verse: 1 Cor 12:7
"But the manifestation of the Spirit is given to each one for the profit of all."

Insights:

- God gives Gifts of the Spirit to every believer
- God must expect something from me
- It is my responsibility to discover what God expects from me

5.2 Five Responsibilities of the Believer

a) Learn how to flow with the Holy Spirit

Key Verse: 1 Cor 12:1
"Now concerning spiritual gifts, brethren, I do not want you to be ignorant."

Insights:

- God expects us to cultivate and develop our capacity to flow with Holy Spirit
- God expects us to be builders, not just receivers of blessings

b) Passionately Desire the Gifts of the Spirit

Key Verse: 1 Cor 12:31
"But earnestly desire the best gifts."

Insights:

- **'Earnestly Desire'** - NT:2206- Zealous to be passionate; to contend to excel; strongly exert yourself in the pursuit of something you want
- Flowing in the Gifts of the Spirit results in the manifestation of the Spirit of God through us. We bring heaven to earth

c) Stir Up the Gifts of the Spirit

Key Verse: 2 Tim 1:6
"Therefore I remind you to stir up the gift of God which is in you through the laying on of my hands."

Insights:

- **'Stir Up'** - NT:329 - to kindle glowing embers back into a roaring fire; to ignite a flame or level or passion
- A fire is usually rekindled step by step by providing fresh fuel and air

d) Don't Quench the Holy Spirit

Key Verse: 1 Thess 5:19
"Do not quench the Spirit. 20Do not despise prophecies."

Insights:

- **'Quench'** - NT:4570 - to stifle, suppress, extinguish, put an end to something burning
- Sinful words, attitudes, and actions grieve the Holy Spirit
- Fear, unbelief, control, and unwillingness to yield all quench the Holy Spirit

e) Don't Neglect the Gifts of the Spirit

Key Verse: 1 Tim 4:14
"Do not neglect the gift that is in you, which was given to you by prophecy with the laying on of the hands of the eldership. Meditate on these things; give yourself entirely to them, that your progress may be evident to all."

Insights:

- **'Neglect'** - NT:272 - to be careless about, to make light of; to place little importance upon so that no effort is made to develop and grow in the gifting
- It takes effort and commitment to develop experience and expertise in moving in the Gifts of the Spirit

f) Excel in Building Up People

Key Verse: 1 Cor 14:12
"Even so you, since you are zealous for spiritual gifts, let it be for the edification of the church that you seek to excel."

Insights:

- Every believer is called to excel in building up the lives of people
- God gives Gifts of the Spirit because He expects us to be involved in ministering the life of the Spirit to people.
- **'Excel'** - NT:4052 - to stand out because of having an abundant impact in building people

6. Three Ways of Supernatural Operation

6.1 Levels of Supernatural Operation

Key Verse: Heb 2:4
"God also bearing witness both with signs and wonders, with various miracles, and gifts of theHoly Spirit, according to His own will?"

Insights:

- There are many different levels and ways of operation of the Holy Spirit
- We need to develop in different areas, and not lock into only one way
- Don't get pre-determined mindsets on how God will move
- Within each of the three ways of supernatural operation below, there many different levels of operation

6.2 The Word and Prayer of Faith

The Word of Faith

Key Verse: Ps 107:20
"He sent His word and healed them, And delivered them from their destructions."

Insights:

- Faith comes by hearing the word of God (Rom.10:17)
- On the basis of the Word of God, we can preach healing and expect people to be healed
- God has given to every person the measure of faith (Rom.12:3)
- Faith grows, as we hear and meditate on the word of God (Rom.10:17)
- Faith grows as we exercise it ie act upon what the word of God says

Example: The Centurion - Matt 8:7-10
"And Jesus said to him, "I will come and heal him." 8 The centurion answered and said,"Lord, I am not worthy that You should come under my roof. But only speak a word and my servant will be healed. 9 For I also am a man under authority, having soldiers under me. And I say to this one, 'Go,' and he goes; and to another, 'Come,' and he comes; and to my servant, 'Do this,' and he does it." 10 When Jesus heard it, He marveled, and said to those who followed, "Assuredly, I say to you, I have notfound such great faith, not even in Israel!"

Example: Paul - Acts 14:7
"And they were preaching the gospel there. And in Lystra a certain man without strength In his feet was sitting, a cripple from his mother's womb, who had never walked. 9 This man heard Paul speaking. Paul, observing him intently and seeing that he had faith to be healed, 10 said with a loud voice,"Stand up straight on your feet!" And he leapedand walked"

Example: Oral Roberts

- People went into a healing line only after teaching about healing had taken place
- After prayer people were interviewed and testified what God had done
- Testimonies of healings caused the faith level to rise

Example: Our Church

- The word of God is preached before people are ministered to.
- People come up for prayer after their faith has been stirred by hearing the word of God

The Prayer of Faith

Key Verse: Mark 11:24
"Therefore I say to you, whatever things you ask when you pray, believe that you receive them, and you will have them."

Insights:

- *Prayer that gets results must be filled with faith*
- *Faith means not doubting in your heart*
- *Prayers are not always answered immediately*
- *Sometimes you must persevere in prayer* **(Luke 18:1)**
- *If you don't have an immediate manifestation of answer to your prayer, persevere in asking, seeking, and knocking* **(Matt.7:7)**

Example: Elders - James 5:14
" Is anyone among you sick? Let him call for the elders of the church, and let them pray over him, anointing him with oil in the name of the Lord. 15 And the prayer of faith will save the sick, and the Lord will raise him up. And if he has committed sins, he will be forgiven. 16 Confess your trespasses to one another, and pray for one another, that you may be healed."

Example: Elijah - James 5:16
"The effective, fervent prayer of a righteous man avails much. 17 Elijah was a man with a nature like ours, and he prayed earnestly that it would not rain; and it did not rain on the land for three years and six months. 18 And he prayed again, and the heaven gave rain, and the earth produced its fruit"

Example: The Widow - Matt 15:28
"Then Jesus answered and said to her, "O woman, great is your faith! Let it be to you as you desire." And her daughter was healed from that very hour."

6.3 The Gifts of the Spirit

Key Verse: 1 Cor 12:7

"But the manifestation of the Spirit is <u>given</u> to each one for the profit of all"

Insights:

- The person stirs their faith to receive and operate in the gift **(2Tim.1:6)**
- God supernaturally imparts revelation and gives faith for a person to operate in the Gifts **(Acts 3: 4-8)**
- When a person operates consistently in the particular gifting it becomes like a mantle residing on the person
- That person can operate in a particular Gift, or Gifts, of the Spirit consistently, with a significant level of accuracy or success eg words of knowledge, prophecy, miracles
- The operation of Gifts of the Spirit releases an increased presence of God, alters the spiritual atmosphere, and awakens faith for miracles to take place

6.4 The Sovereign Realm

Key Verse: 2 Chron 5:12-14

"and the Levites who were the singers, all those of Asaph and Heman and Jeduthun, with their sons and their brethren, stood at the east end of the altar, clothed in white linen, having cymbals, stringed instruments and harps, and with them one hundred and twenty priests sounding with trumpets 13 indeed it came to pass, when the trumpeters and singers were as one, to make one sound to be heard in praising and thanking the LORD, and when they lifted up their voice with the trumpets and cymbals and instruments of music, and praised the LORD, saying: "For He is good, For His mercy endures forever," that the house, the house of the LORD, was filled with a cloud, 14 so that the priests could not continue ministering because of the cloud;for the glory of the LORD filled the house of God."

Insights:

- *The presence and glory of God invaded and filled the atmosphere*
- *The glory of God appeared as a visible cloud*
- *People were unable to stand because of the glory of God - they fell over*
- *This is a much greater level of supernatural operation*
- *The manifestations that take place depend on the level of the presence of God, and what God wants to do at that time*
- *Many people experience the supernatural power of God at the same time*
- *Often there are angels present as ministering spirits. They may be seen by some people*

Example: Jesus' Ministry - Luke 5:17

"Now it happened on a certain day, as He was teaching, that there were Pharisees and teachers of the law sitting by, who had come out of every town of Galilee, Judea, and Jerusalem. And the power of the Lord was present to heal them."

- *God's presence and glory rested upon Jesus*
- *The presence of God's sovereignty filled the atmosphere around Jesus*
- *All who were present in that atmosphere could receive a miracle*

Example: Apostle Peter - Acts 5:14
" And believers were increasingly added to the Lord, multitudes of both men and women, 15 so that they brought the sick out into the streets and laid them on beds and couches, that at <u>least the shadow of Peter passing by</u> might fall on some of them. 16 Also a multitude gathered from the surrounding cities to Jerusalem, bringing sick people and those who were tormentedby unclean spirits, and <u>they were all healed.</u>"

- *God's presence and glory rested upon Peter*
- *The presence of God sovereignly filled the atmosphere around Peter*
- *There was high expectation for miracles to take place*
- *All who were present in that atmosphere could receive a miracle*

Example: Benny Hinn

- *The presence of God fills his meetings and people receive miracles without anyone praying for them*
- *As testimonies of these miracles are given, faith is released for others to receive miracles*

Additional Insights:

- *Often those used to move in this level of operation have experienced a deep personal encounter with the Lord.*
- *This may have come by:*
    - *by extended and the persistent pursuit of the Lord*
    - *by a sovereign experience of him (The Grace of God)*
- *If the person has had as sovereign experience of the Lord , it may be:*
    - *a one-of special experience for that time, or situation*
    - *to launch the person into a ministry God has called him or her to*

7. How Miracles are Released

7.1 Keys to Operating in the Realm of the Supernatural

Key Verse: Gal 3:2

"This only I want to learn from you: Did you receive the Spirit by the works of the law, or by the <u>Hearing of faith</u>? 3 Are you so foolish? Having begun in the Spirit, are you now being made perfect by the flesh? 4 Have you suffered so many things in vain — if indeed it was in vain? 5 Therefore He who supplies the Spirit to you and works miracles among you, does He do it by the works of the law, or by the hearing of faith?"

Insights:

- *There are three simple keys to operating in the Realm of the Supernatural*

i) Hearing............hearing and recognizing the Voice of God

ii) Faith..................an inner conviction based upon Hearing the Voice of God

iii) Obedience.........prompt response to speak and act on what you have heard

7.2 Bible Examples of the Keys

a) Jesus - John 5:19-20

"Then Jesus answered and said to them, "Most assuredly, I say to you, the Son can do nothing of Himself, but <u>what He sees the Father do</u>; for whatever He does, the Son also does in like manner. (v20) For the Father loves the Son, and <u>shows Him all things</u> that He Himself does; and He will show Him greater works than these, that you may marvel."

Insights:

- Jesus continually heard the Voice of God
- Jesus saw into the Realm of the Supernatural
- Jesus was committed to the Will of the Father **(John 6:38)**
- We must learn how to Hear and See in the Spirit

b) Peter - Acts 3:4-8

"And fixing his eyes on Him, with John, Peter said, "Look at us." 5 So he gave them his attention, expecting to receive something from them. 6 Then Peter said, "Silver and gold I do not have, but what I do have I give you: In the name of Jesus Christ of Nazareth, rise up and walk." 7 And he took him by the right hand and lifted him up, and immediately his feet and ankle bones received strength. 8 So he, leaping up, stood and walked and entered the temple with them -- walking, leaping, and praising God."

Insights:

- **'Fixed his eyes'** - NT:816 - to gaze intently: behold earnestly, to fasten the eyes, look earnestly or intently steadfastly, set eyes
- Peter focused his attention and perceived in his spirit the intention of God to heal this man now
- Peter spoke and acted upon what he sensed, and a miracle occurred
  <u>Revelation + Words Spoken + Active Faith = Manifestation of Holy Spirit</u>

c) Paul – Acts 14:8-10

"And in Lystra a certain man without strength in his feet was sitting, a cripple from his mother's womb, who had never walked. 9 This man heard Paul speaking. Paul, <u>observing him intently</u> and seeing that he had faith to be healed, 10 said with a loud voice," Stand up straight on your feet" And he leaped and walked."

Insights:

- **'Observe intently'** - NT:816 - to gaze intently, behold earnestly, to fasten the eyes, look earnestly or intently steadfastly, set eyes
- Paul focused his attention and perceived in his Spirit the man had faith to be healed.
- Paul spoke and acted upon what he sensed and a miracle occurred
  <u>Revelation + Words Spoken + Active Faith = Manifestation of Holy Spirit</u>

8. How to Hear the Voice of God

8.1 The Holy Spirit Desires to Communicate with us

Key Verse: John 16:13

"However, when He, the Spirit of truth, has come, <u>He will guide you into all truth</u>; for He will not speak on His own authority, but <u>whatever He hears He will speak</u>; and <u>He will tell you things</u> to come. (v14) "He will glorify Me, for He will take of what is Mine and declare it to you. (v15) "All things that the Father has are Mine. Therefore I said that He will take of Mine and declare it to you. 8.2 We Must Want to Hear God Speak Key Verse: Mark 4:23-25 "If anyone has ears to hear, let him hear." 24 Then He said to them, "Take heed what you hear. With the same measure you use, it will be measured to you; and to you who hear, more will be given.25 "For whoever has, to him more will be given; but whoever does not have, even what he has will be taken away from him."

8.2 We Must Want to Hear God Speak
Key Verse: Mark 5:23-25

"If anyone has ears to hear, let him hear." 24 Then He said to them, "Take heed what you hear. With the same measure you use, it will be measured to you; and to you who hear, more will be given. 25 "For whoever has, to him more will be given; but whoever does not have, even what he has will be taken away from him." "

8.3 The Holy Spirit Speaks from Within Us

Key Verse: 1 John 2:27

"But the anointing which you have received from Him abides in you, and you do not need that anyone teach you; but as the same anointing teaches you concerning all things, and is true, and is not a lie, and just as it has taught you, you will abide in Him"

Insights:

- The Anointing is a person. He is the Holy Spirit dwelling within us
- The Holy Spirit can be grieved **(Eph.4:29-32)**
- The Holy Spirit can be quenched **(1 Thess.5:19)**
- Your spirit is joined to the Holy Spirit **(1Cor.6:17)**
- The Holy Spirit speaks spirit to spirit

8.4 Bible Examples of Direct Spirit to Spirit Communication

a) Habakkuk 2:1

"I will stand my watch and set myself on the rampart, And watch to see what He will say to me, and what I will answer when I am corrected."

- He positioned himself to be still and quiet
- He took time to wait for God to speak
- He was able to discern the Voice of the Lord Speaking
- God spoke to him by way of a vision, an inner picture

b) 1Sam.3:10

"The LORD came and stood there, calling as at the other times, "Samuel! Samuel!" Then Samuel said, "Speak, for your servant is listening." (NIV) - He positioned himself to be still and quiet. - He took time to wait for God to Speak - He needed instruction on how to recognize the Voice of the Lord

c) Mark 2:8

"But immediately, when Jesus <u>perceived in His spirit</u> that they reasoned thus within themselves, He said to them, "Why do you reason about these things inyour hearts?"

- Jesus continually listened to the voice of the Holy Spirit
- He perceived in His spirit what the Pharisees were thinking
- The Holy Spirit communicated with Him spirit to spirit

d) Acts 14:9

"This man heard Paul speaking. Paul, <u>observing him intently and seeing</u> that he had faith to be healed, 10 said with a loud voice, "Stand up straight on your feet!" And he leaped and walked"

- As Paul fixed his attention on the man the Holy Spirit spoke into his spirit
- He realized the man had faith for a miracle, and acted to bring it about

8.5 Common Ways the Holy Spirit Communicates Directly

a) Seeing

- A spontaneous mental picture or image prompted by the Holy Spirit
- It may come as a **still or moving picture** displayed within the mind
- It may come as a **written word or group of words** displayed within the mind
- It may be instantaneous, or it may develop slowly, like a Polaroid photo
- It may take practice with a brief period of trial and error learning to determine which images are from Holy Spirit

b) Hearing

- God may speak with an **outer audible voice** heard physically by your ears **(1 Sam 3: 4-10)**
- God may speak through an **inner audible voice** that seems very clear and seems to come from within you
- God will most often speak with a **still small voice** in our thoughts **(1Kings 19:11-1)**
- His voice comes from within as a **spontaneous thought** that interrupts our thoughts
- It may be just a single word indicating some need
- Many people struggle with this ie "was that my thought or was that from the Lord?"

c) Feeling

- God may speak to you through inner impressions
- The impression may come as an **inner 'knowing'**
- The impression may come as an **inner peace or as an agitation**
- **Colossians 3:15** – "And let the peace of God rule in your hearts, to which also you were called in one body; and be thankful."
- **'Rule'** - NT:1018 -to be an umpire in a game and blow the whistle; to decide, determine what should happen; to direct, control, rule
- The impression or feeling may be 'release' or 'restraint'

d) Inspired Writing

1 Chr 28:19 "All this," said David, "the LORD made me <u>understand in writing</u>, by His hand upon me, all the works of these plans."

- The Spirit of God gave revelation to David concerning the Temple design
- God did it by **guiding his hand** as he wrote ie inspired writing

8.6 Other Ways Revelation is Received

a) Visions

- **Acts 16:9-10** "And a vision appeared to Paul in the night. A man of Macedonia stood and pleaded with him, saying, "Come over to Macedonia and help us"
- **Open Vision** - like watching a scene open up before your eyes. Your eyes are open and you can still see the natural surroundings, but a spiritual vision is superimposed upon it. It may be still or moving
- **Closed Vision** - your eyes are closed, and you receive a mental picture on the screen of your imagination

b) Trances

- **Acts 10:9-13** "Peter went up on the housetop to pray, about the sixth hour. 10 Then he became very hungry and wanted to eat; but while they made ready, he fell into a trance 11 and saw heaven opened and an object like a great sheet bound at the four corners, descending to him and let down to the earth. 12 In it were all kinds of four-footed animals of the earth, wild beasts, creeping things, and birds of the air. 13 And a voice came to him, "Rise, Peter; kill and eat"
- See also: **Acts 22:17** - Paul

c) Dreams

- **Matt 2:13** "Now when they had departed, behold, an angel of the Lord appeared to Joseph in a dream, saying, "Arise, take the young Child and His mother, flee to Egypt, and stay there until I bring you word; for Herod will seek the young Child to destroy Him.""
- See also: **Gen 37:5** - Joseph; **Matt 27:19** - Pilate's wife

d) Angelic Visitations

- **Acts 8:26-27** *"Now an <u>angel of the Lord spoke to Philip</u>, saying, "Arise and go toward the south along the road which goes down from Jerusalem to Gaza." This is desert. 27 So he arose and went."*
- See also: **Luke 1:28** - Mary; **Acts 5:19** - Peter

e) Visitations

- **Rev 1:12-15** *"Then I turned to see the voice that spoke with me. And <u>having turned I saw</u> seven golden lampstands, 13 and in the midst of the seven lampstands <u>One like the Son of Man</u>, clothed with a garment down to the feet and girded about the chest with a golden band. 14 His head and hair were white like wool, as white as snow, and His eyes like a flame of fire; 15 His feet were like fine brass, as if refined in a furnace, and His voice as the sound of many waters"*
- See also: **Gen 18:1** – Abraham; **Josh 5:13-15** - Joshua

f) Translated in the Spirit

- **2 Cor 12:1-4** "It is doubtless not profitable for me to boast. I will come to visions and revelations of the Lord: 2 I know a man in Christ who fourteen years ago — whether in the body I do not know, or whether out of the body I do not know, God knows — such a one was caught up to the third heaven. 3 And I know such a man — whether in the body or out of the body I do not know, God knows — 4 how he was caught up into Paradise and heard inexpressible words, which it is not lawful for a man to utter."
- See also: **2 Kings 5:26** - Elijah

g) Transported in the Spirit

- **Ezek 8:2-4** "Then I looked, and there was a likeness, like the appearance of fire — from the appearance of His waist and downward, fire; and from His waist and upward, like the appearance of brightness, like the color of amber. 3 He stretched out the form of a hand, and took me by a lock of my hair; <u>and the Spirit lifted me up between earth and heaven, and brought me in visions of God to Jerusalem</u>, to the door of the north gate of the inner court, where the seat of the image of jealousy was, which provokes to jealousy. 4 And behold, the glory of the God of Israel was there, like the vision that I saw in the plain."
- See also: **1 Kings 18:11-12** - Elijah; **Acts 8:39** - Philip

9. Why Some People Struggle to Receive
9.1 Spiritual Sensitivity can be Developed
Key Verse: Heb 5:14
"But solid food belongs to those who are of full age, that is, those who by reason of use <u>have their senses exercised to discern</u> both good and evil."

Insights:

- **'Use'** - NT:1838 - a habit, something practiced constantly
- **'Exercised'** - NT:1128 – to train or practice for an Olympic competition
- This requires that people remove anything that would hinder them performing their best

9.2 Natural Senses

- Every person has five natural senses - sight, hearing, taste, touch, and smell
- With our five senses we connect with the natural world
- Information from our five senses is communicated into our brain where the information is stored in the memory bank of experiences we recall
- As we build up a range of experiences we can quickly identify what our five senses are picking up
- Eg a mother easily recognizes the voice of her child crying in a room full of crying children

9.3 Spirit Sensations

- Human beings are spirit beings living in a body ? Every person has spiritual senses which enable us to be aware of the spirit world around us
- Our spiritual senses can extend beyond the body and can become aware of spiritual atmospheres created by people by demons or by the Spirit of God
- Unsaved people call this the 'sixth sense' - it is really your spirit man

9.4 How You Process Sensations

- Information from your natural senses enters your soul and is processed by your mind through comparing with previous experiences, and by reasoning
- Information from your spiritual senses enters your soul as a spontaneous picture, thought, or impression, and is processed by your mind
- Until the mind has been trained to recognize and yield to spiritual impressions from the Holy Spirit, it tends to reason them away and/or ignore them
- As the mind is renewed by the Word of God it can be trained to be sensitive to the promptings of the Holy Spirit and obey His voice in simple faith
- We need to learn

1. i) to receive impressions
2. ii) to identify and evaluate them
3. iii) to enquire of the Holy Spirit for more detail
4. iv) to take a risk, and speak or act on the impression

9.5 Extreme Responses

- **Extreme # 1:** Highly logical people may reason away all spiritual impressions
- The left side of the brain dominates their mind, and reject all intuitive thoughts
- They may be in bondage to spirits of unbelief, control, and fear

- **Extreme # 2:** Intuitive people may respond to every impression without discerning what is God and what is not
- People who have experienced rejection, abuse, or have been involved in occult practices are often deeply sensitive to impressions
- They may lack discipline in evaluating their thinking processes
- They may hide behind a false spirituality, constantly declaring that "God told me"
- They may be resistant to feedback, and view it as a further rejection

10. How to Activate the Gifts of the Spirit

10.1 Gifts of the Spirit Can Be Activated

Key Verse: 2 Tim 1:6-7
"Therefore I remind you to stir up the gift of God which is in you through the laying on of my hands. 7 For God has not given us a spirit of fear, but of power and of love and of asound mind."

Insights:

- **'Stir Up'** - NT:325 - to rekindle a fire that was once burning brightly
- **'To activate'** means to take practical steps that stir your faith and energize your spirit to be responsive to the Holy Spirit

10.2 Bible Examples of Activation of the Gifts

1. 2 Kings 3:15 - Elisha stirred his gift with the help of a musician
2. Judges 16:20 - Samson stirred his gift by shaking himself

10.3 Gifts of the Spirit can Become Dormant for Five Reasons

1. Fear / Intimidation (2Tim 1:6)
2. Unbelief (Matt 17:19-20)
3. Controlling spirits (Acts 4:15-18)
4. Passivity (Matt 11:12)
5. Neglect (1Tim 4:14)

10.4 Feed Your Spirit Man

Key Verse: 1 Tim 4:14-15

"Do not neglect the gift that is in you, which was given to you by prophecy with the laying on of the hands of the eldership. 15 Meditate on these things; give yourself entirely to them, that your progress may be evident to all."

Insights:

- An important foundation for operating in the Gifts of the Spirit is to cultivate a strong spirit life through
- worship
- waiting on God
- meditation
- reading the Word of God
- pursuing intimacy with God
- obedience to the promptings of the Holy Spirit

10.5 Practical Keys to Activating the Free up your Spirit

1. Pray strongly in tongues to energize your Spirit
2. Pray strongly and fluently until you feel your spirit stirred
3. As you pray in tongues you are praying with your Spirit (1Cor 14:14)
4. As you pray in tongues the Spirit of God is moving through you (Acts 2:4)
5. Faith Expectation
    1. Expect the Spirit of God to speak to you
    2. John 10:27 – "My sheep hear My voice, and I know them, and they follow Me."
    3. Expectation draws the presence of the Holy Spirit
6. Focus
    1. Focus your attention on listening for the voice of God
    2. See Him speaking to you, working through you
    3. Don't let your mind be distracted or wander
7. Feel
    1. Identify the impressions that the Holy Spirit gives to you
    2. Was it a word, a picture, or an impression within?
    3. Focus your attention on it
    4. Look at it; ask the Holy Spirit for more detail
8. Faith Action
    1. Speak out what it is that God has been revealing to you
    2. Step out and act on what God has been showing you
    3. The miracle does not take place until you put yourself in the place of risk
    4. As you speak and act on what you have received, the Holy Spirit will give you more, or will act in a supernatural way
    5. v) At some point you have to take the risk and act upon what you feel the Holy Spirit is showing you

Examples:

- *Matt 14:29 - Peter stepped out of the boat and he walked on water*
- *Luke 17:14 - As the lepers went they were cleansed*
- *Mark 6:42 As they distributed the food it multiplied*
- *John 2:7 Once the water-pots were filled the water changed into wine*

11. How to Test Revelation

11.1 Does It Agree With the Written Word of God?

Key Verse: Gal 1:8
"But even if we, or an angel from heaven, preach any other gospel to you than what we have preached to you, let him be accursed."

Insights:

- Whatever revelation is received must not contradict Scripture
- The Holy Spirit who inspired the Word of God will not contradict himself

11.2 Does It Agree With the Character of God?

Key Verse: Matt 4:5-7
"Then the devil took Him up into the holy city, set Him on the pinnacle of the temple, 6 and said to Him, "If You are the Son of God, throw Yourself down. For it is written: 'He shall give His angels charge over you,' and, 'In their hands they shall bear you up, Lest you dash your foot against a stone." 7 Jesus said to him, "It is written again, 'You shall not tempt the LORD your God.'"

Insights:

- Evil spirits are able to quote the word of God
- God will never tell you to do something that is out of harmony with his character
- God grows us step by step, not by sudden dramatic changes **(2Cor.3:18)**
- The supernatural is not necessarily spectacular

11.3 Does It Produce Good Fruit?
Key Verse: James 3:17-18
"But the wisdom that is from above is first pure, then peaceable, gentle, willing to yield, full of mercy and good fruits, without partiality and without hypocrisy. 18 Now the fruit of righteousness is sown in peace by those who make peace."

Insights:

- A tree is known by its fruit **(Luke 6:43-44)**
- **'Pure'** - NT:53 - no hidden or selfish motives
- **'Peaceable'** - NT:1516 - brings healing and harmony into relationships
- **'Gentle'** - NT:1933 - not pushy, demanding, harsh, or contentious
- **'Yielded'** - NT:2138 - open to reason,, not stubborn, hard, or dogmatic
- **'Mercy'** - NT:1656 - compassionate, kind to people, sensitive to people
- **'Good Fruit'** - NT:2590 - results in right living before God
- **'Partiality'** - NT:87 - no favorites, treats people as being of equal value
- **'Hypocrisy'** - NT:505 - not acting, no pretence; authentic or genuine

11.4 Does It Bear Witness With Your Spirit?

Key Verse: 1 John 2:27

"But the anointing which you have received from Him abides in you, and you do not need that anyone teach you; but as the same anointing teaches you concerning allthings, and is true, and is not a lie, and just as it has taught you, you will abide in Him."

Insights:

- The Holy Spirit dwelling within you is the Spirit of truth **(John 14:16-17)**
- The Holy Spirit gives a witness in your spirit, an inner joy or peace **(Col.3:15)**
- As you gain experience in listening to the inner witness within your spirit, it becomes easier to recognize 'revelation' which is not true, or has a demonic, or human, source

12. Gift of Prophecy

12.1 What Prophecy Is

Key Verse: 2 Peter 1:21

"for prophecy never came by the will of man, but holy men of God spoke as they were movedby the Holy Spirit."

Insights:

- *Prophecy is a spontaneous message given by the Holy Spirit to a believer to speak to a specific person or group of people at a specific time*
- **'Prophecy'** - *NT:4391 - to spontaneously speak forth the mind and counsel of God; to speak under the inspiration of the Holy Spirit*
- **'Moved'** - *NT:5342 - to bring forth a burden; to be carried by a wind*

12.2 The Purpose of the Gift

Key Verse: 1 Cor 14:3
"But he who prophesies speaks edification and exhortation and comfort to men."

Insights:

- The purpose of the prophetic message is for
  a) 'Edification' NT:3619 - to build up; promoting another's growth
  b) 'Exhortation' NT:3874 – to come along side and strengthen
  c) 'Comfort' - NT:3889 - to come near and give hope and/or support in time of grief or pain
- When the Gift of prophecy flows, there is often a change in the spiritual atmosphere, and a release of other Gifts of the Spirit
- The Gift of prophecy can also be used in spiritual warfare **(Ezek 21:14)**

12.3 General Guidelines

- All believers are encouraged to prophesy **(1Cor 14:1)**
- All believers are encouraged to desire the Gift **(1Cor 14:39)**
- All believers are encouraged not to despise the Gift **(1Thess 5:20)**
- Believers filled with the Holy Spirit can immediately prophesy **(Acts 19:6)**
- Often the Gift of prophecy combines with word of knowledge to give revelation about an individual or entire congregation

12.4 Judging Prophecy

Key Verse: 1 Cor 14:29

"Let two or three prophets speak, and let the others judge. 30 But if anything is revealed to another who sits by, let the first keep silent. 31 For you can all prophesy one by one, that all may learn and all may be encouraged. 32 And the spirits of the prophets are subject to the prophets. 33 For God is not the author of confusion but of peace, as in all the churches of the saints."

Insights:

- Since prophecy is an utterance that can be understood, it must be judged
- **'Judge'** - NT:1252 - to distinguish, to separate out what is good

- Judging prophecy includes evaluating
  a) the content of the message
  b) the spirit in which it is given
  c) the reliability of the individual giving the message

- Key Questions to ask
  a) Does it agree with Scripture? (Gal1:8)
  b) Is there an inner witness of the Spirit? (1 John2:20)
  c) Does it lift your spirit or bring heaviness? (2 Cor 3:17)
  d) Does it agree with the Character of God? (Matt4:6-7)
  e) Does it bring honour to God? (John16:13-14)
  f) Does the prophecy come to pass? (Deut18:18-21)

12.5 Cautions in Operating

Don't Use Prophesy

- As a Christian fortune telling
- To scold or rebuke people
- To correct leaders
- To bring forth your pet ideas
- To give direction to business dealings
- To give direction to male-female relationships
- To prophesy healing out of your own compassion

Some Do's

- Speak forth clearly and boldly
- Stop when the anointing lifts
- Use normal tone of voice
- Speak in simple everyday language
- Stay within the boundaries of edification, exhortation and comfort

12.6 Feed Back

- *Welcome feedback on the quality of your prophecy*
- *Feedback enables you to recognize how the Lord has worked through you*
- *Feedback enables you to improve your sensitivity and flow of prophecy*

12.7 Practical Points

- *Free up your spirit (praying in tongues, praising)*
- *Faith - expect God to give you something*
- *Focus – concentrate your attention, listening for promptings of the Holy Spirit*
- *Faith Action*
    - *step out and share simply what you have received*
    - *start with what you have been given expecting to receive more*
    - *example: box of tissues*
    - *example: TV newsreader*
    - *get feedback from the person you ministered to*

13. Diverse Kinds of Tongues

13.1 What is the Gift of Tongues?

- It is a supernatural utterance given by the Holy Spirit spontaneously in a language the believer has not learned
- It is not the prayer language of the believer, but it is an anointed message that should be accompanied by an interpretation **(1Cor.14:13)**

13.2 The Twofold Ministry of the Holy Spirit

Key Verse: John 14:17
"The Spirit of truth, whom the world cannot receive, because it neither sees Him nor knows Him; but you know Him, for <u>He dwells with you</u> and <u>will be in you</u>."

Insights:

- The Holy Spirit empowers believers in one of two ways
    1. the anointing coming and remaining **within**
    2. the anointing coming **upon** for a period of time

- The Spirit was **with** them because he would come **upon** them from time to time to work miracles
- Jesus promised that the Holy Spirit would come and dwell within them

13.3 The Anointing 'In' - Empowers Praying in a Tongue

Key Verse #1: 2 Cor 1:21

"Now He who establishes us with you in Christ and has anointed us is God, 22 who also has sealed us and given us the <u>Spirit in our hearts</u> as a guarantee."

Insights:

- There is an anointing that comes into the believer and abides
- The anointing that abides within gives constant contact with Heaven

Key Verse #2: 1 Cor 14:14

"For if I pray in a tongue, my spirit prays, but my understanding is unfruitful. 15 What is the conclusion then? I will pray with the spirit, and I will also pray with the understanding. I will sing with the spirit, and I will also sing with the understanding. 16 Otherwise, if you bless with the spirit, how will he who occupies the place of the uninformed say "Amen" at your giving of thanks, since he does not understand what you say? 17 For you indeed give thanks well, but the other is not edified."

Insights:

- When you pray in a tongue your spirit is praying
- Praying in a Tongue = Praying in the Spirit **(Eph.6:18)**
- Usually one distinct language is involved
- The language is given by the Holy Spirit
- The person must speak forth
- It requires you to exercise your will
- It is a flow of communication from man to God **(1Cor 14:2)**

Some Benefits

- Strengthen your spirit man **(Eph 3:16)**
- Energise your spirit man **(1Cor 14:2)**
- Praise and worship **(1Cor 14:15-16)**
- Intercession **(Rom 8:26)**
- Decree the will of God for your life **(1Cor 14:2)**
- Sensitise your spirit **(Heb5:14)**

13.4 The Anointing 'Upon'- Empowers Diverse Kinds of Tongues

Key Verse: 1 Cor 12:7

"But the manifestation of the Spirit is given to each one for the profit of all: 8 for to one is given the word of wisdom through the Spirit, to another the word of knowledge through the same Spirit, 9 to another faith by the same Spirit, to another gifts of healings by the same Spirit, 10 to another the working of miracles, to another prophecy, to another discerning of spirits, to another <u>diverse kinds of tongues</u>, to another the interpretation of tongues. 11 But one and the same Spirit works all these things, distributing to each one individually <u>as He wills</u>."

Insights:

- **'Diverse kinds of tongues'** are energized by the Holy Spirit
- It is a divinely given message spoken into the world, straight from the throne of God
- It is dependent on the Holy Spirit **coming upon someone** and empowering them to operate that way
- The Holy Spirit must will it, and energize it.
- It is the responsibility of the individual to speak out when the Holy Spirit comes upon them.
- Paul spoke in tongues (diverse) more than anyone **(1Cor 14:18)**

13.5 Tongues of Men or Angels

Key Verse: 1 Cor 13:1
"Though I speak with the <u>tongues of men and of angels</u>, but have not love, I have become sounding brass or a clanging cymbal."

Insights:

- **'Tongues'** *means different kinds of languages, not just one language*
- **'Tongues'** *could be a distinct language understood and spoken by a particular cultural group of people*
- **'Tongues'** *could be a distinct language understood and spoken by* **angels**
- *Speaking in tongues is speaking in a language that is understood and spoken either by men or angels*

a) Example: Tongues of Men - Acts 2:1-8

"When the Day of Pentecost had fully come, they were all with one accord in one place. 2 And suddenly there came a sound from heaven, as of a rushing mighty wind, and it filled the whole house where they were sitting. 3 Then there appeared to them divided tongues, as of fire, and one sat upon each of them. 4 And they were all filled with the Holy Spirit and <u>began to speak with other tongues</u>, as the Spirit gave them utterance. 5 And there were dwelling in Jerusalem Jews, devout men, from every nation under heaven. 6 And when this sound occurred, the multitude came together, and were confused, because <u>everyone heard them speak in his own language</u>. 7 Then they were all amazed and marveled, saying to one another, "Look are not all these who speak Galileans? 8 And how is it that we hear, each of us in our own language in which we were born?"

Insights:

- People of many different cultures understood what they were saying.
- They heard their own language spoken, and were amazed
- This was a manifestation of diverse kinds of tongues energized by the Holy Spirit
- They were speaking the wonderful works of God - not praying but proclaiming!

b) Example: Tongues of Angels - Ps 103:19-21

"The LORD has established His throne in heaven, And His kingdom rules over all. 20 Bless the LORD, you His angels, Who <u>excel in strength</u>, who do His word, <u>Heeding the voice</u> of His word. 21 Bless the LORD, all you His hosts, You ministers of His, who do His pleasure."

Insights:

- Angels respond to the voice of God's Word ie the voicing aloud in the earth of the Word of God, by God's representative, Man
- The Holy Spirit comes upon a man to give utterance in diverse kinds of tongues
- The diverse kinds of tongues is a language that angels understand
- God speaks his mind and will through a man. and uses his voice to activate angels to perform a task
- Diverse tongues bypass the soul and understanding of man and enable a direct command to be given to the Angels through God's yielded authority on the earth
- Angels excel in strength (vs.19) and are able to subdue and bind wicked spirits

c) The Purpose of the Gift

- A sign to the unbeliever **(Acts 2:6; 1Cor 14:22)**
- Prophetic proclamations in the earth **(Acts 2:11)**
- Releasing Angels in spiritual warfare **(1Cor13:1)**
- Empowering the Ministry of the Intercession **(1Cor 12:28)**
- Supernaturally communicate across language barriers **(Acts 2:6)**

d) Practical Points

- Be sensitive to the Holy Spirit coming upon you as you pray
- Ask for the gift of diverse tongues
- Practice speaking out in a new tongue
- Be aware of changes in the spiritual atmosphere as you speak
- Listen to the flow of the Spirit that comes forth
- Ask the Holy Spirit to give you the interpretation

14. Interpretation of Tongues

14.1 What it is

- The interpretation of tongues is a supernatural ability given by the Holy Spirit, to enable the believer to understand a language being spoken, earthly or heavenly, without having first learned it

14.2 Interpretation is a Gift

Key Verse 1 Cor 12:10

"to another the working of miracles, to another prophecy, to another discerning of spirits, to another different kinds of tongues, to another the interpretation of tongues."

Insights:

- It is not a translation ie not an exact word by word explanation of the message
- It is an interpretation - it catches the spirit and intent of the message
- Used in private and public worship, and public ministry, as led by the Holy Spirit **(1Cor.15:5)**

14.3 Purpose of the Gift

- *Tongues (with interpretation) is a sign to the unsaved (1Cor 14:22)*
- *It energises the spiritual atmosphere*
- *It reveals the mind of the Holy Spirit at that particular time*
- *It can facilitate the release of angelic activity*

14.4 Practical Points

- *Interpretation of tongues is a companion to speaking in tongues*
- *It can help you develop sensitivity to the Holy Spirit coming upon you in private worship*
- *It can bring understanding of the mind of the Spirit*
- *Can reveal what you are praying about in the spirit*
- *In public worship, the gift of tongues and interpretation can bring the church into a flow of the Holy Spirit, not unlike the Gift of prophecy*

15. Word of Wisdom

15.1 What it is

- It is an impression, a thought, a mental picture, or a still small voice of the Holy Spirit showing what to do or how to deal with a specific situation. It is wisdom about that one matter at that one time

15.2 The Purpose of the Gift

Key Verse:1 Cor 12:7
"But the manifestation of the Spirit is given to each one for the profit of all: 8 for to one is _given the word of wisdom through the Spirit,_ to another the word of knowledge through the same Spirit, 9 to another faith by the same Spirit, to another gifts of healings by the same Spirit, 10 to another the working of miracles, to another prophecy, to another discerning of spirits, to another different kinds of tongues, to another the interpretation of tongues.11 But one and the same Spirit works all these things,distributing to each one individually as He wills."

Insights:

- The Word of Wisdom is listed first in **1Cor.12:8**
- It is often included in the operation of all the other gifts
- We need wisdom from the Holy Spirit to know how to carry out what God has revealed to us
- The Word of Wisdom reveals to us
    - how to do something God has shown you to do
    - how to resolve situations
    - how to pray for a person
    - how to avoid dangers
    - how to speak the right words into situations

15.3 Bible Examples

- **2 Sam 5:22-25** David received a word of wisdom, how to fight a battle
- **1 Kings 3:16-28** King Solomon handled the two mothers in conflict over a child with a word of wisdom
- **Hebrews 11:7** Noah received a word of wisdom to build an ark
- **Acts 15:13-21** James received a word of wisdom on how to resolve a church conflict that threatened to divide the church
- **Acts 5:1-11** Peter received a word of wisdom, how to deal with dishonesty
- **John 8:4-7** Jesus received a word of wisdom, how to deal with the accusers of the woman caught in adultery

15.4 Practical Points

- Don't be impulsive in making decisions or giving advice.
- Don't act under pressure of people or circumstances
- Ask the Holy Spirit for insight, for a word of wisdom and what to do.
- It may come as a spontaneous picture, an impression or a flow of thoughts
- You may "see "a picture of how an event will unfold in the future. This gives you confidence as to what steps you should take
- Be prepared to wait on the Lord for wisdom **(Prov.2:6: Prov.4:7)**

16. Word of Knowledge

16.1 What it is

- An impression, a thought, a mental picture or the still voice of the Holy Spirit giving knowledge of facts about a person, or situation, that one could not possibly have known naturally
- It is not accumulated or acquired knowledge, it is **revealed** knowledge
- It is knowledge about past situations and experiences, or about current situations. It uncovers what is happening

16.2 The Purpose of the Gift

Key Verse: 1 Cor 12:7-11

"But the manifestation of the Spirit is given to each one for the profit of all: 8 for to one is given the word of wisdom through the Spirit, to another the word of knowledge through the same Spirit, 9 to another faith by the same Spirit, to another gifts of healings by the same Spirit, 10 to another the working of miracles, to another prophecy, to another discerning of spirits, to another different kinds of tongues, to another the interpretation of tongues. 11 But one and the same Spirit works all these things, distributing to each one individually as He wills."

Insights:

- It uncovers important unknown facts concerning a person or situation
- It uncovers the 'true' situation as seen from God's perspective
- It enables you to minister more effectively to the needs of people

16.3 Bible Examples:

- **2 Kings 6:8-10** Elijah received details about the enemy strategy
- **1 Samuel 9:15-20** Samuel received knowledge about Saul. (16 specific details)
- **2 Kings 5:20-27** Elisha received knowledge about Gehazi's secret sin.
- **John 4:18** Jesus received knowledge about the woman's marriage failures.
- **Acts 5:1-11** Peter receive knowledge about the financial dealings of an Ananias and Sapphira
- **Acts 9:10-16** Ananias received knowledge about Saul, what was wrong where he was living, what needed to be done

16.4 Practical Points

- It may come as a spontaneous picture, an image in your imagination, an impression or flow of thoughts, or an inner 'knowing'
- A word of knowledge may come as a dream or vision
- It may give you sudden insight about sickness, bondage, problems
- To operate effectively in the word of knowledge you must separate your own knowledge from that which the Holy Spirit gives
- As you "see" a picture or feel an impression, focus on it, and identify it clearly
- Ask the Lord for specific details
- Ask the Lord how to wisely use what you know (Word of wisdom)
- It may mean little to you but have dramatic impact as you speak it
- Wait on the Lord daily
    - ask for words of knowledge for family, work, soul winning
    - expect to receive
- When giving a Word of Knowledge consider:
    - Is this word of knowledge for prayer only?
    - Should I share this with a local church leader first?
    - Is this public or private information?
    - How d I give the word of knowledge in such a way that the person is able to receive it eg Jesus drew the woman in (John.4:16)

17. Discerning of Spirits

17.1 What it is

- It is knowledge given by the Holy Spirit that reveals what spirit power is operating in or behind a person or situation

17.2 The Purpose of the Gift

Key Verse: 1 Cor 12:7

"But the manifestation of the Spirit is given to each one for the profit of all: 8 for to one is given the word of wisdom through the Spirit, to another the word of knowledge through the same Spirit, 9 to another faith by the same Spirit, to another gifts of healings by the same Spirit, 10 to another the working of miracles, to another prophecy, to another discerning of spirits, to another different kinds of tongues, to another the interpretation of tongues. 11 But one and the same Spirit works all these things, distributing to each one individually as He will."

Insights:

- *It is a supernatural gift of revelation given by the Holy Spirit and received by faith into your spirit*
- *'Discernment'* - *NT:1253 - a clear discrimination, seeing through to the root causes*
- *It enables a believer to have essential information about*
    1. *The activity of the Holy Spirit or Angels*
    2. *The nature and activity of demonic spirits*
    3. *The motivations of a person's words and actions*
- *it is not the same as natural discernment with the mind or senses which depends solely upon the person's feelings and interpretation of the situation*
- *The Gift of discerning of spirits can*
    1. *Reveal the presence and nature of spirits inhabiting a person's body* **(Acts 16:16)**
    2. *Reveal the geographical location and activity of evil spirits*
    3. *Facilitate deliverance and release for those who are bound by spiritual oppression*
    4. *Give understanding of what is happening in the spirit realm around your life and ministry*
    5. *Identify whether a 'revelation' is from God or not*

17.3 Bible Examples

- **Luke 2:25-27** *Simeon discerned the timing and activity of the Holy Spirit*
- **Luke 13:10-13** *Jesus discerned the demonic source of the sickness*
- **Matt 16:23** *Jesus discerned in demonic source of Peter's words*
- **Acts 8:18-23** *Peter discerned the motives of Simon the sorcerer*
- **Acts 16:16-17** *Paul discerned the spirit of divination*

17.4 Understanding Your Senses

Key Verse: Heb 5:14

"But solid food belongs to those who are of full age, that is, those who by reason of use have their <u>senses exercised</u> to discern both good and evil."

Insight:

- **'Exercised'** - NT:1128 – to train or practice for an Olympic competition

a) Natural Senses

- Every person has five natural senses: sight-taste-touch-smell-hearing
- As a child grows these senses are developed or trained
- A memory bank of all these experiences is formed in the mind

b) Spiritual Senses

- Man who was formed as a spirit being in the image of God has spiritual senses
- These senses are energized and quickened by the Holy Spirit
    1. i) Sight - seeing in the Holy Spirit
    2. ii) Hearing - hearing the voice of the Holy Spirit
    3. iii) Knowledge - revelation knowledge
    4. iv) Understanding - insights into the spirit realm
    5. v) Perception - sensing the various activities of spirits
    6. vi) Discernment - identifying different spirits
- Each of these senses can be developed or trained by practice
- Each time you become aware of a spirit sensation, the memory of this experience is recorded in your mind <u>for future reference</u>

c) The Processing Ability of the Mind

- *Your mind has the ability to recall a number of similar events, sensations and feelings, and to draw conclusions all similarity and difference between them*
- *This comparative ability of the mind includes*
    1. *Information and details about events*
    2. *Senses e.g. different kinds of smells and tastes*
    3. *Emotional Feelings associated with different events*
    4. *Triggers or prompts that recall information and feelings*
- *Each time you have a spiritual experience, your mind will process the information and compare it with previous experiences*

17.5 Developing Sensitivity

Key Verse: Heb 5:14

"But solid food belongs to those who are of full age, that is, those who by reason of use have their senses exercised to discern both good and evil."

- Spiritual sensitivity can be developed through
    1. i) Fasting - food, visual media
    2. ii) Worship - engaging the presence of God consistently
    3. iii) Renewing the Mind - thoughts , images
    4. iv) Personal Honesty - motives, words, attitudes

17.6 Practical Points

- Practice identifying spiritual impressions of 'release' or 'restraint '
- Identify the first impressions you have as you meet people, enter a room, participate in meetings
- Put a name to what you feel, or to the impression you felt
- Ask the Holy Spirit what He wants you to do about what you discern
- Practice repeatedly. Build up a memory bank of spiritual experiences
- Learn to distinguish what comes from your spirit, and what comes from your soul, which may be rooted in insecurity and distrust of people
- Practice repeatedly until you become more sensitive to spiritual impressions and atmospheres

18. Gift of Faith

18.1 What it is

- It is not the normal measure of faith for daily walking with the Lord
- It is a gift that comes in a moment of time that enables you to get the job done
- It is an impartation of ability to confidently know God's provision is sure
- How can you know? - there is an inner knowing that faith gives
- It is the gift of power enabling a believer to obtain supernatural results
- An impossible situation exists. A gift of faith is given. A solution is seen / known and power is released for the person to accomplish the task
- A person with a gift of faith for a specific action will have a boldness and confidence about the outcome that is completely unreasonable
- Different Kinds of Faith we steadily grow and increase in:
    1. Saving Faith **(Ephesians 2:8)**
    2. Walk of Faith **(Hebrews 11:6)**
    3. Faith – Fruit of the Spirit **(Galatians 5:22)**
    4. Gift of Faith – a Gift of the Spirit **(1Cor 12:9)**

18.2 The Purpose of the Gift

Key Verse: 1 Cor. 12:7-11

"But the manifestation of the Spirit is given to each one for the profit of all: 8 for to one is given the word of wisdom through the Spirit, to another the word of knowledge through the same Spirit, 9 to another faith by the same Spirit, to another gifts of healings by the same Spirit, 10 to another the working of miracles, to another prophecy, to another discerning of spirits, to another different kinds of tongues, to another the interpretation of tongues. 11 But one and the same Spirit works all these things, distributing to each one individually as He wills."

Insights:

- It releases power for supernatural acts to be done
- It imparts boldness and confidence that impacts people

18.3 Bible Examples

- **1 Kings 17:13-14** Elijah boldly declares miracle provision of food.
- **John 9:1-7** Jesus knew the man born blind would be healed.
- **Acts 3:1-7** Peter boldly proclaims the crippled man's healing.
- **Acts 27:20-26** - Paul boldly declares that none on the ship will perish.
- **Acts 14:9** - Paul and the cripple. Paul knew he would be healed

18.4 Practical Points

- *Maintain regular time in the Word of God – the source of faith **(Romans 10:17)***
- *Choose to believe the Word of God and to trust it completely **(Romans 4:20)***
- *Practice speaking the Word of God boldly **(2 Corinthians 4:13)***
- *Expect God to honor and keep His Word **(Isaiah 55:11)***
- *Learn to take authority over the atmosphere, and dominion over evil*
- *spirits present so that the heavens open*
- *Learn to step out in faith in your own personal gifting to start a flow*
- *of the anointing that alters the atmosphere and makes room for the gift*
- *of faith to flow*

19. Gifts of Healings

19.1 What it is

- It is a supernatural ability imparted by the Holy Spirit to bring about healing in a person without any natural means i.e. medicine, doctor
- The healing may be immediate (a miracle) or it may be progressive i.e. the person recovers in a way that cannot be explained naturally **(Mark 16:18)**

19.2 The Purpose of the Gift

Key Verse: 1 Cor 12:7

"But the manifestation of the Spirit is given to each one for the profit of all: 8 for to one is given the word of wisdom through the Spirit, to another the word of knowledge through the same Spirit, 9 to another faith by the same Spirit, to another gifts of healings by the same Spirit, 10 to another the working of miracles, to another prophecy, to another discerning of spirits, to another different kinds of tongues, to another the interpretation of tongues. 11 But one and the same Spirit works all these things, distributing to each one individually as He wills."

Insights:

- It releases power to bring healing to body, soul and spirit
- Gifts of healing, not the Gift of healing
- One person may have a high rate of success in one particular area eg seeing deaf ears opened, or blind eyes healed, or cancers healed
- There are many various forms of Gifts of healing, but it is the one Holy Spirit that empowers them

Bible Examples

- **2 Chronicles 30:20** Multitudes of people healed when Hezekiah prayed
- **Luke 4:40** All that were sick with diverse diseases were healed
- **Mark 5:25-34** The woman with an issue of blood was healed
- **Matt 10:5** "These twelve Jesus <u>sent out and commanded them</u>, saying: "Do not go into the way of the Gentiles, and do not enter a city of the Samaritans. 6 But go rather to the lost sheep of the house of Israel. 7 And as you go, preach, saying, 'The kingdom of heaven is at hand.' 8 <u>Heal the sick, cleanse the lepers, raise the dead, cast out demons.</u> Freely you have received, freely give"
- Jesus did not tell the disciples to **pray** for the sick!
- Jesus commanded his disciples **'Heal the Sick'**

19.3 Practical Points

a) Lay hands on the Person

Mark 16:17 "And these signs will follow those who believe: In My name they will cast out demons; they will speak with new tongues; 18 they will take up serpents; and if they drink anything deadly, it will by no means hurt them; <u>they will lay hands on the sick, and they will recover</u>"

- Always ask permission before praying for someone or laying hands upon them
- Do not push or shake them as you pray for him

b) Cast Out any Spirit of Infirmity

Luke 13:11 "And behold, there was a woman who had a <u>spirit of infirmity</u> eighteen years, and was bent over and could in no way raise herself up. 12 But when Jesus saw her, He called her to Him and said to her, "<u>Woman, you are loosed from your infirmity</u>." 13 And He <u>laid His hands on her</u>, and immediately she was made straight, and glorified God."

- Some sicknesses are caused by the presence of an evil spirit
- Speak directly to the spirit and commanded it to leave

c) Command the Sickness!

Acts 3:1 "Now Peter and John went up together to the temple at the hour of prayer, the ninth hour. 2 And a certain man lame from his mother's womb was carried, whom they laid daily at the gate of the temple which is called Beautiful, to ask alms from those who entered the temple; 3 who, seeing Peter and John about to go into the temple, asked for alms. 4 And <u>fixing his eyes on him</u>, with John, Peter said, "Look at us." 5 So he gave them his attention, <u>expecting to receive</u> something from them. 6 Then <u>Peter said</u>, "Silver and gold I do not have, <u>but what I do have I give you</u>: In the name of Jesus Christ of Nazareth,<u> rise up and walk</u>." 7 And he took him by the right hand and lifted him up, and immediately his feet and ankle bones received strength. 8 So he, leaping up, stood and walked and entered the temple with them — walking, leaping, and praising God "

Mark 11:22 "So Jesus answered and said to them, "Have faith in God. 23 For assuredly, I say to you, whoever <u>says to this mountain,</u> 'Be removed and be cast into the sea,' and does <u>not doubt in his heart</u>, but <u>believes that those things he says</u> will be done, he will have whatever he says. 24 Therefore I say to you, whatever things you ask when you pray, believe that you receive them, and <u>you will have them</u>."

- Speak to the mountain (sickness)
- Don't doubt in your heart
- Believe what you say will come to pass

d) Anoint with Oil

Mark 6:12 "So they went out and preached that people should repent. 13 And they cast

out any demons, and <u>anointed with oil many who were sick</u>, and healed them"

- Anoint with oil only as the Holy Spirit leads
- The type of oil used is of no consequence
- It is **faith in the power of God** to heal that causes the healing to take place
- Apply a small amount of oil on the tip of a finger and apply to the forehead of the sick person
- The oil acts as a focal point for their faith

e) Encourage a Faith Action

Matt 12:13 "Then He said to the man, "Stretch out your hand." And he stretched it out, and it was restored as whole as the other."

- Where possible encourage people to take some action of faith

- Encourage them to try to do what they could not do before you prayed
- Some miracles begin to operate when the person acts in faith.

f) Important Safeguard

- Do not encourage people to stop using medicine
- Do not encourage them no longer to see a doctor
- In an emergency situation were medical attention is urgently required
    1. Pray very briefly
    2. Call the doctor
    3. Give whatever assistance you can and keep praying

g) Important Tips

- The gifts operate by faith and not by long prayers
- Keep your thoughts centered on Christ and His Power to heal
- Don't allow unbelief to fill your heart (by focusing on the sickness)
- The person being prayed for must repent of sins and have their heart free from unforgiveness or bitterness
- Low self-esteem, coupled with unbelief and passivity, can hinder the flow of healing

20. The Working of Miracles

20.1 What it is

- A miracle occurs when natural laws are broken by supernatural intervention
- The working of miracles is a specific effect that comes when the Gifts of the Holy Spirit work together to override or invade natural laws; to do something that was impossible naturally
- The working of miracles operates alongside the Gift of Faith and Gifts of Healing

20.2 Bible Examples

- **1 Kings 18:37-39** Elijah calls down fire from heaven
- **2 Kings 4:1-7** The pot of oil keeps refilling – creative miracle
- **Matt 14:25** Jesus walks on water
- **Matt 14:19-21** The five loaves and two fishes feed 5000 people
- **Matt15:30-31** Crippled people are totally healed
- **Acts 8:6** Deliverance is a working of miracles
- In each of these miracles there is a similar pattern: <u>Revelation + Words Spoken + Active Faith = Manifestation of Holy Spirit</u>

20.3 Practical Points

- *Desire to be used in this way by the Holy Spirit*
- *Pursue the presence of God and sensitivity to hearing His voice*
- *Meditate in the word of God, particularly on the nature of God and His mighty acts*
- *Listen to testimonies of miracles taking place. These build your faith*
- *Practice speaking the word of God from your spirit into your circumstances*
- *Maintain strong devotional life in the Bible – the source of faith*
- *Be willing to take risks*
- **Expect** *God to do the Supernatural*

21. Keys to Ministering in the Spirit

21.1 Identity

- God has made you a Minister of The Spirit **(2 Cor 3:6)**
- You are joined to the Holy Spirit **(1 Cor 6:17)**
- You are not there to pray 'nice' empty prayers, but to release the Kingdom of God into the earth to bring about a miracle
- That Kingdom is outside you - it is also within you
- "Look on us...such as I have I give to you." **(Acts 3:4-6)**

21.2 Connection

- Connect with the person
- Don't withdraw because of feelings of inadequacy
- Take hold of the person's hand **(Mark 1:31; 8:23; 9:27)**
- Relax - Don't 'try' to make something happen
- Look them in the eye - connect with your heart **(Mark 1:41)**
- Meditate...become conscious of the presence of God
- Notice what you are feeling? Thinking? Conscious of?
- Keep your mind directed towards God **(Luke 9:16)**
- Be aware of the presence of God within you - and the presence of God coming upon the person

21.3 Attitude

- Your spirit responds to your thoughts and attitude
- Whatever you direct your mind to your spirit opens up to
- Fear and self consciousness will close up your spirit
- As you minister keep directing your thoughts toward the Lord in expectation
- Be yourself - don't try to 'perform' or be 'spiritual'
- God gives Grace to the humble ie those who are dependent on Him

21.4 Verbal Command

- *Power is released by Command*
- *Assert spiritual authority by verbal command **(Luke 10:19)***
- *You must put your inner man into the words you speak **(Mark 11.23)***
- *Command demons to go **(Acts 16:18)***
- *Command sickness to leave **(Acts 3: 6)***
- *Break bondages by verbal command **(Mark 11:23)***
- *Speak words of life **(Acts 9:40)***

21.5 Impartation

- *Power is released by Impartation*
- *Paul desired to impart spiritual Gifts **(Rom 1:11)***
- *Impart = to share something you possess **(2 Tim 1:6)***
- *Impartation occurs as a flow from within you **(Luke 6:19)***
- *You must give from within your spirit **(1 Cor 6:17)***
- *Lay hands on their head and release what you have eg by speaking and/or by breathing on them **(John 20:22)***

22. Practical Guidelines for Ministering to People

22.1 Personal

- Personal hygiene, make sure to use deodorant
- Breath Fresheners. Keep your breath fresh
- Wear light loose modest clothing

22.2 Connect and Relate

- Be honest with them
- Be willing to take time
- Keep confidences shared (unless you need to refer their situation on)
- Treat people with respect
- Where possible, woman pray with women, and men with men

22.3 Prepare people to receive

- Encourage people with words
- Explain their part in cooperating with ministry
- Be willing to confront root sin issues
- Build expectation that God will move
- Ask permission to minister to people - don't presume
- Ask permission to lay hands upon them - don't presume
- Keep your hands in view and ensure touch is appropriate
- Be cautious about where you lay hands eg head, shoulders

22.4 Possible Experiences as you Minister

The person you are praying for may experience some of the following sensations

- Shaking
- Body or hands stiffen
- Eyelids flutter
- Sensation of heat
- Tears /Grief
- Falling - make sure a catcher is positioned to catch safely
- place one hand behind the person's neck to help prevent them suddenly falling backwards and possibly hurting themselves
- Demons manifest
- Don't focus on or require manifestations

22.5 Be aware of 'Blocks' to Ministry

a) Personal Blocks

- Fear - focus attention on the Lord. 'See" Him blessing
- Self Consciousness - focus attention on the Lord
- Pressure to perform - relax and stop 'trying'
- Unresolved issues - deal with these quickly
- Lack of Prayer - expect His Grace - and change!

b) Ministry Blocks

- Unforgiveness - lead them to forgive
- Lack of repentance - lead them to repent
- Unbelief - rebuke demonic spirits
- Control- Rebuke demonic spirits

22.6 Stay sensitive to the Holy Spirit

- Don't lean on methods or experience
- Lean on The Holy Spirit to direct you
- Listen for Holy Spirit promptings
- Respond to impressions the Holy Spirit gives you eg a word, a picture or a sensation
- Ensure a 'Catcher' is standing behind them, and is alert
- Avoid 'pushing' or 'rocking' them, as you minister
- Speak and release the power of God

22.7 Get Feedback

- Where possible get feedback from the person you ministered to.
- Ask what they have experienced, or what they thought took place
- Be willing to pray again
- **Never** instruct anyone to stop taking any prescribed medicine - **the occurrence of a miracle should be verified by their doctor**, who is responsible to determine whether medication should be stopped or not

Video Transcripts

Introduction 85
1. Hearing from God (1 of 5).................................. 87
2. Prophesy (2 of 5) 140
3. Tongues, Interpretation of Tongues (3 of 5) 167
4. Discerning of Sprits (4 of 5) 206
5. Faith, Miracles, and Healing (5 of 5) 243

Vimeo:
https://vimeo.com/channels/spiritualauthority
Video (1 of 5): http://vimeo.com/47753518
Video (2 of 5): http://vimeo.com/45802644
Video (3 of 5): http://vimeo.com/45874811
Video (4 of 5): http://vimeo.com/45951460
Video (5 of 5): http://vimeo.com/45886661

YouTube:
http://www.youtube.com/playlist?list=PLrhZUkV364KPllr1ciOV7jdIPAL0LdLGM
Video (1 of 5): http://youtu.be/E4eGBHCx1Ll
Video (2 of 5): http://youtu.be/62htQXLY42U
Video (3 of 5): http://youtu.be/loLZXw9Fbkc
Video (4 of 5): http://youtu.be/1iuOs5Q9sh4
Video (5 of 5): http://youtu.be/pcCg6HFjdWQ

Introduction (Transcript)

God has created every person to be a supernatural spiritual being, with the capacity to function not only in a natural world, but also to access the realm of the spirit, access where God is, and to bring heaven to earth.

God's desire is that you be a channel for heaven coming to earth, for His presence and goodness and healing and love and peace and prosperity to flow through you, and to manifest in the world around you.

So in the course we'll be teaching about that supernatural dimension. We'll teach about how miracles are activated, what the keys are around that. We'll teach you what the foundational key is, is out of intimacy with God and hearing the voice of God, and we'll give you practical steps, practical keys, how to start from wherever you are right now, and step by step grow your faith, so you can be starting to operate successfully, and regularly and confidently in the gifts of the spirit.

So in the course we'll teach on the gifts of the spirit, we'll give you a little bit about each. We'll also give you some foundational understanding about the spirit man, and how God works in and through us. Also if you're watching this by DVD you'll see demonstrations of the power of God touching people, you'll see demonstrations of how to move in words of knowledge, hearing the voice of God, minister to people. You'll see all of that in this course, and it will inspire you and help you. God's given me ability to make it extremely clear, and I know that you're going to really enjoy this.

Put in the effort. Invest in yourself. Do the course, and put into practice the things you learn, and you'll just be overjoyed when you see God is far more willing to work through you, than you really realize. His plan is that the kingdom comes into the earth through you. All you've got to do is learn how to do it.

In 1 Corinthians, Chapter 12, Verse 1, Paul says I don't want you to be ignorant of spiritual gifts, and this course is to help solve that problem. God bless you. Have a great time on the course and may you extend the kingdom of God boldly.

1. Hearing from God (1 of 5)

https://vimeo.com/47753518
http://youtu.be/E4eGBHCx1LI

Hello everyone, and welcome to our seminar on Activating the Gifts of the Spirit. For those of you who are watching on the internet or watching through television, we want to welcome you too. I trust that you'll download off the internet the manual you'll need, and you can just follow it through with us. I encourage you, if you're in a group, that you just practice with the people are in the group. Remember, it's just a practice. Life is just a practice and so, as you practice, you'll get feedback from the person, and you'll be able to explore what it is to hear the voice of God, and to flow with the gifts of the spirit. So we're going to start in this first session, and the first session we're going to look at the Gifts of the Spirit. In your notes it's Section 2, and we're going to read from 1 Corinthians, Chapter 12, Verse 1. In Verse 1 it says, now concerning spiritual gifts, or concerning operations of the spirit, brothers, I would not have you to be ignorant, so Paul is writing to the church. Notice here's the first thing. God wants you to move in the supernatural. You are designed to be a supernatural being. You are a spirit being living inside a body.

With your body you can communicate with the external world. With your spirit you can communicate with the realm of God, with the realm of the spirit. So you are designed to flow and access with the supernatural realm of God, so you don't have to become a spiritual person. You already are spiritual. You already have a spirit dimension to you. Your natural body has five senses; you can see, you can hear, you can taste, touch, smell. Your spirit man also has spiritual senses. With your physical senses you can interact with the physical world. You receive signals and whatever, and from that you can begin to identify certain things. It's the same in your spirit. Many people haven't developed their spiritual capacity, so the first thing is you are a spirit being, and God wants you to operate supernaturally. That's His plan and so Paul writes, I don't want you to be ignorant of the supernatural realm or how to work with the Holy Spirit.

The word ignorant means having no practical experience or understanding of this, so the reason things are hard is because we don't know how, and over this seminar we want to take away the mystery of how hard it is, and make it so it's actually really simple. Everything that God does is incredibly simple and it requires just an open heart to receive, so you don't have to be highly educated to move in the supernatural. You don't have to be highly educated to flow with the Holy Spirit. He will use anyone who will just open their life up and say God, here I am, I'm available, work through me - so God will work through you. So the first thing then is that God wants us to be empowered and equipped to bring His power to people. The church has long lost the flow of power, but now, in these days, God is restoring power back to the church, and we'll see part of the great commission is that you be anointed with the power of the Holy Spirit, and you are able to lay hands on the sick, you are able to minister to people, you are able to flow with the Holy Spirit.

That makes sense because the world isn't going to come into a church building. The church has to go to the world and bring God to the world, so we want to show you how to do this, and we want to teach you how to work with the Holy Spirit in an environment where you're just practising and learning, then your journey is to develop what you learn and grow it. Don't wait for some revival, and don't wait for some big experience. Take what we give you and teach you, and begin to apply it and practice it, and you'll get better and better and better. God is more willing to use you than you realise. Okay, so this is the first thing.

The second thing is, and we're going talk a little bit about the gifts of the spirit themselves. If you go down to Verse 7, now the manifestation of the spirit is given to every man, to profit with all. The manifestation of the spirit is given to every man to profit with all. So notice here it uses the word 'manifestation.' That word manifestation means very simply this; it means something that's visible, tangible, that people can see, so he's saying God wants to operate through you, in a way that's tangible, that people can experience Him. I prophesied over someone the other day. I brought a word from God to them, and I shared with them things God showed me, that were so personal and so connected to that person, that when I asked them how did this affect you, they said I felt like my whole life was open before God and He was here talking to me personally.

So the gifts of the spirit are manifestations of a person, the Holy Spirit, so it's not like you have some kind of gift. You have a person, and you work with Him to bring His life forth, so it's all about a relationship with the Holy Spirit. Now notice here it says the manifestation of the spirit is given to everyone, so who is left out of the word everyone? There's no one left out. This is for you. Everyone includes you. If you read further down in Verse 11 it says, now these work the same self spirit dividing to every man severally as He wills. So God is very clear in the word. He wants every person to be able to flow in the spirit. Notice this, He gives the gifts of the spirit to everyone, so if you haven't functioned in them or flowed in them or received them yet, it's mostly because you don't know how to. If we show you how to, and you extend your faith, God will work through you. It says He gives them to everyone.

Okay, so next thing you notice about it is this, is it is a gift, so the gifts of the spirit are something God gives you, so you don't have to earn it. You don't have to stay in church a long time for this to happen. As soon as the Holy Spirit empowers you, or comes on you, and you're baptised in the spirit, you are able to operate in the gifts of the spirit immediately, if you will learn how to recognise and work with the Holy Spirit. It's very, very simple. It's never hard. It's just we have to grow this dimension in our life. Have you ever as a man - I remember my wife, we had a whole group of babies in a crèche crying and she said oh my one's crying. I said really? I can hear lots of babies crying, you know, that's what I heard. I could just hear babies crying, but she could hear, that's my child crying, because her ear was tuned in the midst of the noise to pick up the sound of someone she recognised.

So there is a lot of noise that we have going on in our head and in our lives. We need to learn how to calm down and quiet down, and just recognise when God is talking to you, so we want to help you with that and demonstrate that. The gifts of the spirit are given to everyone to profit all, so you notice here it's not an indication you're mature. God will give the gifts of the spirit to any person. It does not make them spiritual. It means they're just listening and responding to God, that's all. So a person can flow in the gifts of the spirit but have perhaps other areas of their life they're very immature, so it does not make you a very spiritual person being able to flow in the gifts of the spirit or the power of God. It just means you've learned how to operate by faith in that dimension, but the rest of your life you may have many issues and many problems.

We tend to put people that can move in the gifts of the spirit on this pedestal, as though they're something special and unusual, because we've got this idea that only special people will God use. We also have this wrong idea that you have to get your life together and get your act together before God can use you. I challenge you to find that anywhere in the Bible. It's just a religious concept, and if you think I've got to get my life together before God can use me, you'll spend all your life focussed on trying to make your life better, rather than focussing on walking with God, enjoying Him, and letting Him work through you. So God wants to work through everyone and the gifts are given to profit, they're given to profit others, so when God gives you a gift, it's not for you, it's for someone else. You're the delivery boy, so the gifts of the spirit, it's like I'm connected to God, I receive something from Him and I pass it on to someone else. That's what the gifts of the spirit are, so I'm just the channel through which this flows. I'm the gate through which God interacts with the person.

So it's good for you to see that you are described in the Bible as, you are a temple, or a house in which God dwells. You are a gate for the supernatural to come into the earth. Getting the idea? So once you see that it makes a huge, huge difference. Okay, now let's have a look at the different categories of gifts. It's in your notes under Section 2.3 and it says, notice how we look down here and we read, in the manifestation of spirits given to each one for the profit of all, for to one is given the word of wisdom through the spirit, to another the word of knowledge through the same spirit, to another faith by the same spirit, to another gifts of healings by the same spirit, to another working in miracles, to another prophecy, to another discerning of spirits, to another different kinds of tongues and interpretation of tongues. The one and the same spirit works all these things, distributing to each one individually as He wills.

So you notice there are nine distinct operations of the spirit there. It helps if we put them under three headings. It just gives you an idea of what they're about, and then we'll explain them more as we go through and teach about them, so here it is. First of all there are three of the gifts are gifts of revelation. That means God reveals to you something you didn't know. Now if I talk to someone and they tell me, then now I've learned it from them. If I've read it in a book, I've studied it and learned it, but if someone just tells me a secret, it reveals something to me. So the gifts of the spirit, three of the gifts of the spirit God just reveals something, you couldn't have worked it out. You just couldn't have known. You couldn't have known, like for example, I prophesied over a woman the other night and said at the age of between 10 and 14 she'd gone through these particular crises in her life, and this is how it affected her, and God was now wanting to set her free from what had happened.

We had some ministry for her. Afterwards she told me that there were two crises in her family, one when she was 10 and one when she was 14. There's no way I could have known that. All I'm doing is sharing what God is showing me, but for her it was like her whole life was opened up to God. Remember the woman at the well, in John 4 when Jesus spoke to her, Jesus asked her a little bit, interacted with her and then He said well why don't you bring your husband? She said I haven't got a husband, and He said to her that's true, you've had five husbands and now you're living with a man. When she went away she said I met someone who told me everything about my whole life. Now why did she say everything about her whole life when actually He'd only said one thing about her life? Because the impact of that supernatural revelation was to cause her to experience the sensation that all of her life was suddenly opened and God could see everything, so when you bring a word of knowledge, or move prophetically, it may not seem much to you.It's like it's very little to you, because it's not for you, but when it goes to the person oh, the person can be deeply impacted; how could you know that? It's like suddenly their whole world is opened up, and so for you it was like a little tentative step. For them it's like oh! This is a big deal, because now you've opened up something in their life. This is so powerful, to flow in the gifts of the spirit. It's wonderful to be able to operate in them.

Okay then, so there are three gifts. They're words of knowledge, word of knowledge, just a little bit of knowledge about a person, some fact about their past or present; a word of wisdom is a supernatural insight about what to do, or how a person needs to act, or what they should do at this time; and discerning of spirits - we'll describe that a little later - is the ability to see right into the root of what is behind things that are happening. It enables us to see the motivations of people; it enables us to see what the Holy Spirit is doing; it also enables us to discern demonic spirits.

There are three gifts of utterance where something is spoken and those are: the word of prophesy, and inspired something, words from God; diverse tongues; and interpretation of tongues, where the person speaks in a tongue and someone interprets, then gifts of power when something supernatural is done, so something's revealed, something's spoken, something's done, and those are by faith miracles are done, the working of miracles and gifts of healing all fall under those power miracles. Okay then, so now if we have a look then the next thing there is I want you to have a look in number four, believers can operate in all of the gifts. So every one of you is able to operate in all of the gifts. Okay, in Mark 16, Verses 17 and 18, notice what Jesus said, and this is associated with the great commission, so it's page six in your notes, number four.

So Mark 16, Verses 17 to 18. Now you know this verse well. This is what it says; These signs follow those who believe: In My name they will cast out demons; they'll speak in new tongues, take up serpents, drink anything deadly, it will not hurt them, and they will lay hands on the sick and they will recover. Now Jesus is giving the great commission. He's sending us into the harvest field, and He's sending people into cultures where the supernatural is well established. Now in a western culture, often people are very dull to things of the spirit or supernatural, but in other cultures, the majority of cultures in the world, there's a high level of awareness of the supernatural realm. You go into Asia, Africa, South America, these different countries, idolatry is practiced openly. Sorcery and witchcraft are practiced openly, and they have tremendous and very real power, so Jesus was sending His disciples into cultures that experience supernatural power. What they needed was something stronger, more powerful to deal with and confront the demonic realm.

As I say, in a western culture it's not so obvious, but in Asian cultures and other cultures of the world, these things are practiced very openly. You go to some villages, they all live in fear of the witch doctor and his power is real. They live in fear of the supernatural realm and so idolatry is practised. In our culture the supernatural's more hidden. It's not so out there, but it is still there, and so Jesus was sending them into cultures supernatural. He wanted them empowered spiritually to be able to do this, so notice what He said; These signs will follow those who believe. It doesn't say these signs will follow pastors. It doesn't say these signs will follow special people. It doesn't say these signs will follow just greatly anointed people. It just says, these signs will follow those who believe for these signs to follow, so God wants you to be a believer. You need to believe for God to work through you.

We believe God will work supernaturally. We believe He'll do it in another country. We believe He'll do it through Benny

Hinn, but what we struggle with is to believe, He would do it through me, and that's what He said: the signs follow believing, so we're going to inform you of the how to. You grow the believing for it to happen and start to stretch out, you'll be quite surprised. So notice several things there; casting out of demons which is discerning of spirits and also working of miracles and faith is involved in that, speaking in new tongues and maybe interpretations. You can see that one clearly. Taking up serpents has to do with wrestling with the demonic, gifts of revelation and prophesy, drinking any deadly thing, again supernatural miracles and laying hands on the sick, gifts of faith and healing.

So Paul made some instructions then, in 1 Corinthians 12. He said it is given to everyone. The manifestation of the spirit is given to everyone, so His desire was that every believer could flow in the gifts of the spirit, and that's my desire too. God wants you to, and we'll show you how to and it'll be great for you to step out and try to. So let me just give you an example of it. An example that can easily be found is the example of Ananias. Let me just find it for you, and we'll just read it for you in Acts, Chapter 9. In Acts, Chapter 9 there's a man called Ananias. Now remember Saul had been persecuting the church, and as he was going to Damascus he had an encounter, a supernatural encounter. He was knocked off his horse and he was struck blind. He went and fasted and prayed for three days. Then there was a disciple - Verse 10 of Chapter 9, Book of Acts - there was a disciple at Damascus named Ananias, and to him the Lord said in a vision - so notice he saw something, and in this seeing, God spoke to him. Now notice what God said to him. The Lord said to him arise, see? The Lord said to him in the vision Ananias - He called him by name - and he said here I am Lord. The Lord said to him arise, go into the street called Straight. Now notice he even was told what street to go to, and then He said inquire in the house of Judas. He's told what house to go to, find the house that Judas owns - He said and then there's someone in there by the name of Saul, so there's another word of knowledge, and he is praying.

Now notice the revelation that's coming, he's being told things he couldn't know, and Saul has seen in a vision a man called Ananias coming to him, so God is downloading to him words of knowledge and revelation. Then He said, I want you to go him and lay your hands on him and he'll receive his sight. Now this is a freaky thing, because he knows that Saul's been murdering all the Christians, and now God's telling him go to this place in this street, inquire, the guy is in there, and he's blind, and he's praying. I've shown him that you're going to come, and you're going to pray over him. Now that takes - remember this guy's life is on the line. Can you understand that all moving in the spirit, there's a point where you have to take a risk? This was a big risk wasn't it aye? He's having to go to the house of a murderer of Christians - that's a step of faith. He probably said goodbye to everyone before he went, just in case [Laughter] you know? [Laughs] And notice what he says, Ananias, I've heard a lot about this man, he does much evil to Your saints, so he started to reason with God about it. The Lord said go, he's chosen unto Me, and I will show him great things he must suffer for My name's sake.

So Ananias went his way, entered the house, laid his hands on him, he said brother Saul, Jesus that appeared to you in the way as you came, sent me that you might receive your sight and be filled with the Holy Ghost. Immediately he was healed and filled with the Holy Ghost, spoke in tongues. Isn't that a great story aye, great story, so there's an example of words of knowledge, works of wisdom, knowing what to do, prophetic utterance, speaking over him, gifts of healing, and faith flowing. It's great. That's a great story of many of the gifts all flowing together with one man. So we see now that you are designed to be supernatural. God wants you to operate in the supernatural. He is willing to do this for you. What is your part? What is the bit you've got to play? There are some responsibilities we have concerning the gifts of the spirit, so let me give you what they are. I'll lay them out for you, and then we'll finish this session, then we'll give you something to do, give you a little activation. This will be quite an easy one as well. Everything's easy, okay. Everything will be easy, and you've just got to step out and do something, it's really simple. So let's have a look there.

Gifts of the spirit are given to everyone, so if God gives it to me, what does He expect me to do? What's my part? There's a number of things that we're called to do, so I'm going to identify them. Now you notice I'm referring to the Bible all the time, because I want you to get a base from the word of God for how to operate in the spirit. If you have lots of spiritual experiences without having a word of God base, you can go all over the place. You'll find we'll continually draw you back to the written word of God as the judge of your spiritual experiences, okay. So here's several things that God requires of us. Number one, He wants you to learn how to flow with the Holy Spirit. He wants you to learn it. Your responsibility is to be a learner, and learning starts tonight and goes on for the rest of your life.

In 1 Corinthians 12:1, concerning spiritual gifts, I don't want you to be ignorant. So God expects you to put in the effort to learn. Nothing comes just easily. You have to put in some effort. You have to do something. We'll show you what kinds of things you do, so He wants us to learn how to work with the Holy Spirit to build others. So here's an interesting thing - God is wanting you to be a builder of people. Many people have got the wrong paradigm, and they have very much a paradigm where you come to church and you get blessed and ministered to, and church is all about you having your needs met. That's only a part of the truth. Actually the real truth is higher than that. God wants to meet your needs or bless you, so you can become a blessing to others, so flowing in the spirit is about discovering how to fulfil my destiny with God in the workplace, in the marketplace, wherever I am. So God expects me to learn and learning is a lifetime thing.

Secondly, we're expected to passionately desire the gifts of the spirit. 1 Corinthians 12:31, earnestly, passionately, oh! Love with the gifts of the spirit! Why? Because when you flow in them, it answers all arguments. If you have a miracle, no one can argue with the miracle. I remember being in a meeting, and there was a lady there and she was born deaf. I prayed for her, and both her ears opened up, and she could hear for the first time. You could just - like the whole meeting all stopped for this woman, and I watched in a moment as first of all there was shock because she could hear, then she started to cry, then she started to laugh. Then she was just bewildered about what was going on. It was quite extraordinary, and no one could deny that God had touched the woman. There was just no answer for it, so in particularly spiritual cultures, people just throng to get a miracle, so when I go into Asia they'll have meetings and they'll expect the power of God to flow. People just get saved, all kinds of people get saved, because you can't argue with the power of God. You just can't argue with the power of God. You get deaf ears opened, blind eyes opened, people get healed and things happen. That's God, and people want the God who does that.

In Pakistan in the meetings there that Dave was at, Pastor David, my son was at, all kinds of miracles were happening, and people just flock to come in and receive Christ. Muslims come in from all over to receive Christ, because they're seeing the power of God. There's something about the power of God that just stops everyone in their tracks. I had one guy, we did the seminar here, and he learned how to pray for the sick, went back to his workplace, and he was working on one of the machines there, and one of his friends walked by. He was obviously in pain in his back so he said hey, what's happening? He said I've got a lot of pain in my back. He said well I've got two answers for you; one, you come to church on Sunday and we pray for you there or two, I pray for you now. Which will it be? Now that's pretty bold to do that, and so he said oh, okay, pray for me now. So he just left the machine for the moment, laid hands on him and began to pray. He said how do you feel? He said well it's a little bit better - prayed again, the guy was totally healed, and everyone's watching.

So the whole of the workplace was affected, because of one miracle that took place. Now of course they didn't all come to Christ, but that guy came to Christ, and favour came on them to start a prayer meeting in the business, to pray for the business and for the workers. Isn't that great? So God wants you to be passionate for this, to really yearn for it. The Bible instructs us: earnestly desire the gifts. Here's the third thing and that is, in 2 Timothy 1:6, it tells us I remind you to stir up the gifts of God which is in you through the laying on of my hands. The word stir up means to kindle a fire, to get something activated and happening, so we're called to stir up the gifts. So this is completely contrary to a passive, waiting around and praying for a revival or hoping that one day God will do something. This says you stir yourself up - and I'll show you exactly how to stir yourself up, and what you do that gets yourself stirred up, and stay stirred up, so you begin to find God working through you. So stir up there.

Here's the fourth thing the Bible tells us in 1 Thessalonians 5:19; don't quench the Holy Ghost. In other words, quench means to put out a fire that God started, so it says don't quench the Holy Spirit. Control, and fear in your life, they go together, they quench God working. Unbelief - oh, I don't think God could do this - that will quench God working in your life. There are things that facilitate the spirit of God working, and some things quench His working in your life; reasonings in your mind will quench the flow of the Holy Spirit. Negative, critical talk will grieve and quench the Holy Spirit, so we're called not to quench Him but to learn how to co-operate with Him. And finally the last one is this; don't neglect the gifts of the spirit. 1 Timothy 4:14, don't neglect the gift that's in you. In other words, don't take it lightly, don't just waste what God has given you, don't despise the little beginnings that you start with. Even if you start with a little and it doesn't seem much, it can grow. It can grow until it becomes a great flow through your life.

So those are some of the first things that we see concerning the gifts of the spirit, that there's supernatural operations, you're designed to be a supernatural being, to connect with heaven and earth, you're designed to move and flow with the Holy Spirit. God wants us to add understanding how to do it. He promises He'll give the gifts to every believer, every person. He desires to work through you, and it's not about maturity, it's about faith, believing for Him to do it, so you will have to extend your faith. Now faith means something like this: I am convinced in my heart God is willing to do this, and so I will step out, and start to put myself in a place where God can work through me. Always there's this threshold you've got to cross where no matter what you've been taught, you have to step out and just do something. That's the point where you start to grow and develop in the things of the spirit [laughs] and you'll find God will always come with you. He won't let you down. He'll always be there.

There are many different realms that we can flow within the spirit. There's different ways we can operate in the spirit. You don't have to copy the way someone does it. God wants to work through you naturally and easily in a very natural way, and as I demonstrate it you'll see it's very natural. There's not any contriving or striving or anything, it's very natural. So we're going to stop now, and I want you to do an activation, okay? So what would that activation be? Well again I want it to be very simple so the first one, who was successful at hugging someone? Okay, great, you all hugged someone or two people so that wasn't that hard was it aye? Had to put your arms out and just hold on. [Laughs] Okay, so here's the next one I want you to do. I want you to find someone you don't know, and find something that you don't know about them, find something about them.

Now how would you go about finding something about someone that you didn't know? You'll have to ask. Now this is quite important when you're going to move in the spirit, you'll need to start asking questions. You ask questions of the Holy Spirit and He shows you things. Okay, so here's a good way to start. Go up and just meet someone that you don't know and find out something you didn't know about them. We'll do that for about five minutes, okay? So you can leave your seat.

Okay, are we ready for this session? Welcome to the next session. Second session we want to talk about hearing the voice of God tonight and I want to show you how you go about hearing the voice of God, how we recognise the voice of God, and I want to first of all give you a context for it. We're going to look in Galatians, Chapter 3 and Verse 2. The reason we want to focus on hearing the voice of God is because this is a major key to the supernatural being released, a major key for the supernatural being released. I want you to read with me if you've got a Bible or the notes - if it's an even page you may not have it, except in the ones you get tomorrow. So this is Paul writing, so just if it's not there that's okay, just focus on listening rather than searching.

In Galatians 3, Verse 2, Paul is writing to the Galatians Church. They started off as a very vibrant Holy Ghost church and now they had lost it altogether, so he's writing and he's bringing adjustment to them. One of the issues he addresses is their loss of the manifestation of the Holy Spirit. One of the key reasons they've lost the manifestation of the spirit was legalism. They came back under laws and rules, do this, don't do that, and they lost completely the flow of the spirit, so he begins to challenge them and he asks them two questions. Now what you've got to see is when he asks these two questions he's actually - each one is to bring about an insight of where they're missing the mark, and the problem he's addressing is that they thought you become mature by obeying the laws. What he's saying is no, you need the power and presence of the Holy Spirit. So notice the question he asks. I want to learn this from you, I want you to tell me this; did you receive the Holy Spirit by the works of the law, or by the hearing of faith?

He asked them a question, how did you receive the Holy Ghost into your life? How did you get born again? How did you get baptised in the spirit? How did you get a supernatural change in your life? Did you get it by working hard, or did you get it by the hearing of faith? Very simple. What is the answer? The hearing of faith. How do you get saved? You hear the word of God, and you believe and respond, and the power of God is activated by your response, see? That's how a person gets saved, so he appeals to the foundation of their Christian experience. How did you get saved? Did you get saved and supernaturally changed, and the spirit come into your life, because you worked hard and went to church and did good things - or did you get it because you heard the word of God and believed, and when you responded the spirit of God came? The answer's really clear. It was never by the works of the law. They were supernaturally transformed when the spirit of God came into their life.

He wants them to get that answer, because now he's going to ask them the real question. So he asks them the first question to get their head clear - how did you start in this game? Did you start by working hard to be a better person, or did you start by believing God? Well believing God. Great! He's asking now the real question he wants to ask, so then he goes on and he said: are you so foolish? You began in the spirit, and you think you'll become mature by the flesh? Have you suffered so many things in vain? He says now, He that supplies the spirit to you, and works miracles among you, does He do it by the works of the law, or the hearing of faith?

So you notice he's asking almost the same question, but he's applying it to something else. So the first one was like this: how did you get saved? How did you get your initial experience with God - work hard, or believe God? Which was it? Believe God.

Now he does it a different way, he asks the same thing. This time he says how does God supply the spirit to you? How does God do miracles among you? So in other words he's saying, how do the gifts of the spirit flow? How do miracles happen? Work hard, or hear God and respond? The answer's really clear isn't it? Now he's framed it up that way by appealing to how they started as a believer. They heard God's voice, heard God speaking to them and they chose to believe and respond, and they were into a flow of the spirit. It was supernatural. He said the moving in the spirit's the same way, it's exactly the same way. It's not by working hard. It's not by trying hard. It's by extending your faith to believe and listen to God, so here is why, if we want to move in the supernatural, we must practice hearing and identifying the voice of God. This is the significant key to operating in the spirit. It is the hearing of faith. I extend my faith to believe God will speak to me, I extend my faith to believe God wants to use me.

Now for some of you that may be a challenge, because it's easier to believe He'll use someone else, than use you, and the core challenge is: will you believe in your heart, actually there's no reason at all why God would not use me. There's no reason at all why He would not want to do this. God loves me, He's justified me, I'm accepted. He wants to work through me. He's designed me to work this way. Of course I believe, and I'll extend now to listen and hear His voice, expect to hear His voice - and I'm going to apply this when it comes to working with one another in the exercises. I'll get you starting to stir your faith to believe, and listen, and then stretch out to see what God does. That's how the activations will work, so for example - so always it involves faith, I must extend out and believe that God will work through me.

Secondly, I need to tune in to hear God speaking to me; and three, I need to step out and actually act on what God gives me. Think about how you got saved. You heard the word of God, faith rose to believe it to be true, and then you stepped out and acted by speaking out, or confessing Christ in some way, so the flowing in the spirit actually works the same way. It all works the same way, and so we just need to practice hearing the voice of God. In John 5, 19 to 20, Jesus answered and said: I tell you, the Son can do nothing of Himself, but whatever He sees the Father do, that's what He does. So He says the Father tells him, or shows Him, everything He's doing, so Jesus' miracles were done by what He saw the Father doing. He just spoke out and did that. Notice He didn't heal every person. Sometimes He healed everyone, but you know there's a guy by the door of the temple, He walked past him every time He went into the temple and never did anything. Why was that? Because He never saw the Father healing on that day, but when Peter went by, after being baptised in the spirit, Peter looked at him and he worked a miracle and the guy was healed.

So was it the will of God for him to be healed? It certainly was, but there was a flow of the spirit that Jesus listened to. So He went to one place by the well, by the Bethsaida [a place reputed for its healing properties] and the porters there, and there's a whole heap of crippled people and one He heals. So why one? That's not very fair. I don't know. I don't understand all the ways God works. All we know is, He saw what the Father was doing, and did that. He avoided or resisted pressure to try and meet every need. He learned how to listen to the Holy Spirit and work with the Holy Spirit, so we're not called to fix all problems. We're not called to solve everything. We are called to learn how to yield, extend our faith, listen to God, and obey Him, and it's in the little things you get the miracles. Let me give you an example.

Before I was a Christian I was raised a Catholic. When I became a Christian I stopped going to the Catholic Church and started to attend another church, a spiritual church. It was a great offence to my grandmother, and she was deeply offended by it. We had some significant issues over that and anyway her birthday was coming up. I thought I need to get her something and my thinking in those days was you better make it up somehow, thought I'd get her a nice gift, so I went downtown. The day came and went and I got so busy I missed it. I thought oh no, double banger. [Laughter] I missed the birthday, and I didn't go to church and I'm going to hell, you know? This is not good [Laughter] so I thought then what I need to do then - my reasoning, which is not a good reasoning, was I need to buy a nice gift to make it up. Actually that would never make it up. You just couldn't appease the thing like that, but I did want to buy a gift anyway so I went to the shops and I was looking and I couldn't work out what to get.

I went past this shop and I felt the Holy Spirit say go in there. It was a religious shop, books and things, and I went in there and I looked around and there was stuff I didn't really like there. It was full of all kinds of stuff, and I was wrestling with God over it. I saw a little picture there and it was the shepherd with the sheep - you know the picture, I'm the good shepherd and there's a picture of a lovely shepherd, robes and Jesus [laughs] and he probably doesn't look anything like that, but that was the picture. Anyway I felt the Holy Spirit say I want you to buy that and I just resisted. I just really - I thought no, no, no, I don't even like those things. So I walked up the street, came back and I thought no, I can't see anything, I'll go back to the shop. So I went back, I thought I've got nothing to lose. I feel God's telling me, I'll just get it, I'm just going to get the picture.

So I bought the picture, and I bought some dried flower arrangement, and I put it all together, bundled it off with a note, sorry I missed your birthday, here's a little gift and blah blah blah. Anyway I met my grandmother a little later and I said to her did you get the birthday gift? She said yes, thank you very much, I really enjoyed the little dried flower arrangement. It was very, very pretty and smelled nice and so on. Oh good. I said what about the picture? She said oh, she said that did bring back some memories, and she said when I was at school in boarding school at the age of 12, a girlfriend and me got into trouble with one of the teachers. We wanted to try and put it right with the teacher, and so we decided we would buy a gift, and we bought that picture for her. [Laughter]

Now only God could come up with something like that. We're talking something like 60 years prior, and God knew what she did, and when she saw the picture it triggered the memory of trying to put something right in a relationship that was wrong, and she associated with my gift a desire to put right with her something that was wrong. Now only God could come up with stuff like that aye, so this is the blessing of being able to listen to the Holy Spirit on different situations. Okay, getting the idea? So we need to hear what God is saying. Alright then, so another example is found in Acts 14, Verses 8 to 10. Paul is in Lystra and a certain man without strength in his feet was sitting, a cripple from his mother's womb, he'd never walked, and the man heard Paul speaking. Paul - now notice what it says - Paul observed him intently, and saw he had faith to be healed. Now that's an interesting statement.

Paul fixed his eyes on the man - in other words he stared at him, and as he stared at him he perceived, that's in his spirit, that the man had faith to be healed. What does it look like if you've got faith to be healed? What would you be looking for? What would you be looking for? He perceived. In other words there was an inner knowing that this man had faith. He went to him and prayed and immediately the man rose up and was healed, so this is he saw something. So in flowing with the Holy Spirit, or hearing the voice of God, we begin to hear that sometimes we see things, sometimes we hear things, sometimes we will just perceive or sense something in our spirit. So let's now have a look, as we've seen how Paul operated, and we see how Jesus operated, and we see that it's by the hearing of faith that we can work in miracles. Now we want to look at how to hear the voice of God.

What does the voice of God sound like? So the first thing I want to do is to point out this, is that when you hear the voice of God, you will hear from within, not from without. God put His Holy Spirit within you. 1 Corinthians 6 and Verse 17 says he that's joined to the Lord is one spirit, so that's like a husband and wife being married. So being born again, your spirit is joined to the Lord, so if you're going to hear the voice of God you will hear Him in your spirit. You won't necessarily hear Him with your audible ears. You won't necessarily see anything with your natural eyes. You will have to develop your spiritual sense. Getting the idea? Okay then, now what I want to do is I'm just going to get three people up, and I want to just do a visual illustration for you to give you an idea of something - I want to put something visual in front of you, to help you understand something spiritual. So I won't refer to all the notes as I do it, but what I've got in the notes I will teach it by doing a visual demonstration for you. That okay?

Okay, so why don't we get three guys to come up. Can we get three guys? There we are, there's one there, Brian, two guys over here. Won't you guys come on up on the stage and just help me out here okay, help me out here. Alright then, so you don't have to do anything, you've just got to stand there, okay, so here we go. See, stand there and face over here, this is perfect. Come over and stand over here, face over here and you face over there. There we are, it's perfect, alright then, you can see everyone. Now God has designed us and we are body, soul and spirit. We're a spirit man; with a soul; living inside a body, so your body has five senses: see, taste, touch, we can interact with the physical world so we have physical senses and they will all feed into the soul.

Okay, I want you to just turn around this way here like this now, put your hand on his shoulders, and you put your hand on his shoulders. That's right - so if I'm interacting with Brian and connecting with Brian I see his physical body, and if I look into eyes I can see there's a person in there, but what is in there is the hidden man of the heart. The hidden man of the heart is found here. It's the soul, the mind, will, emotions, memories, personality and it's the spirit man. Okay. Now his spirit man, and everyone has a spirit dimension - you have a spirit being, a part of you which is spirit - the spirit man also has spiritual senses. So we just all turn around, face this way again. Okay, now the spirit man has spiritual senses. Just stand there, that's right. So his spirit man, dwelling inside him, energises his body. Your spirit is incredibly important.

The Bible says that if the spirit is absent from the body, a person's dead, so this is how important your spirit is. Your spirit energises and gives life to your soul and your body. Your spirit is a vital part of you, but your spirit has many functions, so one function of your spirit is to energise your soul and body. Your spirit quickens your body, because if your spirit is withdrawn from your body, the body dies, so your spirit's very important. If you spirit is wounded or damaged or hurt or injured you tend to get sick much more readily, and the Bible tells that. It says a broken spirit dries the bones, so if your spirit is damaged in some way, then it will affect your body and your body's health. Another aspect of your spirit is that your spirit illuminates your mind. See, it says the spirit of man is the lamp of the Lord, lighting up all the inner parts, so your spirit will illuminate your soul with ideas and thoughts. How many have ever had a hunch that turned out to be right? Where did the hunch come from? Oh, that's sixth sense. No it isn't, it's your spirit. The sixth sense is actually your spirit.

So when we get a hunch or an intuition, actually there's an idea come from our spirit that's come into our mind, that's what we're picking up and if you act on it then you start to find things happen, for example so we now see that we are designed to operate, we're quite unique. The soul area here is mind, will and emotions, and so your soul retains memories, memories of various experiences, so when you have a new experience you reference the old ones and come up with the conclusion. For example - we'll just turn all around this way again, face all this way. Now I went to Singapore one time and when I went to Singapore there was this dreadful smell, and I couldn't work out what the smell was. I had no reference point for it whatsoever, so I could smell, but there was no experience to attach it to. I couldn't recognise it. It was just an unknown horrible smell, then someone said oh - I said what's that smell? They said oh, that's Durian and they brought out this big fruit, and it's Durian, and it smelt! Some people love it, some people hate it and mostly you can't eat it in a building, it smells everything out.

Now prior to that I had no reference point. Next time I came around [sniffing sound] oh, Durian, you see because I could smell and the sense would then register and the mind and memory would raise up them something and I was aware that's what that means. That means Durian. That means a fruit. I had a picture, a smell and an experience to relate this to and so next time round, no trouble, Durian! Now just turn around and face this way again. Your spirit man will also pick up spiritual sensations, and they will go to the same place that the physical sensations went to. They go into your brain, into your memory, inside you, and your mind processes what you get, so as a unique person you can receive from the physical world and recognise things from a memory bank, but you can also receive from the realm of the spirit, and also build up experience so you quickly recognise different things. You quickly recognise a different kind of spirit. You quickly recognise various sorts of things. Why? Because you have developed your spiritual senses and built experience. Get the idea?

Paul writes in (or the Hebrew writer in) Hebrews 5:14 says: you remain immature, because you haven't exercised your spiritual senses to discern. You've got to practice to discern. Do you get it right every time? No. Why do we not get it right every time? Because our mind argues all the time, you know and I'll talk about that in a moment. Okay then, so if you just put your hand on his shoulder now and your hand on his shoulder over here. Right, that's right. So when you are born again the Holy Spirit comes in and becomes joined one spirit with the Lord, so we see in 1 Corinthians 6:17 very clearly, he that's joined to the Lord is one spirit. That's how close you are to Him all the time, so everywhere you go you carry the presence of God, and God knows all things, so in your spirit you know a lot, and you have access to the source of lots of things all the time, all the time. He's never going to leave you, never going to turn away from you. You have access all the time to the presence of God, all the time.

How do you get in tune with that access? You've got to silence all the noise that goes on in your head and tune in to your spirit. So now how am I going to hear the voice of God? Well the first thing it's helpful to think of is where am I going to hear Him? The first thing to recognise is you're not going to hear Him out here saying 'Hello, this is God." [Laughter] You're not going to get that and - just all turn and face this way - so if you go looking for signs and fleeces and all that kind of stuff, you're acting immaturely. That's not where we're to be looking for God outside us. It's not where He's to be found. He can be found inside you, so if you're going to grow in the things of the spirit, you have to develop what's inside you. Getting the idea? So you find many immature Christians are constantly looking for something outside them, looking for something shaking or moving or this or that or a feeling or anything, but they're looking in the wrong place, because the devil can manipulate circumstances, and manipulate everything around you. He can make storms happen. He can do all kinds of things.

So we don't look outside ourselves. We look to our spirit man, because that spirit man is joined to the Holy Spirit, and therefore has access to heaven. Put your hands all on one another like that. Okay now, here we go. So the physical man accesses the physical world, but through my spirit I can access the realm of heaven all the time, free to access the presence of God. I've just got to learn how that happens. Okay, so turn around now. We're going to show you how it happens. Turn around, put your arms on one another's shoulder like that. Okay, so if God is wanting to communicate to me, how will He do it? Very simply, the Holy Spirit will communicate with my spirit. How does He do it? Usually in one of three ways. Now He can do it many ways but there's usually one of three ways that there's direct spirit-to-spirit communication.

Here it is; number one, you see something. You don't see it with your natural eyes. The Holy Spirit puts a picture into your spirit, and that picture in your spirit rises up into your mind, or the Holy Spirit will speak a word into your spirit, and that word will rise up in your mind, or the Holy Spirit will just put an impression. You don't know how you know, but you just somehow know something. If I say: do you know you're saved? You say yes, of course I know I'm saved. How do you know? I don't know, I just know. Well the Bible tells me, but I know. I know. You know because there's an inward knowing. How do you inward know? Inward knowing is the witness of the Holy Spirit with your spirit, you're a child of God. It's an inner knowing. That's how you know you're saved.

Okay, so the Holy Spirit will do this, so if I'm going to be tuning into the voice of God here's the first thing. The first thing is, I have to quiet the noise. You have got noise all the time in your head. That's why I hate having headphones on, just noise in the head. Some people love it, and I don't mind listening to a certain amount of music, but I don't want my head to be full of noise of something else. So what kind of noise is in your head? All kinds of memories, all kinds of pictures, all kinds of experiences, things that have happened, all kinds of things in there. You have demonic voices talking to you, they fill your mind with accusation, condemnation, not good enough, who do you think you are? All that kind of stuff is noise, and the noise is a block to hearing God, so if I'm going to hear God I need to number one, know I'm going to hear from my spirit so I should activate my spirit by prayer, praying in tongues; secondly, I need to quiet my soul so that my mind is not busy and all over the place. Thirdly, I need to tune in to what will be spontaneous.

Now the language of your heart is different to the language of your head. The language of your head is logical, structured, line upon line, and it's thought through carefully. That's how the language of the mind works. Its logic, so for example if you're working out some mathematics you're logical - one, two, three, four. You're trying to work out where to put something, one, two, three, four. If you're trying to create something, now it's intuitive and you start to flow, so the way we're designed is like this. Amazing design God has given to us. We're designed to be supernatural, it's amazing. Your brain is divided into two hemispheres or two parts. With the left side it's the logic side, so if we got him doing some maths I suppose he can - do you do maths or something? Okay, suppose he can do maths, or he's trying to figure something out, and we put a brain scan on him and try to find out what part of his brain is busy, all the left side will be busy. If he's dreaming and imagining or creating it'll be the right side of his brain, so you're designed so that one part of you is logical and process oriented, one, two, three, four, blah, blah, blah, like that. The other part of you is intuitive. It gets ideas, there's flashes and ideas and things like that and it's creative, so if you're a creative person you'll be very active in this part. If you're a logical person you'll be very active in that part of your brain, but both sides exist for every person.

Now when the Holy Spirit is speaking to us what happens is, He imparts into our spirit, and which side of the brain do you reckon it comes up into? It comes up into the right, so what do you get? You just get spontaneous thought. You get a picture just pops into your mind, or you get a word just suddenly comes into your mind. So what happens immediately after that comes in, the other part of your brain takes over and starts to argue it down and dismiss it. Men are often quite bad at that, and their wives are often quite intuitive, so some of you may recognise - and we won't ask for any show of hands - of a decision making process where the husband felt this was the right thing to do and his wife said I don't know, I don't feel very happy about that. He says well why not? It's logical, it all works out and she says no, no, I don't know, it just doesn't feel right. Well I can't work with that, you know, that's just unreasonable. You're right, it is unreasonable - it's intuitive. Then later on you go ahead and do it, and you find actually it was the wrong thing to do, because your wife had this intuitive impression, and it was of greater value in discerning what something was than your (my) mind was.

I'll give you another example. How many have met someone and they look good, sounded good but you just felt something was not right about this person? Something's creepy. That's the kind of language a woman would use - creepy [Laughter] you know, don't like that guy. I don't like him. You know, they say I don't like him, and the man may say what's wrong? There's nothing wrong with him. You know, he can't figure it out, but he's operating out of logic, what he can see, what he can hear and he's working on a reasoning basis. She's picking up intuitively from her spirit there's something not right about this person or situation, I don't feel right about it. Now you think about this in Colossians 3:15 it says let the peace of God be the umpire of your heart, so if you feel troubled and no peace in your spirit, then no matter what it looks like, you know it's going to be a problem. Initially you don't know that but you find out after you've had a number of experiences where you overruled your spirit, did something and then it didn't work out too good. You learn then actually listen to the voice of your heart more carefully.

Now we do need to work things out. We've got a capacity to do that. We should develop our mind and intelligence, but we need to also develop the intuitive side of us, so when

God speaks to us it's very simple. I just calm down and quiet my soul to listen. I stir up my spirit through praying and focussing on the Lord, and as He speaks, spontaneous thoughts, pictures or impressions come into my soul, and I pick them up as an impression. Now you don't just do away with your brain and shoot your brain. You actually then enquire, so I'll give you an example of someone. I was talking to one person, and I had a word of knowledge they were extremely lonely and so I said I just feel an impression that actually you're struggling with a lot of loneliness. No, no, no, no, I'm not lonely. It came again, so I said it again. No, no, no, I'm not lonely. Now that's two denials, but it came again, and so I said in the end I actually feel you're quite lonely. I feel God's laying on my heart you're struggling with relationships and friendships, and you're lonely. God added me a little bit more. She broke down and began to weep, so I was right the first time, but the person tried to pretend that wasn't so, and just the impression kept coming and coming and coming.

So remember it was just an impression that came that I couldn't shake off, so when I gave voice to it then God was able to move. So the impressions that you get, your mind will always argue them. Your mind will act like that can't be so, it couldn't be true. Like you see a person smiling and God says they've got grief in their heart, and you look at them and you think no, sorry, got that one wrong. [Laughter] You see your mind tries to reason the flow of the spirit, so we need to learn how to train our mind to ask the right questions, so my spirit can receive information from the Holy Spirit that my mind would never know. The role of your natural mind then is to enquire, Holy Spirit, what does that mean? How do I work with that? What do You want me to do about that? So you enquire of God, rather than reason it all away. So there it is, it's not quite so difficult.

So why is it some people have trouble hearing the voice of God? Now the trouble that people have with hearing the voice of God falls it seems to me into two categories. It falls firstly into the people who are Dr Spock on Star Trek. They are totally head, and they just reason everything,

everything's structured. Usually with a person like that, there's strong spirits sit around their mind, and they're disconnected from their heart. Often there's issues been in their life that have disconnected them. They many times need healing or deliverance or setting free, or training in how to engage with their heart, because they've lived out of their head and logic all their life, and they haven't developed their spiritual side. So very often there's spirits of rationalism and unbelief, rejection and all kinds of things sit around that person, but they can be set free, and they can develop the capacity of tuning in to spontaneity, to spontaneous ideas, to thoughts, to feelings, to impressions, and learning to recognise and identify and name them.

The other extreme is where you get someone who's often quite broken relationally, and everything is God, God told me this, God told me that, God told me this. Now it's like there's this flow where everything God told them. When you hear that, you know two or three things; number one, God isn't saying all those things. Number two, they're very broken people, and three, they've got major problems relationally, and so they're putting it all out there of God to portray some spiritual hotline. The reality is we don't hear God talking all the time that clearly. We have impressions and we learn to be led by... God gives you wisdom to run your life without Him having to tell you what to do. He doesn't tell you what to put on your shopping list. It's your job to figure that one out. He doesn't tell you what colour you should paint something. He gives you room to be creative. He doesn't tell us everything to do in our life, or we're like a puppet being told what to do. He actually works with us in a relationship where we work with Him, He's the senior partner and He guides us, but He gives us room to participate in life, so you've got to learn to find the things that you yourself have and own them, rather than say it's all God.

When I hear people saying God told me this, God told me that, I know one, God isn't telling them all those things; two, there's just a big show, and I'm not meeting the real person; three, there's brokenness inside. They really need help. A person like that usually is unstructured in their life, and create havoc in a church where you're trying to flow and develop things in the spirit. You have to actually bring them into discipline where they have to learn to structure their life and stop just listening to every impression that comes, because they've got turmoil in the soul, and haven't learnt to filter out what's God and what isn't. So both extremes happen, but none of you are in that extreme. You're all here in that happy group who will just be opened up to listen to God, aren't we wonderful? Okay then, so again just summarising it again: when God speaks He speaks into our spirit, get the idea? And it'll come up as an impression which comes into your mind, and then you just focus on that, and then begin to speak and act on what God gives you.

As you speak and act on it, then the spirit of God moves, and that's when people get touched. Okay? Well let's give them a clap and thank them for helping out. [Applause] Good stuff, thank you. Okay, so are you getting an idea now about how all of this works, because I want you to understand it clearly and [laughs] there, we'll see. Now I want to just give you two or three examples out of the Bible just to support what I've been saying, then we'll get you to do an activation, how about that? [Silence] Oh, there was a lot of enthusiasm there, that's right! [Laughter] Okay, so again this is not in your notes today but it will be there tomorrow, so let me just give you a few examples. You might want to just jot them down if you wish to, but let me just give them.

The first one is found in Habakkuk, Chapter 2, Verse 1. He said I will stand on my watch, and set myself on the rampart, and watch to see what the Lord will say to me. Notice this word, I will watch to see what God will say. So he did a couple of things. Number one, he positioned himself to be quiet. This is important to hearing the voice of God, you've got to quiet yourself down, so when I get to do activations with you we'll get you to do a couple of things. One of the things we'll get you to do is to pray in tongues so your spirit becomes energised, alive with the flow of the Holy Spirit. The second thing we'll get you to do, is just be quiet and focus your attention to just listen for a flow of spontaneous thoughts that come, then the third thing is we'll get you to then identify what you're thinking or feeling or what's happening, and speak it out.

Okay, so Habakkuk positioned himself to hear God, quietened himself, and then he focussed on intuitive flow of seeing, hearing. That's how he got it, and he was able to discern it. God spoke to him by a picture. In 1 Samuel 3:10, you remember the story of Samuel, and Samuel was lying down, and the Lord came and spoke to him and said Samuel! Samuel! And he jumped up and ran to Eli. Why did he jump up and run to Eli? Very simply, he heard something so strongly he thought it was Eli. He didn't recognise that it was God's voice, so it takes time to recognise the voice of God speaking to you. You've got to practice until you get used to oh, that is the voice of God, I'm recognising Him speaking to me. I know that's God speaking - and there are a number of ways we can get that. A third example there is in Mark 2, Verse 8, it says Jesus perceived in His spirit that they were reasoning. He perceived in His spirit they were reasoning, so it was He knew something. Now what was going on, get the picture, Jesus is speaking - now get this - He worked out what they were thinking. How did He figure out what they were thinking? He felt it in His spirit what they were thinking.

Now you've probably had an experience like that, where you were talking with someone, or they were talking, and then suddenly you felt something about that person, a thought rose up. You just perceive it in your spirit. You can't shake it off, you just know you can feel it's there. So the third example is the one we saw at Acts 14:9, where Paul looked at the man intently and saw he had faith to be healed. How did he see it? He perceived it in his spirit. There was a knowing inside, so you'll discover then that all of the moving in the spirit, moving in the supernatural, comes out of intimacy or connection with the Holy Spirit, where we learn to recognise His voice and act on it. The more you act on it, the easier it is to recognise. The more you practice walking with God and listening and responding to His impressions, the more easily it comes to you. It's like Jesus said, if you have ears to hear, more will be given. If you don't have ears to hear, even the little you have you lose, so it's like you have to use it or lose it. You've got to continually develop listening to God in your personal private life, so it flows out of devotion.

Okay then, so the last thing I'll finish this session with, and then we'll get you to do something. There are other ways that people receive revelation of course, but what I want to show is just some things about the revelations God gives. There are a couple of checks that you want to run by anything that you think God has given you, and here's what they are. Number one - so these are tests of revelation. If you think you've got something from God - you'll find this on Page 19 in your notes - number one, does it agree with the Bible? If it doesn't agree with the written word of God, the Holy Spirit wrote the written word of God; will He who wrote that Bible tell you something different to what He wrote? Not going to happen, so if you come up with a revelation, and you say that God has spoken to you this thing, but it's contrary to what the written word of God says, you got it wrong. You've actually just got it wrong, and it's come either just as a random thought, it's come out of your own desires or thoughts and perhaps that's how you got it - but you got it wrong.

If it disagrees with the Bible it didn't come from God. You've got to have the Bible as your standard for testing all revelation, so you know, if you find that you've got something, and you think God's told you to do this and you find it's completely the opposite to what the word of God says, you got it wrong. If you keep getting it wrong, you should go and get some counsel to sort out if something's going on inside you. Getting the idea? So if people come to you and say: God told me to do this and it's very clear, you know, God told me it was okay, we're in love, we can sleep together, you know, hello, give me a break! [Laughter] You're not married, you know? The Bible says those that commit fornication shan't inherit the kingdom of God, so He's not going to tell you that it's going to go good for you, personally, if He's told you in the written word something different. Use the Bible. You've got to become familiar with the Bible, load yourself up, read the Bible, get familiar with the Bible and automatically you'll be filled with thoughts of God that are useful in ministering to people - very helpful.

Okay, the second thing is does it line up with the character of God? Is that something that God would be likely to do, you know, like the devil took Jesus up into a high mountain and said come on, the word of God says cast yourself down, there's angels will take care of you, you want to jump. In other words, I'll put it another way - he was standing on a high place and said go on, jump, it'll be okay, you'll just float to the ground. You see this is contrary - it may have been what the words said, but actually it was a misrepresentation of the nature of God. Interesting thing, God seldom takes someone and suddenly moves them from here up to some big thing. God grows you step by step, so it's not the nature of God to want you to suddenly show yourself off in some big way or public exhibition, or to make a big scene of any kind, or to do something spectacular. He just grows you little by little by little, so if it doesn't seem like it's the nature of God, it probably isn't.

Then finally - or two other things - does it produce good fruit? So one way of testing a revelation is if the fruit of it is good. That's why we'll teach you to ask after you've prayed or ministered to someone hey, how did that go? What did you sense as a result of me sharing with you these things? In other words just get a bit of feedback. The person says well that was great man, it really helped me, touched me - you get feedback. If there's fruit from God it's always good. Fruit from heaven is gentle and reasonable, open to reason. If for example you get someone who says well just God told me, and you can't reason with them, that is definitely not God, because the Bible says in James, the wisdom that comes from heaven is quite easily entreated. You can appeal and talk and interact, so we'll teach you when it comes to ministering a word from God that, just do it gently, don't say well God told me like you're the authority in the earth. Just hey listen, I just sense this or I just felt this or I had an impression, maybe God, about this. In other words just do it much more low key. It's easier for you to interact with the person, easier for them to receive as well, not so dogmatic, okay?

The final one is, if it comes from God it will bear witness with your spirit. When something is right your own spirit bears witness to it. How many have had someone tell you something - I taught Michelle what to do but Michelle had some guy come up to her, said oh God's told me that I'm going to marry you. Now what does she feel straight away? Now this is the dilemma when some guy carries on like that. A good Christian girl wants to please the Lord, now he's saying God's told me this thing and she doesn't feel it in her heart, but she wants to please God. You throw people into turmoil with that kind of stuff. It's very manipulative. I said to her tell him just straight, God didn't tell me that, so goodbye. [Laughter] In other words own your own life. I said he can think what he thinks, and he can say what he says, but actually if it doesn't witness with your spirit, don't go with it.

I've seen many people trapped into relationships, into business deals, if they'd listened to their spirit, they'd have never been happy about it, but they kind of got impressed that someone was very prophetic or very spiritual. How did they get impressed? Because they projected it out that they were, but the wisdom from God is easily entreated. It's gentle and pure, and it produces good fruit. One of the things it'll witness with your spirit, so if something doesn't register as being right, then just say well thank you very much, but no thanks, I'm not going to go with that. You can thank the person, be polite, you don't have to be rude, but we don't need to receive things that aren't right, so let your own spirit bear witness with that, whether this bears witness of good fruit or not. Okay now, why don't we just stop now and I'll get you to stand up and turn around and sit down and we're going to give you an activation.

Okay then, now what I want to do in this session, first of all I want to get you all to do an activation. I'll just show you what it is in just a moment, and then I'll introduce you to activations and how they work. After that we're going to talk about how to activate the gifts of the spirit in your life, so I'll do the teaching session how to activate the gifts, after we've actually got you to step out and have a try, so we'll get started first of all and then we'll talk about the specific things. Then we'll have a chance for some questions and hopefully just finish around about 9.30. So I want to just do a simple activation. Now this is a very, very simple one, and in this one here what we're going to do is we want to just pray an inspired prayer so I could just - Henrietta, just come on up here please. Can I just practice on you? There we go, so Henrietta comes up, there we go and so this is the kind of process.

Now with all of these activations, the thing to remember is now we're just practising. Practising means we're stepping out to have a turn. We're getting on the bike to see if we can ride it, and even if we wobble eventually we'll get going and we'll be riding the bike, so we're just having a practice. The first thing I'd like you to do in any activation is to ask with a smile, hey, can I practice on you? Great, that's right, so you get a very positive response, yeah, great, go, do it! Great job, you know, I want, because hunger and expectancy from a person can draw from you, can help you when you're learning how to flow in the spirit, see? Always remember this, that God wants to speak to them and bless them and help them because He loves them - so it's not about you. It's actually about God being loving and the person needing to be touched by God. It's not about you at all. You're just actually the channel through which it happens, so what we're going to do, I could ask her something like well what would you like me to pray for and ask what her need is and get her to tell me her need. That's one way we can pray. You're used to doing that, well what's your need and so forth.

Or what I could do is just ask the Lord to drop into my heart a simple thought that will be the basis of what I will pray. It could be a picture, could be a word, could be just an impression to pray about a certain area, okay? So I need to do, so the steps that we'll take is number one, we just say hey, can I practice on you? Yeah, a very positive response, that's great. Now I'd like to take the persons hand, just make a connection with them. So the first thing it's helpful to do is just if you begin to exercise or stir up your spirit. The key in this remember is listening, just listening to your heart, so I'm going to break it down very, very slowly because if I do it slowly then you can see what's going on inside me. I'll explain it and then you'll see me doing it, okay, so we'll try and pull it apart for you.

So the first thing I would do is just, at this stage, I'll just begin to pray in tongues, and as I'm praying in tongues my inner man is starting to come alive, so I'm becoming stirred up. I become aware of God see, because when you pray in the spirit your spirit comes alive. Your spirit is praying. Your spirit is being built, so if I was to just - so I need to now close off my mind to busyness. I've got to stop thinking you're all looking at me and what if I get it wrong stuff, you know, all that sort of stuff, the what ifs. You've got to shut down what-if messages in your head. They stop you receiving God. The way to shut them down is to just redirect your focus. If I focus on myself then I'll start to fill with fear and my spirit will close, and now I'm not going to get anything, because I need to get it from my spirit, but if my spirit's closed because of fear I'll get nothing. I need to stay relaxed, and the best way to stay relaxed is not to focus on me, but to focus on how much God loves this person.

I might just begin to meditate on how much God just loves her, how important she is. I'm sure that God who loves her, really does want to talk with her, so I just keep my attention fixed, and I'm expecting God to give me something, see? So ask for permission, calm yourself down, stir up your spirit man with expectation, then begin to reach out for God to give you something, and you're looking for a spontaneous word or thought or impression. Then you're going to turn that into a simple prayer, so you have to start at some point - so right now I'm still trying to get something. [Laughter] But it's okay because I'm very aware and I totally believe God knows all about her, God knows exactly what she needs right now. I'm convinced God wants to do this. I just have to relax and wait on Him. Now I'm slowing the whole process down, so you can see it taking place see, then in a moment I'll just get an impression will just come, and just as I was talking an impression came just then. One word just dropped into my mind; I'm talking to you, suddenly a word just drops into my mind like that.

That word is a seed. When God gives you something, He only gives you the seed. You have to actually step out with what you've got and start the journey, trusting God that as you share what you've got that He will give you more, and a flow of the spirit will take place. That's the risky bit isn't it aye? That's the bit, but if you've got nothing to lose, it's only a practice, so I can focus instead of worrying about whether I pass/fail I can just focus on being kind and praying for her, see? So now because I've got a word God expects me to use a measure of intelligence. He doesn't want me to be a puppet, so therefore He expects me now having given me an insight what to pray for, that I would pray with some sense about that, so I'll have to start praying, well just I'll pray generally, and then I'll start to pray about what God has given me, okay? So I'm just going to start, you know, so you start to say something - you've just got to start a flow, and as you start the flow and remain just fixed on the Lord, you'll get the words will start to come.

Alright then, so I have in the moment just one word so I'll just put my attention on that word, and I'm starting to feel things now, so I'm just going to pray for her. I could prophesy this but I'll actually just turn it into prayer, because I want it to be really simple, because every one of us can pray, and mostly if you ask people if you can pray for them they'll say yes. Okay, so here we go. Father, I just thank You for Henrietta. That's a good way to just get started, see, quite easy to start the flow, something simple like that. Then I'll start to move to what I felt God give me, and as I stay focussed on that and relax and let my heart flow to her, there'll be a language just come forth. Don't try and work it out in the head, just let my heart flow to her. Alright then, so just again just focus - I can see the word again. Father, I just thank You for Henrietta, thank You Lord You love her, and that Lord, You will never leave her to be on her own and alone. Lord, I ask that You will just touch her in the depths of her being, and heal the loneliness that she's been experiencing and feeling for some time. Pray Lord she'll feel Your presence loving her, comforting her, and reassuring her, that You are always with her. Lord, let Your presence and love just flow over her right now, in Jesus' name. Oops, have to hold on to you, you'll be going over. Alright then, now did anyone work out what the word was that the Lord gave me? Loneliness, okay, so you see how I just started generally, and as I began to meditate in that word I could just feel all this grief around her, grief of loneliness and that's been something around her life, and God is wanting to heal the loneliness and just have her reassured He's there. [Laughs] What are you feeling? Just tell us what you're experiencing just as a result of doing this.

[Henrietta] [Laughs]

[Pastor Mike] Okay, just take your time, its okay. It's alright to cry, because God is touching her in a real area of her life. What did you feel or sense?

[Henrietta] That God is with me - and that's what I needed.

[Pastor Mike] Right. You needed to know tonight God is with you.

[Henrietta] Yeah.

[Pastor Mike] Isn't that wonderful. Has there been loneliness or struggle, a sense of being on your own?

[Henrietta] There's been a sense of it and in it though I have - I'm aware that He's there. I just needed more of an awareness of that, a deeper, greater level.

[Pastor Mike] Right, you need a deeper, greater level that...

[Henrietta] Of knowing that He is...

[Pastor Mike] ...He is there, alright then.

[Henrietta] ...right in the middle of it all.

[Pastor Mike] Okay then, well why don't we just help you with that now? Peter, get ready to catch her in a moment, because I could feel the spirit of God coming on you. As you close your eyes, I want you to just use your imagination to see that Jesus is just there, right in front of you. He's there with you right now, and His presence is going to come and just touch you, just in a moment. Thank You Lord, You're just coming on her life right now, Your presence just touching her. Lord, just fill her with love. Let Your peace just come on her now. Receive - there it is, very simple, whoa, wonderful presence of God just over her. Just enjoy the Lord.

So when we move this way, people start to experience God. Nice to feel that isn't it aye? [Laughter] Nice to do. That's why we come along. It doesn't matter about all the teaching, we just want to feel God. [Laughter] Okay then, so I pulled it apart, and kind of broke it down into bit by bit by bit so you can sort of see it, but actually when you work and operate it's altogether like that, and it's just relaxed and natural. So the biggest problem in flowing in the spirit is becoming focussed on yourself, and on yourself failing. If your mind goes there, I can tell you now, your spirit will close, and it's very difficult to function, so part of the discipline is to realise the gifts of the spirit are given to us to profit others, so if your attention is on the giver, and the other, and away from yourself, the flow takes place more easily.

So here's what we will do. We'll get you all to pair up with someone you don't know that well, take their hand and smile, can I practice on you? They will say yes! [Laughter] Yes, do your best! [Laughter] Make it a very positive encouraging experience, okay, then what we'll do is we'll just pray in tongues quietly together, then go quiet and you just focus. You're just waiting to receive something, an idea, a thought, a picture, an impression - no big thing, just something simple. Then when you've got that something, just focus on it, then launch out and start praying for the person around what God has shown you, right? I'll just do it one more time. Come on Brian, come on up. Could I practice on you Brian?

[Brian] Sure can.

[Pastor Mike] Awesome, that's fantastic, great, so let me take your hand then. Again I just begin to reach out, and begin to start to focus on the Lord, let my attention be set on Him. [Prays in tongues] Begin to pray in tongues and become conscious of the presence of God, then I'm looking for something, and immediately a word came to me just like that, just a word just dropped into my mind. So now that I know the word's come, now how do I use that? What does God want me to do with that? So I'll start generally, and as I start talking, just relax and lead into what God gave me expecting it to grow and get more - Father, I thank You for Brian. I thank You love him and Your hand is upon his life. That's the general bit see? It's getting started. [Laughter] Father, I just thank You love him, I thank You Your presence is with him. Father, I just pray for an increase in confidence in his life, confidence in hearing Your voice, confidence in flowing with You. I pray Lord in his walk with You, he will greatly grow in his ability to hear Your voice, grow in the confidence of Your power and presence with him, that Lord, he will become bold in moving and ministering in the things of the spirit. Father, let that boldness and confidence just begin to come over his life right now. In Jesus' Mighty name, touch him Lord.

Notice the presence of God just coming on him now - ooh! [Laughs] Because once you speak, the presence of God comes upon your speaking, in Genesis it says the spirit of God brooded over creation, then when the word came, then the spirit of God began to move, so you've got to learn to speak with confidence. Father, I just thank You for him right now - just lift your hands up to the Lord and [laughs] the power of God is here tonight! POWER of God touch his life right now, and there it is. Alright then, so we can teach you how to do that too [Laughter] tomorrow, tomorrow, tomorrow. All of these things can be learnt. I would not have you be ignorant, or just not know. God's plan is that we know what to do, and we'll help you over these two days, tonight and tomorrow, how to do it, but I need you just to step out and have a practice. Now whether you get it right or wrong is not important at all. There's no right and wrong, or worrying about it.

What I want you to do is have the experience of reaching out to pray and minister to someone, and you're leaning on listening to God to get what to say. He will only give you a bit of it, and you've got to actually take the step and put some language with what you've got - so what was the word that God gave me? Confidence, so what is it about that? Did he lack it? Did he need it? That's what I was asking God. Well he lacked it, and he needed it, and God wanted to grow him in confidence; what area? Around the operations of the spirit. Okay, so how was that for you? Was that okay? It was right on? Isn't that good aye, thank You Jesus. [Laughter] Like I say, we're all practising. [Laughter]

So there's no pass/fail in this, there's just try, try and try again and we'll practice. So remember the first and most important thing is to say: can I practice on you? And we do want a smiley face you know. [Laughter] Yeah, come on, encourage me, I'll do the best - and then we'll pray together, I'll lead you through it step by step, and then you go for it. Okay, are we ready? So let's get someone ready to go, come on, get someone to practice on. [Background chat] Have you got someone to practice on? If you haven't got someone to practice on raise your hand and then look for someone who's got their hand raised. Down there, two people. Okay, we all ready? Okay then.

Alright, now I want you all just to listen and walk with me step by step okay? So the first thing is smile at the person and say this: do you mind if I practice on you? Give a nice smiley response. Okay. Anyone missing someone to pray for them? You could - mm? You can go in threes or you can pray for me. [Laughs] That'll be great. I'll come down. Okay then, so are we ready? Everyone's asked if you can practice? Alright, now take their hand, just make the personal contact, take their hand and then when you've taken their hand then we close our eyes and begin to just pray in the spirit, pray in tongues or pray whatever way you're able to. Set your attention towards the Lord. Keep your eyes open so you can see. Okay, praying in tongues, [Prays in tongues] yeah, you pray for me.

So what you do is you then focus your attention on the Lord. He loves this person so much, He just loves them. They're very precious to Him. He wants to give you something, make you aware of a need or something to pray for, so listen now, expecting Him to give you something, a word, a picture, just a thought, an impression. Don't try and work it out, what does this person need. Just God, You speak to me. As soon as you get something lock on it, just focus on it. Thank You Lord. Thank You Lord. Then when you're ready, just one person starts out first in a short prayer, no big long prayers, just use what God gave you to pray a simple short prayer, then change over. Okay?

[Person praying for Pastor Mike] I just thank You for Mikes willingness to serve You and to give his life to help to strengthen us in the Lord. Lord, I just thank You that You have given him this passion in this teaching, and I just pray that You'll bless him mightily, that You'll continue to work through him Lord, and show him new ways and revelations of how he can strengthen the church in the Lord, how he can strengthen all of us in You Lord and that You may empower him and enable him in his ministry Lord, to do even greater works than he's ever done before, that You Lord will be glorified through him. Lord, we just pray that You'll continue to strengthen him in the Lord, Lord and through that he can strengthen us and we thank You in Jesus' name.

[Pastor Mike] Amen, thank you, wonderful. Very good.

[Person praying for Pastor Mike] Ok, all I got was 'strengthen us in the Lord'...

[Pastor Mike] That's right.

[Person praying for Pastor Mike] ...oh gosh, that's new.

[Pastor Mike] Okay, but it's all you needed to do, is just you take what you feel, and always start to work with that. Did you notice once you started it started to flow?

[Person praying for Pastor Mike] Yeah.

[Pastor Mike] Yeah, so just relax. You don't have to be so fast. You can just relax in it all, and feel the flow, okay?

[Person praying for Pastor Mike] My mind usually goes quite fast...

[Pastor Mike] I know, yeah.

[Person praying for Pastor Mike] ...and I speak fast then...

[Pastor Mike] Okay and then you speak fast, okay. Well if you just keep your mind relaxed and centred on Him, and you'll get the flow quite easily, but that was good. That was good. Thank you very much. Now let me pray for you. Can I practice on you?

[Person Pastor Mike's praying for] Yes.

[Pastor Mike] Okay, you'll want to watch then.

[Person Pastor Mike's praying for] I pray with my eyes open, yes.

[Pastor Mike] [Laughs] Good, good, good. Okay. Thank You Lord, thank You Jesus, [Prays in tongues] I'm praying in tongues. [Laughs]

[Person Pastor Mike's praying for] I don't know if I recognise the language or not [Laughter]

[Pastor Mike] You're brilliant. Thank You Lord. Father, I thank You for my sister. I thank You Lord for her humility, and her desire and hunger to learn, and You see her heart and You know the desire she has to be effective for You. I pray Lord You would unusually gift her with revelation, so she would accurately and precisely get insights and words of knowledge about people, and words of encouragement to pray for them. Father, I release Your presence around her life to do this, in Jesus' name, Holy Ghost, amen.

[Person Pastor Mike's praying for] Thank you. Wonderful aye?

[Pastor Mike] Yes. Okay...

[Person Pastor Mike's praying for] We had an odd number...

[Pastor Mike] Yes, sometimes that happens, maybe an extra one tonight or tomorrow. Okay, have you all had a turn now, all practised? Ask the person how did that feel to you? Get some feedback how it went. How did it go? It was good.

[Female participant 1] She did good. She's a very new Christian.

[Pastor Mike] Oh right, excellent.

[Female participant 1] but she did really well.

[Pastor Mike] That's okay, you did well. Well done.

[Female participant 2] Really when you did what you did it really touched me. I found it hard but a word came to me there that I hope was right for her.

[Pastor Mike] Wonderful. Well, it was?

[Female participant 1] Yes, yeah.

[Pastor Mike] Very good. Isn't that good?

[Female participant 2] Can I tell him what the word was?

[Female participant 1] Yeah.

[Pastor Mike] Yes?

[Female participant 2] It was Love.

[Pastor Mike] Oh good.

[Female participant 2] I don't know what the reason was but...

[Pastor Mike] Very good.

[Female participant 2] I'm just touched by it all, quite emotional.

[Pastor Mike] Yes. Yes, well you're feeling the presence of God touching you, and we feel it's not in the head, it's in your heart. You'll feel His love, and so when you feel that, you begin to start to weep. It's not uncommon for people when they start to feel God to start to weep, and they don't know why they're weeping, it could be many reasons, just because we feel loved. Most people go through life struggling to be loved, to be good enough to be loved, but when it suddenly comes without anything, it's just undeserved, you're just given, it actually can just cause you just to weep and weep and weep and not be able to stop, not know why. So don't try and work it out in your head. Just enjoy that you're feeling God touching you, see?

[Female participant 2] I've prayed the last 18 months - because I'm a new Christian, I've prayed the last 18 months to feel and hear the voice of God and it's been in my heart...

[Pastor Mike] And here you are. How wonderful. Why don't you come over here and let me just pray for you. Okay, just stand behind her, that's right. I want you just to close your eyes and as I pray for you you will start to feel the presence of God come on you. Lord, I just thank You. I thank You for my sister's love for You, and her desire for You. Lord, let heaven open over her tonight, and day after day in this next season ahead, let her begin to feel the presence of Your wonderful love. Touch her Lord right now, in Jesus' name. Fill her with that love, in Jesus' Mighty name. Let it overwhelm her - and I feel the Lord showing me that growing up you had to work so hard to be good enough. It was like it was a constant struggle ever to be good enough, and I see words being spoken over you, and the words seem to be no matter how hard you try, the words were so critical of you. It's like someone's finding fault in every little thing, and it was heartbreaking, because no matter how hard you tried it was just as though, I'm never going to be good enough, and you've struggled and wrestled with this for years. So the way you've worked to deal with that is by serving people and doing things for people, but no matter how much you've done, it feels like it's still never enough. God wants you to know He loves you. He loves you, He embraces you and celebrates you. He cares about you. Amen.

[Female participant 2] Thank you. Gosh, you are so right.

[Pastor Mike] [Laughs]

[Female participant 2] Now I know it's God.

[Pastor Mike] Yes, see?

[Female participant 2] That's incredible.

[Pastor Mike] Yeah, this is actually word of knowledge, and then prophetic word flowing together, so God showed me the pictures and I could see you as a younger girl, and someone going like this and speaking words, and how difficult and painful it was. Then as you've grown I can see how you've struggled in this area, and God wants you to have it freely that He loves you. I'm so glad you came. [Laughs] Okay, let's just draw everyone in. Alright then, so if we could just get you all just to be seated again, just gets out of the camera line. Great, okay then.

Now how many experienced that the prayer that was prayed for you, was just so right for you, it was just the right thing? How many had that experience? Whoa! Look at all those hands. Come on, let's give you all a clap. [Applause] That's really wonderful. Okay, how many felt emotions as the person prayed for you, that really touched your heart? How many felt that? Whoa! Look at all those hands! Come on [Applause] that's fantastic, wonderful. Okay then. So how many, when you stepped out to pray, you were thinking, it just seems like it's just me but I'll do it anyway? [Laughs] How many had that happen? Come on, be honest about that, that's right. Okay and there's a part in which it was you, because you've had to give expression to something God was giving you, so it was a thought in your head, so you identified it as your thought, and you had to speak it. That's why you think it's just your thoughts, but we can receive thoughts from our heart, we can receive thoughts from the Holy Spirit, we can receive thoughts which are demonic - but we're in an atmosphere of faith and expectancy, and so even though you may have doubted that it was God, and didn't recognise it was God, I got everyone to put their hands up to say that they were touched by what you shared. So you know that even though it felt like it was just you, for the person receiving, they got a touch from God, through your prayer.

So you come to realise God could be speaking through me and I don't recognise it, because I didn't sort of feel anything big. Remember, it wasn't for you. It was for them, so that's where there's this faith element in it, where we're trusting

God because God is good, God loves people, God wants to help and encourage people, God is willing to use any person to do that. We believe that, therefore without us feeling any great emotions, God can work through us, and we don't necessarily feel anything except maybe later on, oh, I wish I hadn't done that [Laughs] But actually God touched someone in spite of that, and after a while you'll learn to work with the Holy Spirit without needing to feel any great feelings or experiences. We operate by faith. Getting the idea? Okay.

How many enjoyed that as good starter exercise? It wasn't to hard was it aye? See, so what we'll do is we'll gradually grow the experiences you have, but it all works off the same thing; activating your spirit, settling your mind, listening for the spontaneous, identifying it, and then sharing what you have, and allowing if there's more comes to let the more come, and then when you feel it stops flowing just stop. We'll get you to do more and more of that. You might be quite surprised how easily you'll receive. Remember, you're made for this. This is not foreign. This is only a little unusual because you haven't done it, but it's actually how you are designed - that's why we laid the Bible foundation, you're designed for this, okay? I had the privilege of praying for a dear lady here tonight, and you got quite touched too didn't you? Yeah, felt the presence of God. Why don't you come up and just share with everyone what happened? Come on, just come on up here where everyone can see you, that's right. You were telling me how you're a new Christian, is that right?

[Female participant 2] Yes, I am, yes. I did an alpha course at the Village Baptist in Havelock North, and I was brought up a Catholic.

[Pastor Mike] Wow.

[Female participant 2] I had a faith that never really grew. I believed in God from being born...

[Pastor Mike] Right, yes.

[Female participant 2] ...being a little girl, and I was in a strict family, and never quite good enough. I was married and again, in that relationship, I could never quite match up to what I was expected to be. As a new Christian I've now got a faith that's a living faith, and it's within me, rather than fear of hell and damnation and it's alright...

[Pastor Mike] Wonderful.

[Female participant 2] ...if you give to charities and live a good life, but that's not what it's all about. It's a warm contented feeling now...

[Pastor Mike] With God, yeah. So she was sharing with me how she's a Christian for 18 months and had been praying to hear the voice of God and experience Him, for 18 months. She's come tonight wanting to hear the voice of God and experience His love, and she was feeling emotional after I prayed for someone else, so I offered to pray for her, and when I prayed for her God began to give me some words of knowledge.

[Female participant 2] I'm getting very hot. [Laughter]

[Pastor Mike] Hot is good. [Laughter and applause] Hot is good, hot is the spirit of God resting on you, yeah. Okay - and the word that the Lord gave me, was that she struggled to be good enough, and that from when she was very young she was criticised and was never found to be good enough and had struggled all her life to be good enough. God wanted her to know He accepted her and loved her. Isn't that wonderful? Now only God could know those sorts of things, and of course as I spoke then she began to be quite touched - and you're still being touched at the moment...

[Female participant 2] I am, yes.

[Pastor Mike] ...yeah.

[Female participant 2] Apart from the fact that I've got the most beautiful and caring and loving husband now that's helped me find the Lord, given me peace and contentment which I've never known, and he has helped the Lord...

[Pastor Mike] Let's give him a clap shall we? That's fantastic. [Applause] Good on you. I'm so glad you came - so undoubtedly over tomorrow there'll be a lot more of this happen, and that's what we came for. We came to hear the voice of God, and to be able to flow with the Holy Spirit, and you see the tremendous blessing you can be, if you can interact with people and get something from God, that only God knows, that can touch their heart. I'll practice with you tomorrow and whatever I ask you to do I'll do it for you first, so you can see it operating, then you practice and have a turn at it, okay?

Well we're getting near the end of the evening, so perhaps rather than do any more, perhaps we'll just give an opportunity if any of you had some questions you wanted to ask. We may cover it tomorrow of course, but some of it we may be able to cover just right now, so if you have any questions you wanted to ask - I think one or two had some. In the break they came up to me, so if you had a question to ask and if you could stand and speak it out, and I'll repeat it so that the camera picks it all up, and do my best to answer it. There's no bad questions, but there can be inadequate answers, so I will do the best I can to answer well, as best I can. So anyone who had some questions they wanted to ask before we finish this session? Yes, okay then, thank you.

[Male participant 1] My question is about the soul.

[Pastor Mike] Yes.

[Male participant 1] When you were talking, you interchange the words soul and mind...

[Pastor Mike] Mm-hm.

[Male participant 1] ...and memory. Now to me mind means brain...

[Pastor Mike] Right, yes.

[Male participant 1] ...which is where memories are stored.

[Pastor Mike] Yes.

[Male participant 1] But when you die and your brain dies and goes into the ground, that means your memory's gone, but according to scripture it persists.

[Pastor Mike] Exactly.

[Male participant 1] So presumably then the memory is somehow bound up in spirit.

[Pastor Mike] Yes.

[Male participant 1] So that means soul is spirit, so that man has to...

[Pastor Mike] No, no. No, the Bible - yeah...

[Male participant 1] ...so could you explain what happens to memories when a person dies? Is it material, or is it spirit? If it's material that's gone forever, if it's spirit and those memories are in your soul, then a spirit is soul and its like two spirits. Can you explain a bit more about that?

[Pastor Mike] Sure. Firstly although it's useful to consider spirit, soul and body as three separate things, they are actually quite integrated together. In other words you separate your spirit and soul from your body, then your body dies. The Bible talks that it requires the word of God to separate your soul and spirit, Hebrews 4, so clearly the soul and the spirit are quite closely bound together. When Jesus talked about the rich man and Lazarus, the rich man died and was buried, and the Bible says he awoke in hell virtually. Now in hell he had memories. He remembered his family, he remembered his brothers, he remembered Lazarus, he remembered the experiences. There's no indication it was a parable, so it's quite likely it was a real person, so the insight that we would get from that, is that when a person dies, their soul which is separate but connected to their spirit, carries with it the memories of their life.

Your spirit and soul use your body to interact with the physical world, so my understanding of memories, is that experiences that we have are imprinted chemically in the brain, and so there's a chemical imprint left from experiences. In fact actually your memories are made up of the chemical imprints that go into the brain, but there must be a retaining of them. There must be a mind of the spirit, there must be some way that all of these things are retained in such a way that when you die, even though your brain now ceases to function and returns to dust, the person still has all their consciousness. So it would appear to me as though, according to scripture, your soul and spirit are separate but strongly connected, requiring the word of God to separate and work out the difference. It seems to me as though the soul, when you enter the spirit life, your spirit man, the soul is the person residing therein there, the body seems to be used by spirit and soul as a way of engaging and living in the physical world - quite interesting that demonic spirits, when they enter a person will enter in and get involved in the body part of the person, or around the soul in some kind of way, seems to affect both areas.

So the Bible isn't clear on all aspects of how it works, but it does seem to indicate that spirit, soul and body are quite distinct, yet they are integrated to work together. They will separate at your death, but be reunited in resurrection. How God does it all I really can't answer, I can only give as much as I have learnt from the Bible, or learnt through some of the stuff we've looked at in the science field. Science has been able to identify that your memories for example, form like physical trees inside your brain, and that actually memories, when they shift the shape and formation of those neuron trees will change. Really interesting research has been done lately on that, but beyond that, there's a lot that God doesn't say and I don't know either. So I think, you know, we need to research and look into those areas a bit further - but that's about where my understanding of it is, so see spirit, soul and body quite separate.

The bible refers to each one - you may be sanctified spirit, soul and body. It seems to refer to each one as a separate thing, but I don't think soul and spirit are easily separated.

So my understanding is when a person dies and goes into eternity, their form as their spirit man is identical to the form of their physical body and the soul somehow is directly connected into that so the person's like a living person, except they're not living in a physical body. They have their existence in the spirit world now. That's the best I can explain it I think - hope it helps. [Laughs] Okay, anyone else like to ask some things just about what we've covered tonight? Okay then, we've got time for one more practice, otherwise if anyone else has got a question we'll go for the question or we'll get another practice? Okay, you're all going to have another practice? [unclear 01.55.27]

The thing is you're going to get good if you practice, and keeping on practising, so basically you want to take this position: every time I get a chance to pray for someone I will, and I'll look for the chances. When I get an opportunity to pray, if I know the need the person has - just because they tell me their need doesn't mean that's their real need, or all that God wants to say. I'll listen to God for something for them. We should make it our practice that we're going to do it. Now the thing that seems to be the trouble for everyone is something like this. [Just come on up here] This is where the crunch point comes for almost every person, and so it helps if you can be aware of it. It helps you to realise it's normal to go through this. If I - come here. Can I practice on you? Wonderful. Can I take your hand? Thank you. Alright then, now at this point now, the dilemma is, am I conscious of God or not? If I'm conscious of my failures, I suddenly feel terribly distant from God right now, and I've got to do something, and so now I feel under pressure to perform.

Now when a person's under pressure to perform, they don't flow from their spirit. They will just try to perform, and there's no life in it, so what I'll do is I'll be religious: oh God, just bless her. Father, you know her needs Lord. You just help her tonight and touch her. Now it sounds nice, but there's no life in it whatsoever. I'm actually not engaging her, and I will talk about that tomorrow in one of the sessions, about engaging with people as you minister to them. So what I need to do is just direct my attention to the Lord. Now if you build a devotional life, and you maintain your intimacy with the Lord, and increase your awareness of Him in day to day life, what happens when you come to minister is, it's only a short thing to just relax, just drop into your inner man, into your spirit - oh, thank You Lord, You're there. Now Lord, You know her needs right now. Well just pour out Your spirit upon her. Holy Spirit, just come on her right now, Jesus' Mighty name - become conscious of God, and the presence of God comes on her, and she's starting to feel the presence of the Lord.

Now I could reach in - just come back a little and let's do it again. So now I'll just become conscious of the Lord. All I've got to do is just to stop and begin to think well Lord, You know where she is, You know her need, just show me how to help her. What do You want to say to her Lord? So I'm enquiring of the Lord. I'm in a place not of struggling, but of listening and enquiring. Holy Spirit, I know You love her and You know all about her. What would it be that You'd want to say to her? How would You want to help her? Oh - then immediately a word came to mind, so now I've sort of got one word, I know that God is - if you've got the seed you've got the tree. It's just growing it that's the thing, okay? So I've got one seed, so I'll turn it into - I'll begin to pray, and as I pray I'm not struggling to make anything happen. I'm just allowing my heart to flow to her, towards her with love, allowing myself to just be aware God loves her very deeply.

Well thank You Lord that You love her, very precious to You, and You know the struggle that she's been having recently, and I'm asking Lord, that You would bring around her life a refreshing awareness of Your presence, that You'd bring Your peace around her life, and that she would rest from the struggles of trying to do so many things. She'll begin to learn the things that You want her to do, and learn how to say no. Lord, today I just release Your peace into her life. Let the peace of God flow like a river to her now, in Jesus' name. [Laughter] Okay. I know what you think the word was that the Lord gave me. [Peace?] Peace was one word, yes. That didn't come first. The first one was? [Struggle?] Struggle, okay. Can we talk about that? Okay, so what impact did that prayer have on you? Was it relevant for you?

[Female participant 3] Yes.

[Pastor Mike] Okay, has there been a struggle going on?

[Female participant 3] Yes.

[Pastor Mike] There has been a struggle. I asked the Lord because all I got was one word, struggle, and then I thought I've got to do better than that. What is the struggle about? So I asked the question - as I'm talking I got the word so I'm asking the Lord what is that struggle about? So many things to do and so many pressures, so many things to be done, and of course it leaves you then drained and strained see? So then the flow came out that way, yeah, then with the word from God came the presence of God which you started to feel and get touched. You're still feeling it, is that right?

[Female participant 3] Yes.

[Pastor Mike] Yeah. [Laughter] Do you want some more?

[Female participant 3] No. Yeah okay, why not.

[Pastor Mike] See, that was a silly answer wasn't it aye? [Laughs] No, no, it's alright. [Laughter] I want you to lift your hands up to the Lord. There it is - so again in ministering to people we are ministers of the spirit, so what we're doing is we're receiving from God, reaching into God, reaching to inner man and just - power of God just touch your life. So we're receiving from God and releasing to someone. We are a channel. We stand on earth between earth and heaven to bring heaven into earth. How about that? Jesus said pray Your kingdom come, that Your will be done on earth as it is in heaven, so what we see in the spirit or hear or feel God doing, we release it to the person. What I've done is I've tried to put it in ways which are visual so you can literally see it happening, but you do need to understand even if you don't see that, the same thing happens. Even she never fell over this is what's going on, so I've asked the Lord to help me have demonstrations which help you see it, so you sort of - almost like you could see something just flow like a river like that, whoa, it's amazing isn't it? But what really is going on is, it's just from being joined to the Holy Spirit, His presence comes out to touch people.

Okay, ready to practice on someone? Come on, you've just got another three minutes, just about time to fit in one more practice. Come on, let's do it. Find a different person - can I practice on you?

Alright, can we just get some feedback from you now? How many people were quite touched by what was prayed, it was just right for you? Just raise your hands if that was you. Well that's fantastic, absolutely wonderful. Let's give you all a big clap then.

2. Prophesy (2 of 5)

https://vimeo.com/45802644

http://youtu.be/62htQXLY42U

Good morning to those who are watching on the internet or looking at it through a DVD. We're so glad you could be a part of what we're doing, and I encourage you as we do activations that if you're with a group watching this in a room, you practice these same activations and interact with one another to see how it went. So let's get started.

Today we'll look at the gift of prophecy and we're going to pick up in a section in your notes under 12, so first of all what is prophecy, the gifts of the spirit? Remember we saw different gifts of the spirit? Go back to it and look at it in 1 Corinthians 12 and Verse 7. See if we can find it in our Bible, 1 Corinthians 12 and Verse 7. It says this - let's go back to where we were yesterday - the manifestation of the spirit is given to every man to profit others. So God's desire is you build other people, and the gifts are given to help you do it, so it's God's plan we all build up people, and the gifts of the spirit are a help to do that. So we saw a list of the gifts of the spirit, to one by the spirit, the word of wisdom, another word of knowledge by the same spirit, faith, gifts of healing, working of miracles, prophesy, discerning spirits, diverse tongues and interpretations. In all these works the one and self same spirit dividing to everyone severally, so God's willing not only to let you operate in one gift. He will let you operate in any of the gifts. It's quite amazing.

Severally means several, it means more than one, so all of us, it's God's plan we operate in more than one gift. We saw the gifts were divided up into or could be grouped as gifts of revelation, God shows you something; gifts of utterance where you speak something, gifts of power where the power of God flows forth. We shared with you the key on how to flow in that. We'll come back to that shortly, so first of all we're going to look at the gift of prophecy and in 2 Peter 1 and Verse 21 it says: now prophecy never came by the will of man, but holy men spoke of God, spoke as they were moved by the Holy Spirit. Moved means that they were inspired, there was something stirred inside them. So when we speak of prophecy it's not necessarily telling the future. It is an inspired utterance. We read it in 1 Corinthians, Chapter 14, Verse 3, means literally whoever prophesies speaks for edification, exhortation and comfort to men.

So prophetic or the gift of prophecy, God gives you a small inspired thought. He gives you a thought that bubbles up from inside you, and it is inspired. In other words you're not trying to work it out with your mind. It is something God is giving to you, and it flows through and expresses through you, so you receive an inspired thought, picture, impression. You begin to speak, and as you speak there is a flow of God's words through you, and when God flows through you, it sounds just like you. It's not sort of something artificial or weird. It's just like you're talking, and there's a flow of thoughts coming through. It'll also take on something of who you are, and how you would speak, so God works through people. He is happy to work through people. There's no perfect way of prophesying or perfect way of doing it. God just is willing to use you and flow through you.

So notice that it tells us then, that the purpose of the gift of prophecy is three-fold, so number one is edification. That means if you're going to bring a prophetic word it is to build someone, it is to encourage them, to lift them up. The second purpose of the gift of prophecy is the word exhortation, to come alongside them and strengthen them, or stir the person, so the first person is to build them up. So if someone gives a prophetic word, it should build the person up. A second thing is, it could exhort them or comes alongside them, and after the person's had a word of prophecy, they feel like God came alongside them and strengthened them. The thirdly, it is for comfort so when the word of prophecy comes sometimes it will bring such a presence of God to the person that they begin to weep, and they feel God touching them and loving them and comforting them.

I remember last night as I prophesied over one person, that they began to feel touched, and began to feel the love of

God, began to feel tears, and unexplainable sensations that can only be interpreted that God has actually touched their life. So when you bring an authentic word of prophecy or flow in a gift of the spirit like this, the impact on the person is to feel like God came really near them and touched them, and God - I knew God loved the world, now I know He loves me. That's the sensation often that people have, and so it can affect people in very many different ways. So when you prophesy, often when there's a release of the Holy Spirit to touch the person, and spiritual atmosphere can shift, so prophetic words are amazing. Just you can speak to people, and God touches them, and they often say how did you know that, or how could you possibly have known that? It's a wonderful, wonderful gift.

I want to show you several things about the gift of prophecy. One of them first of all is all believers are encouraged to prophesy, so 1 Corinthians 14, Verse 1; follow charity (or love), and desire or passionately hunger after spiritual gifts, and rather than you may prophesy. In other words God highlights prophecy, highlights prophecy. All believers are able to prophesy. Verse 39, 1 Corinthians 14, it says this: brethren, covet to prophesy, and don't forbid speaking in tongues. So the Bible says passionate, be passionate to prophesy. Why? Because we're called to build people up and this is one of the best gifts for building people up, so whenever you have been filled with the Holy Spirit you can prophesy, so all believers can prophesy. Now tell someone next to you you can prophesy you know.

The response probably then is well, really? How? [Laughs] Well we'll get to that. I'm glad you asked that. We'll get to that in a moment, so there are some guidelines around prophesying which I want to share with you, because prophecy like all the gifts can be a great blessing, but also it can be misused, and create a lot of problems, so the misuse of the gifts, or immaturity in operating in the gifts, can create a lot of problems for people, so we need to have a few guidelines around it. So the first thing I want to point out is we're going to read in Verse 29 of 1 Corinthians 14, notice what it says there; let the prophet speak, two or three, and let others judge. So here's an interesting thing about prophesying. It says in Verse 33, God is not the author of confusion but of peace, so when there's confusion there is something else at work other than God. If God is ministering to you, I notice this; He doesn't use lots of words, and He's incredibly sharp and clear, so when something is confusing they may have got an idea right, but something is filtered through it, and it's actually not right.

God does not bring confusion to you, so if someone speaks something to you, and it leaves you confused or feeling flat, the chances are highly likely it did not come from God at all, and the person has just got it wrong, or injected in their own thoughts and ideas into what they're saying. So with prophesying it's okay to judge it, and when you say judge it, it's not judging the person. We're just checking to see whether this really - how much or what of this comes from God, so that means what is the content? Does that feel right? What's the spirit of it? If someone prophesies harsh and judgemental, immediately you can pick the spirit of that's not right. That doesn't come in the attitude that Jesus would come, that's one of love and building people up. So we can assess then a prophetic message in a number of ways. Here's some key things, if someone brings a word of prophesy, you could ask. Firstly, does it agree with scripture? If it's not in agreement with scripture it's wrong, just don't even receive it. No, I can't receive that, it violates scripture.

The second thing is what does it do to your spirit? Does it witness in your spirit? Remember if it comes from God, it will energise or lift up your spirit. You'll feel strengthened or aware of the presence of God, so inside your heart, you must ask, what did you really feel about that? Please be honest, and if you're honest you'll have a witness in your heart about that message, all of it or some of it. So does it lift you up, or bring you heavy after the person's ministered? So if someone's spoken something to you, and you feel a lot of heaviness around you something's not right in it, just say well Lord, I just let it go to You and I don't receive anything didn't come from You, just receive what You have for me. So does it agree with the character of God? So those are some kinds of questions. I tend to work off the content; does that sound right? Does it sound like it's line with the word of God? Does it lift my spirit and bring life? Those are the kind of key things I use on it.

Now there are some guidelines around prophesying I want to give to you, and these come from years of experience, where I've seen the gift misused, so please notice these very carefully, and bear them in mind also when you hear someone else prophesying. So here's some cautions about it and then there's a few do's, and some things that don't - so here's some don'ts about prophecy. Number one, don't use it for Christian fortune telling. [Laughter] People all want to know their future, and you can't believe the number of people that come up to me at various times, and what they want is for me to bring a prophecy about what God's telling them to do. You are responsible for listening to God. You are responsible for your life. If you come to me to tell you what to do, you're letting go responsibility for direction in your life, and for choices in your life. God calls all of us to the journey of faith, relating to Him, trusting Him and planning our way.

Trust the Lord with all your heart, don't lean on your own understanding. In all your ways acknowledge Him. He will direct your paths, so all of us are called to a faith walk. Don't lean on someone to prophesy what you should do. Don't lean on prophesy as fortune telling for you, waiting for God to tell you from someone else what you ought to do with your life. You are failing to be responsible when you do that - a very, very important one that. Better this way, that you make your decisions and then let God confirm, them and the prophetic word will often speak confirmation about what you already knew in your heart God was saying to you. That's a better way of dealing with it. Now can prophecy tell the future? Yes, it can, but not generally the operation of this gift. It's more the person operating in the prophet situation or prophet office, so we're talking here just about the gift of the spirit that all believers can function in.

When a person gets very good flowing in the gift of prophesy, they have a resident mantel over their life, and often they flow effectively prophetically wherever they are. Then God can establish them in an office in the church, which is for the equipping of people for operating in prophecy, and the person operating in an office of a prophet will often be able to bring quite directional words, quite specific words about things that will come and things God is wanting to do, and quite completely unravel what will happen in the future, so that's a strong revelatory gift over the office of a prophet. Now we're not talking about - we're just talking about believers functioning in the gift, so I encourage you to avoid seeking either to tell someone where to go and what to do, or to seek for someone to prophesy then over you. It becomes manipulative.

In the world of the occult people want to have their fortune told. There's a whole realm of the spirit with spirits of divination that operate to try and then impress their thoughts on people, so if you're going to move into that realm, take responsibility for your own personal direction. Let personal prophecy confirm it. That a good idea? That's pretty sound stuff. Here's the second one. Don't use prophecy to scold people. If you're getting a prophetic word that's telling you off, there's something wrong. Don't inject your own disapproval of someone. If we're prophesying, we prophesy love to build them. If it's not going to exhort them and build them, keep quiet. Okay, don't use the gift of prophecy to try to correct leaders, because you've got an issue in your heart about them. Don't use prophecy to bring out your pet ideas. [Laughter] It's not about us, it's actually about listening to God, and building up the other person. That's what the whole flow of the spirit is.

Now here are three other areas which are really important so note these ones. Don't prophesy and give direction over business dealings. There has been immense harm caused when people have wanted someone to prophesy about a business deal. Again this falls in the category of letting go responsibility for decision making, and this time trying to put it into God's hands, when He says you must take responsibility for your life. So in business you don't wait for someone to prophesy what you do. You have to work out a business plan, you have to pray over what you do, you listen to wise counsel, you follow practical wisdom and at times God can confirm things. If there's going to be prophetic words around business let them confirm what you'd already decided to do, or planned to do, or thinking of doing, rather than tell you some new thing you should do. It will inevitably end with loss, financial loss and problems, because it's operating outside the sphere God gave to operate in.

Okay, here's another that's a very important one. Do not prophesy over personal male/female relationships. Well I believe God's going to get you to marry this one, or going to get you to marry that one. [Laughter] This is a no no. Don't do this. Again it violates personal responsibility. If two people feel that God has joined them into relationship, they must take responsibility for their decisions in it, not look to someone to prophesy. Prophecy can confirm it, but don't look to someone to kind of give a direction that way. There's a normal process if a couple - they should find out, or should look out for someone who has similar values, that they feel there's a chemistry between them, they are flowing in harmony with God together, similar kind of direction in their life, and there's a witness from either parents or those around them who love them, that they see the fruit of God on the relationship, but prophesying that you should marry this one, this is well and truly outside the boundaries, and can only end up in harm.

As I shared with you last night, one of my daughters had I guy tell her they were going to get married, and of course that's what people use - God told me. Great, he didn't tell me! So I just told her if anyone tries that on you, just say well He didn't tell me so forget it. [Laughter] The guy was very persistent, God told me you're going to marry me, and she was also quite persistent, and in the end he just wasn't listening, so I rang the Pastor and said would you have a talk to him? He's totally out of order. He's manipulating with the gift of prophecy, trying to bring emotional spiritual pressure on my daughter. This is wrong. Please confront him, so they did that, and that was the end of that. Okay, so [laughs] alright then, so here's another one; don't prophesy that God is going to heal someone. I've seen so many problems over this one, of people prophesying that God is going to heal another person.

Does God heal? Yes, He does. Can God heal? Yes, He can. Will God heal? Well that's always the uncertain bit, and when you prophesy that God is going to heal someone, if you have not heard from God, you have produced a false hope. Now what happens in this situation, is people feel compassion when someone's not well, and they confuse the feeling of compassion, with the direction of the Holy Spirit. So then they prophesy the person's going to get well, and what happens is it brings a tremendous spiritual confusion when the person doesn't get healed. I'll give you an example of it and look, I've had this several times and I believe that people who prophesied this, should be confronted about the misuse of gift, because it produces a false hope. It's like saying what everyone wants to hear. It's not what the gift's about.

The gift is about encouraging people with real hope, so I had a situation where I had a friend in another nation who's a senior business leader, a very important person in the nation, a leading Christian in the nation. His wife also is quite a leading person, and his wife got cancer. I went to visit him, and all these intercessors and prophetic people, everyone without fail, had prophesied that God was going to heal her. Spiritual battle, and all the kind of stuff that goes with it. I felt in my heart she's got six months and she's going to die, so it's very difficult to know how to manage that, when all the popular prophetic thing is all saying she's going to be healed. I feel in my heart that she's going to die, so I put it to him that he had six months, and then there would be a major tsunami, a storm in his life, and he needed to be preparing for it. It was clearly his wife's death, and so the six month - now here's the thing. He himself didn't want to believe she would die - of course you don't, and so he wanted to believe these other words.

Six months went, she died almost to the day, six months later, and so this was a huge problem. Here's why it was a problem. It was a problem because everything had been built around the hope that she would live, and now she died, so you've got tremendous confusion took place, and no one's talking about it. So I went to him and I said that there are two problems you face. I said number one, your wife has died, and this happens in life, that when people come to the end of their life, we've got no power over that. People die, and sometimes they die of cancer, and so you've got about two years to recover from this tragic loss, and it will take a little bit of time. I gave him some practical advice. I said the deeper thing is this; your wife has died but the rest of your future depends on your relationship with God, and right now that's breached seriously because you think God has let you down, so you've lost your trust in God because you listened to all the wrong prophecy.

He was very open to me now because he remembered out of all the people who had prophesied, I was the only one who said she was going to die, so he was very open and I counselled him how to restore his faith, and how to rebuild his life over the next two years. Then we were very, very glad a little later on to be able to see him massively restored, and then ultimately introduced us to a lady and asked what we felt about this lady. Everyone else said she's not the right one. [Laughter] I said she's exactly what you need, and here's why. He was asking for help in making that decision, but you've got to be so very, very careful. Do not take over someone's responsibility that God has given them. Everyone is responsible for the decisions in their own life. Do not let anyone take that over, and make that decision for you by prophesying something around your life. You've got to recognise, it's just immaturity or ignorance of how the prophetic gift functions.

If you've got those safety measures around you you'll be fine. You can just function, stay within the boundaries, comfort, exhortation, edification, building people up. Getting the idea? So when you are prophesying, here's a few practical things to do, and then we'll get to speak on activating your spirit, you'll get an exercise to do together. So here's a few practical things. If you're going to speak on behalf of God and that's what you're doing, speaking to encourage, speak clearly, don't mumble. Speak clearly, speak naturally. Don't put on a spiritual voice. Oh, Oh, OOOHHH! [Laughter]

If you read in the Book of Genesis, when God wanted to connect with Adam, He said Adam, where are you, you know? Who told you you were naked? Have you eaten the fruit of the tree? Very simple language. There's no whoo-ho-ho. [Laughter] That's just people's way of just putting stuff together [Laughter] It's an unnecessary distraction from listening to God. It focuses you on the person, rather than on where we should be focussed, on what does God have to say. So just keep a normal tone of voice, and speak in simple language, you don't have to use King James language. [Laughter]

It turns out that God is a 21st century god [Laughter], and people will hear God speak to them in their own language, or their own way, or their own style, so if you're a highly educated person you'll hear God speak to you in a way that you would recognise. A person that's not well educated, they would hear God speak in a different way through them, so every person will hear God speak in a way which is appropriate to them. So when you speak and share, just speak naturally. I just sense this, or I felt this, or I had an impression of this. Don't go in sort of adding 'God told me'! [Laughter] God told me! Because what you're doing is you're positioning yourself out of accountability, and into some kind of thing where you've got this hotline with God, and now you're an authority over what's about to be said, and no one can challenge it, whereas actually we are to judge the gift. So if someone said God told, they're kind of just stopping you even well no, now wait a minute, wait a minute, God told? You know, I don't feel so right about that - so don't go saying God told me this! Just speak naturally; I just felt this as I was praying for you, or I had this impression while I was praying for you.

It leaves you more transparent and open. It leaves it easier for there to be dialogue about what was said, and if it's God, God can stand up for Himself. He doesn't need us to help Him, so if something came from God it will bear witness in the person's spirit, and if it doesn't, it doesn't mean it was wrong. It just means perhaps they weren't listening. If they were wrong they'll register actually that was God speaking to me at that time, so just share. That's all your job is, to just have a heart to love people, listen to God and share what you sense God giving you and showing you, then stop when you feel the flow stop. Don't keep going. If you're in a meeting then please be sensitive to the flow of the meeting, and also be yielded to the leader in the meeting where he gives permission to flow and to operate, so in a meeting like a church meeting, which is mostly in a house group or something like that, small group, cell group, in a thing like that, then just be aware that you're functioning under authority, and don't kind of take over from the leader because you've got this hotline to God.

This violates chain of command. It just violates what God's set in place, and it puts you right out on a limb, and unable to be connected, and it's spiritually completely out of order, so no good fruit comes from that. Even if you've got it right, it produces a problem - so always the spirit of the prophet is subject to the prophet. It tells us that in 1 Corinthians 14; the spirit of the prophet is subject to the prophet, so how you deliver, when you deliver, and what you say is subject to your spirit. You don't have to feel any great thing. You don't have to wait until you're [inhales] you know, wound up. Initially as we move in the gifts we can be a little nervous and get a little wound up. Oh, I'll give you that right now - 1 Corinthians, Chapter 14. I don't think it's in there so let's see if I can find it - 1 Corinthians, Chapter 14, Sprit of the prophet, Verse 32. The spirit of the prophet is subject to the prophet, so in other words whatever you can manage yourself, it's under obedience. That word means literally to be properly positioned under your own spirit, so you don't ever have to get out of control prophesying.

Verse 32, the spirit of the prophet is subject to the prophet, so if you have something that violently interrupts a meeting and then you try and tell the person, hey, that really disrupted the whole meeting. Oh, well God told me! This is being unaccountable, and it's violating that scripture which actually, the way you deliver, and how you deliver, when you deliver, actually is your responsibility, so it puts it back on the person actually you can learn when and how to flow. You can approach a leader and say actually, I feel I've got something from God for the group, can I share it? That would be a good way of doing it, or they may just open it up and say it's okay for everyone to share something that God has given you, but you always stay subject to order. God always operates with order, and although at times it can look chaotic what God is doing, it is always in a divine order. So again, getting the gift of prophecy, how are we going to get flowing in the gift of prophecy? How can we activate the gifts?

Now remember I shared with you, that you can stir up the gifts of God? I'm going to just go back and just show you how you stir up the gifts of God, then we're going to get you just - I'll give you the practical keys, then we'll get you started doing activation again together. How about that, okay? So just go back in your notes, how to activate the gifts of the spirit. You can literally stir up the flow of God in your life, and so 2 Timothy 1, Verses 6 and 7, I remind you, stir up the gift of God which is in you, by the laying on of hands. So that word stir up [found in Number 10, item Number 10, 10.1] Gifts of the spirit getting activated, stir up the gifts of the spirit, right? So that means rekindle or fire them, so there's something you can do that fires up or energises you, and there's many examples of people activating the gifts of the spirit.

Elijah in 2 Kings 3:15 got a musician, so music can cause your spirit and soul to be stirred, so you can flow in the gifts of the spirit. In Judges 16, Verse 20, Samson would shake himself, and as he shook himself, the Holy Ghost would come on him and he had tremendous strength, so he did it that way but we've got a different way that we can do it. We can pray in tongues, stir the gift up that way. God gave us the Holy Ghost. We can speak in tongues, and activate and stir our spirit man, so there are reasons why gifts can become dormant. Often it's because of fear or because of unbelief, we just don't believe God would work through us, or because we're under control, there's a lot of control, no freedom to flow. Passivity can cause gifts to shut down, or just straight out neglect, where we just don't do it, so gifts can become dormant, but you can activate them again if you begin to re-energise your personal spiritual life, so there's a number of ways we can do that.

I want to give you some practical keys on what I've found is a big help to stirring your spirit man up, so you can begin to flow in the gifts of the spirit. A key part of it of course is your personal devotional life. Building a life where you're in the word of God, reading the word of God, praying the word of God, spending time with the Lord, worshipping Him, sharing with Him, building your spirit man, praying in tongues, all of this is the normal devotional life of a believer, so we need to be feeding our inner life, feeding your spirit man, so you've got something to give. If you don't feed your life spiritually there's not much to give, so we can make it a practice that we feed our spiritual life, hungry for God, hunger - God, use me today God, today I just wait on You. Lord, today give me something for someone or bring someone into my life that I can minister to and share with. That kind of praying, you're stretching out for God to do something.

Now here's some simple things you can do in our environment, and this is a way of breaking it down so it's very easy to do. Number one, free up your spirit. You can't prophesy and flow in the gifts if your spirit is all uptight with tension, so free up your spirit, relax, laugh more and pray in tongues, because praying in tongues actually energises your spirit. When you pray in tongues, the Holy Spirit is speaking through you. He's speaking language to your spirit, and your spirit is expressing, you are flowing with Him. It's a great way, pray in tongues, stir your spirit man and it starts to energise you, and we'll do some exercises on that a little later. The second thing is expect faith, expect God to speak with you. You've got to reach out expectedly. See if I'm going to pray for someone and I'm full of doubt, not that much happens when there's doubt, but when you come, you say God, I just expect You to give me something for this person. I'm believing that when I get myself in that place, You will give me something I need.

It sounds a little risky, but actually what faith does is it steps out trusting God. What am I trusting, that I'm good enough? No, I'm trusting that God is good, God loves them, and God's willing to help them. I'm just here available, so it's a faith that God is willing to do something. The third thing is, so we stir up our spirit, reach out our faith, then just focus your attention. One of the things that people find very difficult to do, is to just focus their attention to listen. You know if you want to hear someone, you've got to stop and listen. There's too much distraction, you can't hear, so the key thing we saw in flowing with the gifts of the spirit is hearing, being able to pick up the small impressions of the Holy Spirit - and they're very small, so I've got to get the noise out of my head. Now for some people that's a problem, because there's a lot of noise, and the noise comes from unresolved personal conflicts, spiritual, emotional conflicts. The noise comes from the voice of demonic spirits speaking into our mind, condemning, judging, accusing, belittling, pressuring, confusing. That's one aspect.

They also come from your own beliefs in your heart; I'm no good, God wouldn't work through me, or I've just blown it, or I'm not - you know, all of those sorts of beliefs of the heart, which are contrary to the word of God, demonic spirits use to stir up and energise confusion and turmoil inside you. It's normal for us to be at peace and rest. In the kingdom of heaven there's righteousness, peace and joy in the Holy Ghost, so turmoil inside your emotions have to do with what you believe in your heart, and that in turn is activated on by spirits to keep you in a state of turmoil so you can't be useful to God. Getting the idea? So we need to be committed to the journey of growing, growing inside and in our freedom and peace on the inside. He's promised to give us peace, so one of the things I have found - there's a lot of things can help in that, but one thing I've found I've learned to meditate, to take the scripture and to picture it, and hold it in my mind and begin to pray, and just keep my imagination fixed on that picture, locking in around that. I've learned, I've trained my mind to stay focussed and you can do the same.

When you have your mind all over the place, sometimes it can be hard to pick up the voice of the spirit, so quietness and peace. I don't like lots of noise in my head or around me, I like quietness, because I've found in quietness it's easier to pick up the voice of the spirit of God. It's a very still, quiet voice. If you're hurried or agitated for example - I don't have time for prayer - your mind's going all over all the things to do. You're not at rest and in a place to hear. You have to do something about that; write it all down, get it out of your head, relax and just be in the presence of God. So number one, free up your spirit and start praying in tongues quietly in an even spirit; faith, expect God to give you something; focus, begin to just give your attention to listen to the spontaneous impressions, then feel, identify what God gives you. Just try and identify the thought, word, picture He gives you, and then when you've got that, focus on it, then step out and speak. That's how it all works and all the gifts of flowing in the spirit all work out the same way. They work on your spirit being alive, you are focussed to receive something from God, you identify what it is and you begin to act on what God gives you.We saw that God gives it to you in a little picture, a word or a thought or some kind of thing like that.

Okay, so what we need to do now is we'll just stop the session now and we're going to now look at giving you an activation to do. How about that? Well that was really exciting. [Laughter] Great, I know you want to stretch out. There's only so much - I can teach you all the stuff but at the end you've got to stretch out and do, so if you don't stretch out and do, then nothing's going to happen. So would you like to come up here? Can I pray for you? So what we'll do first of all is we'll look at the activation we did yesterday, and keep going back into that again alright? So the first thing we did - can I pray for some of you? Great! He's so positive.

That's really good. Okay, can I take your hand then? Alright then, so what we're going to do is just going to pray an inspired prayer, then from that, we'll move to bringing an inspired thought. I'm not going to call it a prophecy because then you'll freak out and think I've got to do something hard. [Laughter] Just an inspired thought, I think everyone could have an inspired thought couldn't they? Could you have an inspired thought? [Yes] How many had one last night, God used you? Great! There you are. Okay, we can do it again today.

So what we're going to do now, I'm just going to ask the Lord to give me something that I can just use as a basis for praying for her. Remember that as you do this, you just free up your spirit and relax. If I focus on trying to do something, what's going to happen is I'll stress out, and then I'll get uptight. My spirit will shut, and what I feared will happen - [Inhales sharply] nothing! So just relax. Take time, just pray quietly in the spirit, [prays in tongues]. Just allow your spirit to relax and just come to a place where I'm open to now extend my faith and believe that God will give me something. So immediately I did that I got one word just came. I don't know what all that means, but I've just got one word to start with, and I'm expecting though that if I will just stay here focussed on that, God will help me understand what that's about, and then I'll begin to pray. As I pray, I will use that word or what God's showing me in that prayer, and there'll be a flow of the spirit of God to touch you. Alright, so now another word's just dropped into my mind, so how did that happen? Just a word just dropped in spontaneously while I'm in the middle of talking, and I've learned to recognise that's most likely the Holy Spirit.

Okay, so I'll just wait again, pray and stir your spirit, relax, extend your faith, ask the Lord to give you something. Now you're listening to your heart, not your head. If you're listing to your head, you'll look and try to figure out now what possible needs could she have, you know? You'll try and figure it out, so that's the language of the head. The language of the heart is spontaneous, it's a flow, it just is a thought or a picture just comes to mind. Okay, so go back there again to check I got it, and thank You Lord, just thank You Lord, You love her. Thank You Lord that You really care about her. Lord, I just thank you to give something just to help her. Alright, so that same word just is sitting there, so I'll just now begin praying. Father, I just thank You for my sister. Thank You, You love her. Thank You Lord that You are working in her life to stir up passion to reach people for Christ. I thank You there's a fire burning in her heart, to win people to You. There's a fire burning in her heart for the lost and the broken. There's passion, that You are igniting, to bring Your power to people who are broken and damaged.

I thank You Lord, You're going to help her to enlarge in her spiritual capacity to minister to people. I pray Lord that Your Almighty power would come around her life today, filling her to do that work in Jesus' Mighty name. Thank You Lord. Holy Spirit, come over her now. Amen.

Alright, now - so the word I got was Passion. Now I had no idea what that referred to. It could refer to lots of things, but what I felt as I said it, it referred to a passion for people, and a great desire to reach out to people, and see people saved. Would that be right?

[Person Pastor Mike prayed for] Bingo. [Laughter]

[Pastor Mike] ...and I also felt, so as I was praying I'm also listening to what's coming out, because it's a flow from the spirit, not from my head, so my head can just be quiet and listen to what's being said. As I'm listening I get to know her, and as I was praying I could feel this passion for the lost, a desire to be able to reach them, a desire to be able to bring the power of God to them, to touch them. That's what I could feel was there and God wanting to do that through you. Amen.

[Person Pastor Mike prayed for] Amen.

[Pastor Mike] Awesome. Okay, well there we go, so praise the Lord. Give her a clap. [Applause] Right, now it's your turn, it's your turn, so remember, this is just a practice. It's very important just to ask the person: can I practice on you? The person - give a very positive response - yes, do your best, see? That's it. It's nice to be encouraged. It's good to have an environment which is easier to learn and practice in, but after that we can go into any environment and do it. So then take their hand, quietly pray in the spirit, if you can pray in the spirit. If you can't, just reach out and meditate on the Lord, asking Him to give you something. Now that's the point, if you're going to go through turmoil, you'll be feeling the turmoil. Calm yourself. This is not a win/lose. This is not right/wrong. This is just we try to ride the bike [laughter] okay? I'm behind holding on a little bit to give you a bit of guidance to make sure you don't get too many wobbles and fall off.

So what you would do, if you feel tension rising, you are centring your attention on performing to make something happen. It will only get worse if you keep in that frame of thinking. Just shut that thinking down, and just begin to meditate. Just allow yourself to see, the Lord Jesus, You're there, You're my friend and source. Focus on the source, not the problem or the fear. Focus on the source, see and as you focus on the source, just relax beforehand. Just a firm thank You Lord, You love her. You love her. You're just so glad to work through me, so I just wait on You. Maybe You will speak to me. That's the language you use in your head. It's an affirming faith kind of language. If you allow your mind to drift, and go on and think you're having to get something, immediately you'll disconnect from the Lord and shut down with anxiety and fear and tension. Then the more you focus on that, the harder it gets, then you'll just try and make something up to get the heat off, and think I wonder if I can slip away at morning tea time. [Laughter]

[Female participant 1] [unclear] [Laughter]

[Pastor Mike] The doors are locked. [Laughter] So there's no way you can explore flowing with the Holy Spirit unless you do something, so these exercises are to get you doing something to explore what it feels like, and it'll feel great, and there's also some turmoils around it. It's all part of the journey of working with the Holy Spirit. The turmoils are inner and outer conflicts. The joy is when the spirit of God flows through you and you see the person - you open your eyes up to what you thought was just you, and there's tears coming down, and God has touched them - and you thought it was just you. Remember, it will be your thoughts in your head, and it'll be your voice. It'll feel just like you because it's God working through you now. So you wait for a picture, thought, impression, and then just turn it into a prayer. Start generally, and then pray. Let's do it. We can do that, and then we'll graduate, and we'll do something just another level up after you've done that, okay? Last night everyone did it okay, so come on, you can do this. You know you can do it. Find someone, break into a pair, and then stand up wherever you'd like to. Let's do it.

[Background chat] Right, pray quietly. Focus your attention. Reach out expectantly, expecting God to give you something. Receive what you've got, then begin to turn it into a prayer. [Background chat] Alright, let's just stop right where we are now, and let's just get some feedback. How many people, the prayer that was prayed was just right for you? Great, that's wonderful, okay. How many of you felt touched by the Holy Spirit when that person prayed the prayer? Wonderful! Come on, give yourselves a great clap. [Applause] How many of you felt it just seemed like it was just me, I'm kind of thinking maybe it's just me, I'll just do it anyway? How many had that experience? There's a few like that, okay. How many of you, it was really a struggle? How many felt tense and uptight when that magic moment came when you're sort of waiting for God to give you something? How many felt a little bit uptight then? Okay. Was there anyone unable to overcome that? You got stuck at that point and just froze? Anyone freeze? No-one, that's great. Okay, very good. You've done very well.

Right then, what we're going to do now is we're just going to extend that exercise a little more. If you just sit down for a moment, and I'll show you how you can extend that exercise now a little bit more, then we'll just take it a little further. So first thing is, we should just - why don't we just give a clap, everyone did so well. [Applause] A number of you were quite touched by what happened, because when someone speaks an inspired thought from God, there is a flow of anointing, a flow of the person of the Holy Spirit and it just touches your heart. For some people they feel inspired, some people weep because they feel God is near me. That's why it's so powerful.

Now what we did was we made it a prayer, because a lot of people, the majority of people, if you say can I pray for you will say yes, and if you would just stop for a moment, and listen quietly, God will give you what to pray for, and it can deeply touch their heart. I remember I was out and I saw two old ladies by a garden and I stopped and I thought I've got to go over to them. I said I just felt to help them with the garden, and then I said I'm a Pastor. Can I pray with you? They said yeah, that's fine, so I put my arm on both their shoulder and thought God, You've got to show me what to pray, and then I got an idea and I began to pray. When I opened my eyes one of the ladies is just weeping. The other lady moved away. I thought that's fine, you know? Just what is God doing? God's not working on her, He's working on this lady. I said tell me what's the trouble, what's happening? Just asked her to talk about what's happening. She said oh, my husband died only two weeks ago, and so we were able to talk. I got her to talk about her husband, then I was able to lead her to the Lord. So just the prophetic prayer opened the door, when loving care was expressed, for her to come to Christ. She just was at a point and the prayer opened her heart and brought God into her life, then she opened up her life to come to Christ, so there it is. How about that? Just a simple thing, just oh, I should go and help these ladies and that's how the gifts flow, very, very easily, very natural.

Right, then now what we're going to do as we move from prophetic or an inspired prayer, we're going to go to an inspired thought, an inspired thought. We don't call it a prophecy because otherwise you'll think it's too hard. [Laughter] Okay, so we'll just call it an inspired thought, and so what we're going to do is we're going to follow exactly the same kind of format. Ask the person to come up, can I practice on you? Yes, do your best. Just pray in tongues quietly, wait expecting God to give you, and look for something, just a thought from God for that person. We're not going to foretell the future or anything like that. There's nobody prophesying like that, it's just something that God gave to you, just an inspired thought that would do these things: encourage them, exhort them or stir them, or comfort the person okay? So I'll need a volunteer for that again. I'll have to stretch out and do it for you, then you'll see what it looks like okay, so I need someone, so who do I get? Someone over here, one of these ladies over here. [Laughter] You were pointing to someone - why don't you come on up here, come on, that's right. Never point to anyone else. [Laughter] Okay, so first thing, can I practice on you?

[Person Pastor Mike's praying for] Yeah!

[Pastor Mike] Wonderful, that's great. Okay, so we're all ready to go. Can I take your hand? Okay, so it's not necessary to do this, but it can create a sense of connection, so it can be quite a positive thing to do this. It's helpful if you ask the person's permission. It just respects them, and some may not want you to do that, so it's helpful to show respect for a person when you minister to them, by not trying to do something that they don't want you to do. Okay, so I've been at meetings, had a word to someone, and they didn't want to come up. So I said do you mind if I come to you? I went down and then didn't touch them, just shared what I felt God giving me, so it didn't highlight or make it too embarrassing, you've got to respect people's dignity. Alright, so we begin to pray in tongues. [Prays in tongues] So I'm just reaching out, I'm just reaching in my spirit, focussing my attention for God to give me a thought. Now it's up to Him what kind of thought He gives. One of the things that we could start - since all of you are Christians, one place that you can start practising in this, is looking for a thought from the Bible, just a story from the Bible, a person from the Bible, some act, a thing that happened in the Bible.

Is it Old Testament or New? Just reach out, and if you've read your Bible, God's able to drop many things into your heart, so what I'll look for is a person or a situation in the

Bible. Then I'll say well, in what way does that relate to her? What aspect of that do You want me to bring out? Okay, so we'll just see what happens. So of course there's that initial tense thing; oh God, I haven't got anything, what do I do? So you've got to overcome all of that. [Laughter] Remember, that's normal so just stay relaxed, just breathe gently and relax. Thank You Holy Ghost. Thank You Lord that You love her, You know all about her. I thank You Lord, You have something to inspire and to encourage her with, something Lord that You just want to speak into her life. Thank You Lord.

Now immediately I saw, or it came to mind, a story in the Bible, so I need to now just focus on that story. I just saw a picture, and I saw a picture of two men, and Jesus with them, and they're on the road to Ammaus. I knew exactly it was the story of the two on the road to Ammaus. That's all I got, a path, two people, and Jesus with them, and I knew immediately it's the road to Ammaus. Now what possible way could I share that with her? I could just share it like I've done that. I want to now minister, so this is what I will do now. I will just close my eyes and just go back, just become aware of God again, and aware of that story. Now what aspect of that story, so I just look at the story and then I can see it, so now I'll just begin to share. So while I was praying with you I sensed - I'm not saying 'God told Me'. I just felt while I was praying, this is what I felt. I saw a picture of the disciples on the road to Ammaus, and Jesus was with them, but they were unaware He was with them. They were so caught up in their own issues, and their own disappointments, and their own struggles and problems, and He was right there alongside them, walking with them, and they didn't even realise that their eyes were closed to Him being with them.

This is like you in your journey at this point, that you're so caught up in the things that are happening in your own life, that you're not realising God is with you. He's been walking with you quite a long way. He's with you. He cares about you, and His plan when He talked with those disciples, was to turn them around and get them filled with vision and direction and fresh passion, so He walked with them. He let them share their heart, their struggles and their pains. He fellowshipped them, and then He began to put faith into their heart again, began to put vision into their heart, and they realised it was Him. They were restored and went back to their whole faith journey again. What I see is God's doing this in your life. You've been walking with the Lord, but you haven't felt Him. You're caught up in the things that are going on in your life, and can't see that He's with you and loves you, that He's with you and He's wanting to help you engage your heart, like He got them to engage their heart. He was quite happy for them to share their disappointments, and as they did that, He then put faith in their heart again. That's what God's doing with your life right now, and the journey was an uncomfortable one for them, because all they could see was disappointment, but they ended up seeing Him, and being passionate again, and that's what's happening in your life. You're on that phase of the journey at the moment. But there's a great end in that story. [Laughs] There we are. Now how did that go? Does that sound like you?

[Person Pastor Mike's praying for] Yeah. [Laughs]

[Pastor Mike] That's good and I can see the tears in your eyes as well. It just fitted you like a glove.

[Person Pastor Mike's praying for] Yeah, perfect.

[Pastor Mike] So thank you very much for being part of it. [Applause] So it helps if you've read the Bible and know some of the Bible. [Laughter] You've got something to draw from. If you haven't then you have to find another thing, so we'll forgive you there. We'll try it another way a little later in the day, but why don't we just try this to see if God will give me something, just something, a person. If it's a person, what is there about that person? Is it an event? What is there about that event? That's all you've got to ask. I mean we're just here to hear, and then to pass on what we saw, or felt, or sensed. Now it doesn't need to be as substantial as what I had, it can just be quite simple. Okay, you all okay to have a go? All ready to have a go? It could be fun.

Remember, just relax, Lord, where is it, the Old Testament, the New Testament? Usually there's a person - who? What person? And a name comes to mind or what event comes to mind? Let it come to your mind and then focus on it. Well God, what is it about that you want me to bring? This is a great place for Christians to start because you can work with another Christian, they've probably read the Bible, know a little bit about it. But you find the Bible is full of events and people and situations that would be really helpful. It's a good place to start. Okay, let's get someone, break into pairs and then start. Lets start with: can I practice on you? [Background chat

Okay, let's just get your feedback. How many people today were really blessed by what was shared, you felt touched by God? How many were really blessed? That is very good. Give you a clap then. [Applause] How many of you felt as the person shared with you wow, how did they know that? Wow, that's great, look at that. Wonderful! Okay then, so it surprised you that they would know that, or be that relevant to you. That's because it's come from the Holy Spirit, see? Okay then, how many of you were quite touched by the Lord, with what was shared, actually touched you and you felt affected by it? That's wonderful, look, it's the majority of people, wonderful - so that means all of us are picking up the flow of the spirit and speaking in a way that's encouraging or exhorting or comforting. It was just inspired thought by the way, it wasn't prophesy [laughter] and how many of you experienced a block or a struggle at that crucial point where you were reaching out to God? How many felt struggles then? Okay, that's several of you there. Right, was there anyone unable to overcome that struggle, it was just overwhelming? Okay, so you all overcame. That's interesting, so there is a point of faith conflict, where you're stretching out for God to give you something and all kinds of turmoils start to go on around you.

That's quite normal but if you will stay focussed and committed you can break through all of that, so it's just great. I want to commend you there for pushing through. Let's give them a clap the ones who pushed through that. [Applause]

So you've had an inspired thought and that's how God works with us. With prophecy we just get an inspired thought or picture. How many got a picture that was a person, a story about a person in the Bible? Okay. How many it was an event, something that happened in the Bible? So some got that. Usually most people get a person. It's quite easy because you've read the Bible, read the person. How many of you, when you started to focus on that person, there was one aspect stood out to you about them? That was the bit you knew you had to talk about? How many had that happen. That's wonderful.

Now you see what happened in the process is you just reached out expecting. God gave you something, and as you enquired, you got more. That's how the prophetic goes. Have you ever seen a newsreader on TV, they only have a couple of lines that they're reading, and as they read the second line it changes, and then there's another line. There's another line drops in and that's how it works prophetically, so the newsreader has only got two lines at a time, but if he will read them then more will come. If you have a tissue box and you don't know how many tissues are in there but if you take one out, you think if I take that one out that's it. But no, low and behold there's another one turns up! [Laughter] And you take that - whoa! There's another one - and so it goes on. So the prophetic flows like that. You will take the first two lines and read them, then God will give you some more if you stay looking. If you pull the tissue out, another tissue is there if you'll stay looking, so if you stay focussed, looking and expecting, it begins to flow like a river from inside you and it's just all these thoughts, one after the other.

Okay, now how many of you found that you were listening to what you were saying, just kind of like, I know I'm talking but I'm actually listening to what I'm saying as well? How many had that happen to you? That's quite interesting. How many of you found that you were quite interested to hear what God had to say to the person? [Laughter] That's awesome. Okay, alright then. Now Sargin, have we got a morning tea break sometime around about now?

[Sargin] Yeah.

[Pastor Mike] Alright then, I wonder if we could just fit in one more of those in, just before we go for a break aye, if I keep squeezing it in? Alright then, so I'll get one more volunteer, just one more to come up. No one's pointing at any more. Hands coming up [Laughter] After a while you learn it's quite a good move to volunteer. [Laughter] Okay, we'll try it again. This time I won't look for a Bible passage, let's look for something else and just let God speak in any way He wants to. Can I practice on you?

[Person Pastor Mike's praying for] Yeah.

[Pastor Mike] Okay, great opportunity to practice, this is fantastic. Of course every day's a chance to practice. Okay, now let's take your hand. Thank You Lord. Now just again breaking it down into steps, in reality you've just got to flow into that quite quickly but we'll just break it into steps. The first part is just energising the spirit. Thank You Lord. [Prays in tongues] Thank You Lord - again just worship the Lord and set your mind and heart on Him, so begin to set your attention on Him. If I focus on myself I shut down. If I focus on Him I shut down. If I focus on the source, I'm connecting what I need - so thank You Lord that You know him, and You care about him. Father, I'm just asking if You would give something that would be encouragement and a blessing. Thank You Lord. Alright then, now I just got something just dropped in like that. Okay, now I've got to focus on it, and then I'll have to at some point begin to start to share it. Thank You Lord. So go back there. If the thoughts come from the Lord, the moment you just drop back into focussing on the Lord, or into the spirit again, what'll happen is you'll start to pick it up again, so you don't have to worry about trying to remember it all.

If God gave you lots, you get to the end of it and say, now how did that start again? So if He only gives you a couple of lines or a little bit of a picture - okay, so here we go, that'll be it. So now this is what I sensed as I was just reaching out the Lord for you. I saw a picture of a man running a race, and the way he's running it's like a sprint, and I could see him run and he would run and then he would lose breath, stop for a little while, then he'd run again, lose breath, stop for a little while because he's running the race like a sprint. I felt the impression I had was that the race you're running is a marathon, not a sprint, and the temptation or the tendency that you seem to have is that you will run at things for a while, and then you lose energy and motivation and have to take a break. Then a new thing will inspire you, you'll run at that for a little while, and then you've run out of steam, and then you'll run at the next thing again. The Lord wants you to know it's a marathon, and you need to learn how to pace yourself, and just keep a steady journey, progressing through this walk with Him. It's more about the marathon, setting the long term in sight, and starting to work your way, and just steadily move towards it, rather than short bursts of energy, followed by sort of quietness and not doing anything. So how does that relate to you?

[Person Pastor Mike's praying for] Yeah. There's some personal experience there, with the aspects of running...

[Pastor Mike] Yes - oh, so you've done both? You've done a marathon and you've done sprinting?

[Person Pastor Mike's praying for] Yeah.

[Pastor Mike] Oh wow, so this is a very good picture. [Laughter] I'd never have known you'd done both of those. [Laughs] So you'd understand with a sprint you've got to put in high energy but if you run out of puff...

[Person Pastor Mike's praying for] Yeah, verifying you've got to plan, you've got to strategise

[Pastor Mike] And that's what God's saying about your life, your walk with Him.

[Person Pastor Mike's praying for] Yeah.

[Pastor Mike] How about that? Awesome. [Applause] Alright then, so would you all like to have another go? Come on, before you go to break, before morning tea, alright. So find someone, can I practice on you? Let's go.

3. Tongues, Interpretation of Tongues (3 of 5)
https://vimeo.com/45874811
http://youtu.be/loLZXw9Fbkc

I want to talk about diverse kind of tongues, and interpretation of tongues. For some of you you may have a little insight around this - I want to help you with this - and there may be some who've got no understanding at all about the gift of tongues, and then wouldn't understand perhaps that there are two dimensions that God wants us to understand. One is personal prayer, and the other is the operation of the gifts, so what I'm going to do is first of all talk about the Baptism in the Holy Spirit and Speaking in Tongues. I'll be focussing on the personal devotional gift every believer can receive. Then we will move, and we will look at the ministry gift or the manifestation of speaking in tongues with interpretation.

We saw that list in 1 Corinthians 12, Verse 7, that one on the list, the gifts of the spirit was speaking in diverse tongues with interpretation. But what I want to do, because some people aren't baptised in the spirit, I want to help you in this session. Anyone at the end of this session who is not baptised in the spirit, we want to pray with you so you get filled with the Holy Spirit and speak in tongues and have the devotional tongue. Then we'll do some exercises speaking in tongues, but also I want to help you understand about tongues and interpretations which go together. So this first part we will talk just about being baptised in the Holy Spirit, filled with spirit, speaking in tongues, what it is and how to get it. Those of you who are already filled with the spirit, I appreciate just your patience for the ones who aren't. Perhaps there are some who are watching over the television or the Internet, not baptised in the Holy Spirit, and today you'd like to be, it'd be great. We will pray with you as well.

Okay then, so firstly I want to just open up several scriptures - so they're not written down in your notes - you can just jot them in somewhere when you get to diverse kind of tongues, and in Section 13 you could just, in the corner there on the left hand side at the bottom, just jot a few scripture notes down. So I want to share with you something that Jesus did and taught, so first I won't teach you all the scriptures on it, just enough for you to get an outline. Jesus made it very clear, when He was about to depart from this earth, that He would leave another comforter, the Holy Spirit. He made it very clear He was going to give them a person. The Holy Spirit would be released to them. He said in John 14, you've seen Him with you. Soon He will be in you. So Jesus made a promise, before His death on the cross, that the disciples would receive the Holy Spirit. He's the spirit of truth, He's the comforter, He will guide them into truth, He will reveal things to come, He'll reveal Jesus. He said I'm not going to leave you alone.

So John 14, He tells us I will not leave you alone, I will send you another comforter, the Holy Spirit. He's been with you, but now He will be in you - very, very important. Now following from there we know Jesus died and rose from the dead, and then He appeared to His disciples. We're going to read and pick it up from there and we're going to look at some things Jesus did, some things He said. So here we are, in John Chapter 20 and Verse 21. He said as He appeared to the disciples, He said peace to you! As my Father sent Me, even I send you. And when He had said this - Verse 22 - He breathed on them and said: receive the Holy Ghost. He breathed on them and said: receive the Holy Ghost.

Now I want you to understand He didn't just blow on them. [Makes blowing sound three times] He actually imparted - just as God breathed into Adam the breath of life, Jesus imparted into the disciples His Holy Spirit. He released into them the spirit of God - at that point they were born again. He breathed on them, and said receive, or take into yourself, the Holy Spirit. Now if I can just - I just need someone to come. Why don't you just pop up here just so I can just demonstrate for you what I'm talking about here. Okay, just Brian, would you like to come just there? So if you can just give me a hand. I want you to close your eyes, and look up, and open yourself to the Lord. Now what Jesus did was He didn't just breathe [makes blowing sound three times] He didn't do something like that. What He did was He imparted from His spirit, see? It's from His spirit, from the depths of His being, He released what He was unauthorised to release. He released the Holy Spirit to come into people, so He went [releases one long breath] like that, and something happened. There was impartation. They received an impartation. The Holy Spirit came into them. Thank you very much, see? What did you feel when that happened by the way?

[Female participant 1] Peaceful.

[Pastor Mike] You feel peaceful? Isn't that great. Okay, thanks very much. Now you notice I first of all just went [makes blowing sound twice] and nothing happened. Then I imparted. That's what impartation is. Something is imparted. Something someone has, they release it to someone else. Jesus said in John 7:37, He said out of your belly will flow rivers of living water, and He was speaking about the Holy Spirit, so God wants you to have a flow from your spirit, but first you've got to be born again. So at this point the disciples were born again. Now I want to share with you two other scriptures. One is found in Luke, Chapter 24, and Jesus again appears to the disciples and - Verse 49 - and He said: behold, I send the promise of My Father upon you. Now notice He's already breathed into them the Holy Spirit. Now He says something else; the promise of the Father. He said: I send to you the promise of the Father upon you. Wait in Jerusalem until you be clothed with power from on high. So He's already breathed into them, and they're born again. Now He's saying wait until you be clothed with power from on high, okay?

Now let's have a look in Acts, Chapter 1, around about Verse 4. It said being assembled together with them, He commanded them they should not depart from Jerusalem, but wait for the promise of the Father. Now they're born again, He's saying there's something else to wait for - for John baptised you with water, but you will be baptised in the Holy Ghost, not many days hence. When they were come together they asked: well when will this happen? When will you restore the kingdom to Israel? And in Verse 8 He says this. You shall receive power, after the Holy Ghost has come upon you, and you shall be witnesses to Me in Jerusalem, Judea, Samaria and the utmost parts of the earth. So notice He has breathed and imparted into them the Holy Spirit, they're born again, now He's talking about a second experience, where the Holy Spirit comes on them, and He uses words like baptised. That means you - like when a ship sinks, it's baptised, it's totally immersed. It's immersed in water.

If you had a garment, and you put it into a tub of water, it's baptised. It's immersed or soaked or saturated, so He's saying you'll be baptised in the spirit. You will be immersed into another dimension of the spirit. Okay, He uses another word. He said you'll be clothed with power. He said there's something will come on you, you'll have the Holy Spirit come on you, and your life will be clothed. Before it's like you were unclothed. You were trying to do the job without the power. He said when the Holy Spirit comes on you, you'll be clothed with power. You'll be wearing something. You'll be equipped for something, see? So notice He's quite clear what He's talking about. Now let's have a look when it happens, what actually happened. In Acts, Chapter 2, Verse 1; When the Day of Pentecost was fully come, they were in one accord in one place, there came a sound from heaven like a rushing mighty wind. It filled all the house where they were sitting, and there appeared cloven tongues like fire sat on each of them. And they were filled with the Holy Ghost - notice this - and began to speak with other tongues as the spirit gave them utterance. Isn't that amazing?

Verse 12; Everyone was amazed, and were in doubt saying to one another what does this mean? And some mocked saying they're full of wine, full of new wine. He said in Verse 15, you're not drunk as you suppose. This is that spoken of by the prophet Joel. It will come to pass in the last days, said God, I will pour out My spirit on all flesh. Your sons and daughters shall prophesy, young men see visions, old men dream dreams. So what has happened is the spirit has come upon them, and the first thing that happened is, they were filled up with the Holy Ghost, and they began to speak or express from inside, because what you speak, your words flow from your heart - out of the heart the mouth speaks. So being filled with the Holy Ghost, they gave voice to a language they had not learnt. It was a language given to them by the Holy Spirit, and they were so overwhelmed by it, some of them were staggering around laughing, and they were obviously like they were drunk.

You look at someone, if they look drunk, then they're behaving a certain way. Okay then, so we see now that He's imparted in the Holy Ghost, the Holy Ghost's now come onto them in power, and the first sign is that they began to speak in tongues. In Acts, Chapter 10, Verse 44, the Holy Ghost came on the Gentiles. They also began to speak in tongues - quite a common thing to find happening. In Acts, Chapter 10, the Holy Ghost came on the house of Cornelius, and we find they began to speak in tongues. Let's have a look and we read it now, Verse 44; While Peter spoke these words, the Holy Ghost fell on them which the word, and the Jews which believed were astonished, as many as came with Peter, because the Gentiles were - also the Holy Ghost was poured out on them, for they heard them speak with tongues and magnify God. So there's at least two instances in the Bible - there are others, another one there, where the Holy Ghost came on people, they were filled, they began to speak in tongues, and they began to magnify God with that expression or experience they had.

So what is this speaking in tongues, because this is a gift that they all received. It was something that God gave to them, as part of being clothed with power. If God has a gift to give you, then it must be important, and we need to understand a little bit about it, so what is this speaking in tongues? We'll go down and have a look in 1 Corinthians, Chapter 14 and get a little bit of understanding about speaking in tongues. So we'll read it in Verse 2; He that speaks in an unknown tongue, speaks not to men but to God, no one understands him. In the spirit, he's speaking mysteries, or things pertaining to the kingdom of God. Verse

4; He that speaks in an unknown tongue builds up himself, but the person who prophesies builds up the church. Verse 14; If I pray in an unknown tongue my spirit prays, but my understanding is unfruitful, so I'll pray with the spirit, and pray with my understanding as well.

Now let's just look at the gift of tongues. The gift of tongues is a language. In order to communicate, you need language, you need language. Our ability to communicate is really a lot dependant on the language we have to communicate with, so if you don't know many words, like I went to Taiwan and apart from 'Ni Hao' I knew very, very little language. I could not express myself in that culture without an interpreter, someone who could give me language, see? So in interacting in a new culture, I needed another language to enter into it, into that dimension - so God gives you a gift, because you are about to be immersed into another culture, into another realm, the realm of the spirit, and you need greater expression. It's hard to just keep telling Jesus you love Him - I love You, I love You - you run out of words, so God gives you a language that never runs out of expression.

So the gift of tongues is the Holy Spirit. They spoke, as the spirit gave them the utterance, so your Holy Spirit imparts into your spirit the language, and then you let go and surrender and allow that flow to come out. You are speaking in that language. So notice what it says in Verse 14; when you speak in tongues, your spirit is praying, so your spirit has a voice. Remember we talked about the different aspects of your spirit? Your spirit has a voice. Your spirit has a mind. Your spirit can speak. When you're speaking in tongues, you're not working it out with your head. You are letting your spirit yield to the Holy Spirit, and speaking out a language. It's a real language. Notice what happens, there's a whole number of benefits with that real language. Notice what it says in Verse 4; When you speak in an unknown tongue, you are building up yourself like a house being constructed, so praying in tongues strengthens and builds and develops your spirit man.

When you pray in tongues you are co-operating with the Holy Ghost directly, and your whole spirit man starts to energise with life. It's a wonderful gift, wonderful gift. It's very neglected, speaking in tongues devotionally. You can pray anytime in the spirit, because you just pray [Prays in tongues]. The flow of the language just never stops. The Holy Spirit is the spirit of prayer. He's always willing to pray through you, so you can pray in tongues anywhere, everywhere, any time of day or night, wherever you're going. Keep your eyes open if you're driving - but you can pray in tongues, okay? [Laughter]

When you're doing this you are building up yourself, is one thing it tells us. It tells us another thing: you are energising your inner life with the Holy Ghost, so when you pray in tongues strongly for a while, you'll feel your whole body start to energise up, because you are expressing the life of your spirit. Remember what we talked - one of the functions of your spirit is to give life to your body? So start to pray in the Holy Ghost, you come alive with spirit life! It's fantastic. Okay, another thing we notice there, is that when you're speaking in unknown tongues it says in Verse 2 you are speaking mysteries. Well that seems weird. It's a mystery because you don't know what it is, but when the Bible refers to mysteries it's referring to the things of God's kingdom that He's wanting to bring into clarity for us, so one purpose of praying in tongues with your devotional tongue is to magnify God, to praise Him. Another is to build yourself. Another is to speak out what God has for your life, so praying in tongues is a very powerful gift, a wonderful, powerful gift.

In Romans 8 and Verse 26, it says that we don't know what to pray, nor how to pray as we ought. How many know that experience? But the Holy Ghost helps us, and that word help means, He comes in and begins to join in with us as we make the effort. He energises, takes over and empowers all our praying. We don't know what to pray as we ought, nor how to pray, but the Holy Ghost helps us making intercession on our behalf or for us, so this is a work of the Holy Spirit. So there's a level of praying in tongues, [prays in tongues] - I can pray quietly. [Prays quietly in tongues] I can pray strongly and stir my spirit man up, or as I yield to the Holy Spirit He may take over, and then there's a whole different language of groaning in the spirit, of travailing in prayer. There's whole dimensions of prayer available, so when you get baptised in the spirit - baptism in water was meaning the end of your old life, the beginning of a new life, so you bury the old because he's died. There's a new person begun. Baptism in the spirit is immersion into the realm of spiritual things, of spiritual experiences, of prophesying, of having dreams, of flowing in the supernatural. This is what the gift - that's why God wants to have people baptised in the Holy Spirit.

The reality is many people, having had an experience, just peter out and don't persevere to get more, to reach into more. There's a contending for these things, because there's no way the devil wants you to operate in the supernatural, so there is the gift of praying in tongues. So how could I receive the baptism in the Holy Spirit? There's some very simple keys, I'll give them to you out of Mark. So we'll just find them in Mark, Chapter 11. It's like everything you get, you get pretty well the same way. Mark, Chapter 11, Verse 24, there's a great scripture here. Here it is. Whatsoever things you desire, when you pray, believe you receive them, and you shall have them. What could be clearer than that? Jesus' own words. Whatsoever things you desire - so notice now the keys in here. Number one, desire: I must want. I must want something. When someone is hungry and thirsty and wanting something, there is a draw and a pull into their life. Even when you're ministering to one another, if the person's hungry for you to help them, it draws out of you. It draws the life of God from you, so first thing is, if I come to God, I must come wanting to be filled with the Holy Spirit.

Number two, when you pray, whatsoever things you desire when you pray. You've got to ask Him. Now you don't ask Him like this: Oh God, if it be Your will then give me this. You know what will happen? He'll just say - without you hearing it - you really don't know what My will is, so how can you really expect to get anything? You actually need to know, it's the will of God for you to be filled with the spirit, so I need to know that, so I don't come to God saying well, if You want me to have it, I'll have it. That is passive. It's religious. It's not how you receive anything from God. If you're going to receive anything from God, I have to extend my faith and believe it's for now, it's for me, now. See? Now that's a decision to push aside all the things, I'm not good enough, whatever. Listen, that's all your history talking to you. That's the demons talking to you. That's your brokenness talking to you. What is God saying? He's saying I love you, I've accepted you, I want to fill you with the Holy Ghost. The gift is here. Will you believe?

That's how He works. Oh, I don't know, Lord, if you want me to have it. I can see you're double-minded and a double-minded man doesn't get anything, so when you ask, you've got to ask believing, and our believing is based on what we know God's word says. So Jesus said wait, you'll receive the promise of the Father. Peter stood up and said: this promise is for you, for your children, and all who are far off, so this Baptism in the Holy Spirit is for every person, and the gift of tongues is for every person. Why? Because it's to empower us internally, to help us in our spirit dimensions in our life - so here's the keys then. Whatsoever things you desire, when you pray you've got to ask - desire, ask. Number three, believe you receive it. Believe that when you reach out, God will respond to you, He WILL give me this gift. Believe you receive it, and then He says: you shall have it. So don't keep ask, ask, ask. Just say God, I believe Your word says that I can be filled with the Holy Ghost, I can have the gift of tongues. I choose to believe it. I believe You'll give it, and You'll give it to me because You want me to have it. You want me to be a strong believer.

The gift is to build you up. Now to approach it oh well, I just think I'd rather have one of the greater gifts. Well this is nonsense. It's just nonsense. God has got a gift to help you. I don't care how little the gift is, I'll have the littlest one, and then I'll have more, but if I ignore the little things He's giving me, it'll probably be very difficult to get more. So one of the things about praying in tongues is God gets a hold of your tongue, so that now instead of your tongue being turned to all kinds of things, it's turned to magnifying God, and turned to speaking a spiritual language - very, very powerful. So number one, desire; number two, ask; number three, believe; that as I ask then - four, receive. I've got to consciously do it, Lord I just receive and now Lord, I just begin to speak in that new language - and I've got to take a step.

Now when you step out to speak you don't stop to try and think now what could I say? I'll make a sound like this. That's your head talking to you. No, praying in tongues, you've got to tell your head stop arguing with me. You've been running my life all my life. I'm flowing in the spirit now, and the proper balance is to live from your spirit, with your head co-operating with your spirit, not ruling your spirit. When the language of the mind is, when your mind talks to you, it argues. It's like a lawyer - oh, who do you think you are? Why do you think that? Blah blah blah blah blah - ooh, sorry. See? So when your mind is talking it dominates, it argues, it reasons, it belittles, it judges. You've got to put your mind in it's right place, which is oh, thank you, I see the word of God says that, I'll receive that, and I won't try and evaluate it because it's from my spirit. I'll just let my mind focus on the Lord, and I'll just begin to worship Him.

So this is what we're going to do. It's probably best if we do this right now as a whole group. Some of you - I don't know which ones aren't baptised in the spirit, speaking in tongues. This would be a great time to get filled with the Holy Spirit. Why wait any longer? Why wait any longer? Oh well I need to pray about it. No, you don't need to pray about it, you've read the scriptures. We've read them. You just need to receive, okay? Aah, some reasoning's going on. See, here's an interesting thing that Jesus said: except you be converted, and become like a little child, you don't enter the kingdom of heaven. Now what He's saying is very simply this, that to enter the kingdom is to experience the benefits of what God has. To enter those benefits, He said you need to be converted, or to have a change, so you become more childlike, not childish, childlike.

A child is trusting, so for a child, if they're up on the bench and daddy says jump, I'll catch you, they say YAY! [Laughter] But when you're an adult, you don't approach it like that. You see if you're an adult and someone says jump, I'll catch you, you say ooh I doubt it! [Laughter] No, I don't think so. [Laughs] See, why do we say it? Because we've had a lot of experiences which flavour what we think, and we've lost simplicity and trust. Everything in the kingdom is about simplicity and trust, see? So coming into this is just a simplicity and trust, so I'm going to do this. In a moment, I'm going to lead everyone through a prayer to receive the Holy Ghost, and what we're going to do is were going to follow through simple steps. It doesn't matter if you received or not, you can still all help us. We'll all work together on this and if you're out there watching it on the television, wherever you are, you can all just do exactly what we do, and the Holy Ghost is going to come to you, you'll get filled with the spirit, speak in tongues wherever you are. It'll be fantastic, because God's not limited.

Okay then, so this is what we're going to do. In a moment we'll stand, and then we'll close our eyes. Close your eyes, you can forget about yourself, and forget about the people around you. They're not looking at you, they've got their eyes closed too. Then you can focus your attention on the Lord, who's the giver of a good gift for you. Just set your attention on the Lord. He's a generous, loving, good giver. Now remember, how do you receive or minister things of the spirit? By the hearing of faith. If you'll just believe what we've read and shared from the word is true, it can happen to you. So how we'll work it is this; I'll lead you through a prayer, and it'll go like this. We will ask the Lord for the Holy Ghost, we'll ask Him for the gift of tongues, then we will receive by faith and thank Him. Then we'll all begin to speak in tongues together, so practically, I'll lead you in the prayer, you follow, we'll get to the end of the prayer, then just take a deep breath like you're receiving. [Inhales deeply]. It's kind of like a physical action, like a faith action that you're doing something physical, but the reality is a spiritual thing - I'm receiving from God now, and I'm going to just speak in tongues. [Speaks in tongues] I'm going to just tell Him how much I love Him. I'm going to let that language of love just flow and flow and flow.

Now if your mind steps in, it'll argue and shut the flow. You've just got to tell your mind no, no, be quiet, just be quiet. Shut up! Just don't talk to me. Just, I'm wanting to flow with the Holy Spirit and worship God. We okay to do that? Why don't we all stand up, and we can help those who haven't got filled with the spirit yet. You don't know who they all are. I don't even know who they all are, so therefore it's not going to matter. [Laughs] Are we ready? So why don't we close our eyes. Let's lift our hands up to the Lord. If you're watching on television, you can lift your hands up to the Lord and all stand together as well. I want you just to follow me in this prayer, and when we get to the end of the prayer take a deep breath, and then receive the Holy Ghost, receive a fresh anointing, and lets all begin to speak in tongues, okay? Just follow me in this prayer.

Jesus, I come to you now. I want to receive the Holy Ghost. I want to be baptised in the spirit. I want to receive the gift of tongues, so today by faith, I receive the Holy Ghost. I receive the gift of tongues. Thank You Lord for this gift, to praise and thank You. Amen. [Repeated by congregation] Take a deep breath - receive the Holy Ghost! Let's begin to pray. [Prays in tongues] That's right, let the gift rise up inside. [Prays in tongues (for about a minute)] Okay, just stop. Just stop. We're going to start again in a moment. You can turn this gift on and off as you will. This one goes on and off at will. If you decide to pray, you can pray straight away. Now it requires - the Bible says 'they' pray, 'they' spoke, so it's no use waiting for God to make your mouth go. He won't make your mouth work. You make your mouth work. You yield; you speak. You say well I feel a bit funny doing that. Well no one's listening except God, just be funny in front of God, don't worry about it.

Just let go, and just stop being uptight and in control. Just let go, and love on Him. [Prays in tongues] See? I remember when I first started to pray in tongues, my mind was arguing saying you're an educated man, and you're babbling like an idiot, stop! [Laughter] And my spirit was saying YES! Oh joy! Glory! I could feel this battle going on inside, so I was walking around a block in Mount Eden. I remember stopping, and saying mind - be quiet! This is doing me good. I haven't felt so much joy in a long time - not without a glass of wine anyway. [Laughter] It was a different kind of joy. It's a joy that bubbled up from inside, not a joy you had to tank up and then you got a hangover. This is great stuff - so are we ready? So all again, on the count of three, we're all going to pray in tongues strongly, loudly. You choose, come on, pray, let's pray strongly, loudly. Give yourself a voice. Let yourself be heard. All these years of put down and held down, come on, let's have a voice to speak out in the gift of tongues!

[Prays in tongues (for about a minute)] Thank You Lord, thank You Lord. [Prays in tongues] Thank You Lord. Let's give the Lord a clap shall we? [Applause] Thank You Lord. Great stuff - now when you're in the shower, there's no one around, you just pray in tongues. [Prays in tongues] You can sing in the spirit as well, and start to give expression as much as you can to that language, and you'll find it becomes a flow like a river. When you're in that flow your spirit comes alive, you come alive. Don't let heaviness, and kind of inferiority shut you down. Whatever you do in God, do it strongly and boldly. I'll just show you what I mean. Let's just give the Lord a clap shall we, just - ready? [Applause] Okay, alright, stop now. Okay, that's good. Now that's the base level. Now the Bible says: clap your hands all you people, shout unto God with a voice of triumph. Now this time I want you to put everything into it, not sort of [claps quietly] polite clap, an English clap. Let's give - come on - just a great shout of victory and triumph, and clap the Lord who CONQUERED SIN AND DEATH and ROSE MIGHTILY FROM THE GRAVE. COME ON, LET'S APPLAUD THIS KING OF KINGS! [Applause and victorious noise] Halleluiah! YES LORD, Halleluiah! Okay, whoa, okay, that's much better.

Now you notice that the whole atmosphere changes when everyone, united, begins to express the life of God, everything changes. You see anything that's done half-heartedly never has any life on it. It's always got a death on it, feels like it's - oh, you know when people have Happy Birthday and they all sing it, but they don't sing it really strongly? You feel almost embarrassed for the person. One, they're singing to them and two, they're singing so badly you think oh God, this is shocking. Anything done half-hearted, no one's pleased by it, not even God, see? So when you do it with a whole heart, passionate and you're just under Him, there's a life comes in it. You can sing songs for 45 minutes or an hour and have no release. You just do this for 30 seconds with all your heart, the whole atmosphere changes, because our body and our soul hold back our spirit flowing, and so when you start to clap and shout, and shake, yes, yes, yes, and start to let go and start to GIVE to God, then your spirit just rises and flows.

So most people in New Zealand live under passivity and apathy and heaviness, so they get in any kind of group, and you can feel it in the group. You can break it easily. Let's keep on doing what we did now, shout - do it one more time shall we? [Yeah.] This time shout and pray in tongues as well, do all you can, just make a big noise. If you want to go like that, stamp your feet, you can stamp your feet as well. Want to shake your head - whoa! Come on, just go wild, for just 30 seconds. You know, we won't remember you were ever here, we'll shut down [Laughter] the camera has only got the back of your head, it's not seeing your face, so you can just go wild for 30 seconds, just worshipping God, okay? Ready? One, two, three - HALLELUIAH! [Praying in tongues, applause, shouting] Yes Lord! Yes Lord! Halleluiah! [Prays in tongues] Halleluiah! Halleluiah! Wonderful.

How many feel the energy level's just shifted in your body straight away? If you're half asleep you wake up, just like that see, because it's really quite simple. Just work your body so it yields, let your soul focus on the Lord, just let your spirit flow, speak in tongues. Fantastic, because what happens is, the power of God starts to flow in you. Your life becomes energised. You practice doing that in your prayer times, instead of just head down and [makes mumbling noises] Go on! Get alive! Speak strongly, and pray strongly, passionately! You don't have to do it very long and you come alive, see? You can pray in other ways as well, but this will get you alive, and get you going. Amen - and not only that, the power of God starts to flow in and through you. Your whole life becomes energised. The atmosphere begins to change. If the whole church does that, the whole atmosphere's completely different, but if they're all passive and shut down, it's just dreadful. I just scream inside, can't stand it, that heaviness and shut down religiosity, and you know the Bible abounds with noise and celebration.

David ushered in a whole new dimension of expressive praise and worship and dancing and rejoicing and celebrating. In the New Testament, James prophesied - God would do that again, so that is - see, so sometimes we just bring our cultural baggage in, and we think that because that's our culture, that's normal. But heaven's full of shouts and trumpets and noise and rejoicing and celebrating. There's joy unspeakable, see? It's expressive, full of life, so just practice praying in tongues, and giving more expression to your life with God, okay? So we'll do it one more time, 15 seconds this time. You ready? One, two, three - YAY LORD! Hallelujah. [Praying in tongues, applause, shouts] Hallelujah! Wonderful Jesus. [Laughs] Whoa! Great stuff, hallelujah. Okay, great. Give someone a hug and let's sit down then. You'll get too excited now.

Isn't that great? Okay, we still haven't got to where we want you to get to, so we've done baptism in the spirit, and speaking in tongues. Now you can pray in tongues all the time. That's your personal devotional language, and it builds you up. So we're going to go back now into 1 Corinthians 12 and Verse 7, and we're in Section 13, diverse kind of tongues and interpretation. I'll move through this part reasonably fast now, but in 1 Corinthians 12 and Verse 7 it talks about these - the manifestation of the spirit is given to every man to profit with all: word of wisdom; word of knowledge; faith; healing; working of miracles; prophecy; discerning of spirits; diverse kinds of tongues; and to another, interpretation of tongues. Now this is not your devotional language. This is a gift. This is an operation of the Holy Spirit, like the other gifts, for a specific a person or specific group, so not all may flow in tongues, interpretations as a gift. Do you understand that? Everyone has a devotional language; but not all might flow in it as a gift, and tongues with interpretations comes as a package usually, so if there's one there should be the other, otherwise you haven't got a clue what's going on.

So if someone prophesies, you know exactly God's building the church. If there's tongues you can't understand it, unless it's interpreted, and so this is not your prayer language. This is actually a manifestation of the Holy Ghost, diverse tongues as the Holy Ghost wills. Now we'll go and have a look back into 1 Corinthians - let's see if we can find it in Chapter 13. Though I speak with the tongue of men and of angels - isn't that interesting? So the language that, when the Holy Spirit comes on you, and you manifest the gift of speaking in tongues with an interpretation, it is a language of men, or it's a language of angels, so it's a language you're given - so example, I was talking with Doug, and he had prayed among a group of Chinese. There was someone there who knew Hebrew, and he said you have spoken in fluent Hebrew. He knew exactly what he was praying, so this is a specific demonstration of the power of God.

In the Book of Acts, they began to pray in tongues, and as they prayed in tongues, for some of them they were manifesting the sign gift of tongues, and people could hear them and understand them in their own language, so when the gift of tongues - it is a language. It is a real language, so it has expressions, so don't pray in tongues, or any gift operation, in a monotone boring way you know? Language needs to be interesting, and be alive and have expression, have you in it, not [speaks in monotone] just we're talking like this, and there's no expression. Let life and vibrancy - put yourself into it, see?

So the tongues of men and angels - so tongues means a different kind of language. It's a distinct language. Sometimes the gift of tongues with interpretation, the tongues may be a language someone could understand. Sometimes the tongues may be a language understood by angels, so clearly He said: if I speak with the tongues of men or angels, so quite possibly He spoke with the tongues of angels at times. I'll give you a couple of examples of this. In Acts 2, they began to speak in other tongues, and everyone heard them speak in their own language. Now you had people from all over the world, and everyone who came there understood something someone was praying, so how did that happen? That is supernatural. They've never learnt the language, yet they're speaking, and they're speaking from their spirit a language they didn't know, and someone understood the language. A most amazing gift really isn't it? We don't see much of that. We need to believe for more of that, just to be able to pray and speak, and someone from another language there and they - whoa, you were speaking something I understood. Do you know my language? No, don't have a clue, I just spoke in the Holy Ghost. Ha!

So people in different cultures did understand Him. It's quite an amazing gift, and I've heard of people going into places, overseas particularly, and having prayed in tongues, and actually someone understood what they were saying. It was their language. They recognised it, and were quite astonished they'd never learnt the language, so the gift of speaking in tongues with interpretation is a manifestation of the Holy Spirit, that comes on you at a certain time. It's for a purpose, to build the church. It could possibly also be a language of angels, and there's a number of things in scripture that talk about angels being activated. In Psalm 103, it says: the Lord has established His throne in the heaven - Verse 19 - His kingdom rules over all. Bless the Lord, you angels who excel in strength, who do His word, harkening to the voice of His word. So when God's word is spoken on the earth, angels can respond to that voice. I don't think we can command angels. I think that's an area where there's not a lot in the Bible on it, so people have different views, but I do believe that there can be a ministration of speaking in tongues, where angels understand what it is, and can be activated because of it, so speaking in tongues can be a very, very powerful gift of the spirit.

So what is the purpose of speaking in tongues? In 1 Corinthians 14:22 it says: it's a sign gift to the unbeliever, so a person who has no understanding of anything spiritual, and you speak in a language and they understand it, boy, they know that's God! That's definitely a supernatural sign. It can be also, I think, for prophetic proclamations, we can begin to speak out in the spirit and decree and declare things. I think angels are released many times by the speaking in tongues and activating that gift. It can cross language barriers - so again, for that gift to come on you, you'd need to desire to operate in that gift, and then practice. I'd practice at home, letting the Holy Ghost come on you, then begin to speak out, and so on. So we should ask the Holy Spirit to give us the interpretation. In 1 Corinthians 14, Verse 27, it says: if any man speaks in an unknown tongue - they're talking about in a church meeting or in a group meeting - let it be by two or at the most three, one after the other, and let one interpret. If there's no interpreter, let him keep silence, and let him speak to himself and to God.

So that's quite an interesting verse, so you notice there He's talking about two different things. He's talking about the gift of tongues, in a group setting, needs to have interpretation for it to build and benefit everyone, so we can all speak in tongues and just worship God together, but when there's a sign gift of tongues, like prophecy, there's a gift, when we have that gift, someone needs to interpret it, or it doesn't have any meaning for anyone. So if a man speaks in an unknown tongue, let it be by two or three, so don't have everyone doing this, just one, two or three, and there needs to be an interpretation. If there's no interpreter - then that's the interesting thing - if you've spoke out, you should pray you get the interpretation, and you interpret it - so how about that?

He said if there's no interpreter, keep silence, and speak to himself and to God, so clearly when you are speaking in your normal language of tongues you're speaking to yourself, and you're speaking to God, very, very clearly. So what about the interpretation of tongues? It's a gift that God gives you, it just comes on you, and you can actually - do you translate what was said? No, you don't translate it. Translating, you listen and phrase by phrase, you make sense of it. This is actually God gives you the inspiration, you just get the message, and you just share what God has given you - so it's not a translation. It just catches the spirit of what God is saying, and so a person may give a tongues message, but the interpretation's quite short, or the tongues message could be quite short, the interpretation could be a little longer. It's got nothing to do with translation. It's actually God is saying something by the spirit, and here's what it means by the spirit. Together the two build up the church, and they can activate things in the realm of the spirit.

So it's quite an interesting thing, because when you flow in those gifts, it energises and activates and creates atmosphere, because God is released through the moving in those gifts. Great gift to desire, great gift to begin to flow in. Not so many flow in it, and for a whole number of reasons, so what I want us to do is, were going to just do some activations together, and let's have a look, what time are we now? We're running out - we'll just get you back on your feet for a moment, and I'm going to get you to do two or three activations and praying in tongues. I want you just to stand with me and we're just going to give you a couple of activations and praying in tongues, and I want you to experiment with what you feel, and what you sense, as we do this. Then we'll go back into our next session, I want to teach you about words of knowledge.

Okay, here's what we're going to do, so you can make a bit of space for yourself. I'm going to give you a few exercises just in praying in tongues, and what I want you to do is, I want you to experiment with what you sense and feel as you do this. I want you to feel the flow inside, so first of all we saw, that praying in tongues, you pray as the Holy Ghost gives you the word, so you can pray and we're going to pray. On the count of three we'll pray. We won't pray more than 30 seconds, just 30 seconds, and when you're praying in tongues, I want you to put your hand on your belly, I want you to pray strongly in tongues, building up your own spirit man. And as you pray in tongues and speak strongly to yourself, I want you to sense what happens inside you, what you feel in your body as you do that. Are we ready? Okay, one, two, three. [Praying in tongues]

Okay stop, just stop now. Okay, now what did you experience? What did you sense as you prayed? What did you feel? Lots of energy, okay, very good. Something rising up inside you, yes. Something - like you were rising on the inside. Anyone else? Something you felt? Bubbling on the inside. How many did you feel like you were expanding, like you're sort of growing larger on the inside? Okay, that's quite a common experience to have that one. Alright then, now this time what I want us to do is, I want us to see if we'll all pray strongly in tongues, and we just focus your thoughts on the Lord, and we're worshipping Him, we're just honouring Him and thanking Him, I want you to see what happens in the atmosphere in the place as with one mind we set our minds on the Lord, just fix on Him, hold Him in your mind. You mean to pray in tongues strongly, again 30 seconds and we'll do it as strongly as we can, and let's just see how the atmosphere is affected by that. Ready? One, two, three. [Praying in tongues]

Okay, stop. Alright then, what did you sense or notice as we did that? [Breaking through.] Yeah, breaking through, great, yes. Okay, anyone else? Breaking through. What were we breaking through? Yeah, we were breaking through the atmosphere that's present, or spiritual atmosphere that sits over our nation, over our areas, over our region. When you begin to give expression to the life of God, suddenly you feel release, and you've actually broken through an invisible but real resistance. So what happens for many people, is there's something sits around them, that just holds them down. It's working on the beliefs of the heart, and it's usually demonically operated around those beliefs of the heart. It just holds you down, gets you in turmoil. When you decide to pray in tongues, it's like it all breaks off you. Now lasting freedom requires usually deliverance and change in the heart beliefs, and freedom from bondages, but if you will pray in tongues I tell you, you can stir your spirit man up and become full of life.

When you become full of life, then power - there's real power. I'll just show you what I mean. Just come on over here again. Okay, if you stand there. Brian, you can stand alongside her. I need a couple of catchers this time, because there's two people there. Now I just want to show you something. If I was just to begin to pray strongly in tongues [prays in tongues strongly] I can feel my spirit rise up, and instead of being conscious of myself, become conscious that God is within me. So if I - just lift your hands up to the Lord, just expecting to receive - and so I can then reach, and God is with me, and the power of God is there to touch people's lives. See? Mighty power of God, so I just put my hand on her head and touch her, and I believe that I am charged and full with the Holy Ghost, and so POWER of God can touch her life - like that. And I let go something from inside me and you could see it visibly. Notice I did not put my hand on them. I did that intentionally, didn't my hand on, so there'd be no pushing. You could see something is coming out of this person. There is a life of God, the hidden life of the spirit is designed to flow out of us.

Like to come on over dear? Just come on over, just come, just close your eyes, close your eyes. So just lift your other hand up to the Lord. As you expect to receive from Him, then I open my heart and inner life, and I just sense the mighty power of God just flowing - POWER of God just touch her life. You can just stay there, and you'll feel the presence of God over you. Now it can be strong, it can be gentle. I've done it in a dramatic way, so you get something visual that gets you thinking about we connect with the realm of the spirit and we bring from within us, from the gateway of our heart, we release the life of God. Could you come over? I'll just pray with you, if you'll come there. See many times when people pray, or we minister to someone - we'll get onto this later on this afternoon - when people pray and minister, it's like because of inferiority and rejection and the lies of the devil we tend to oh, we'll just leave it all up to God. Well God, just You do it all. Now God wants to work through you, so you have to give yourself, so you are joined one spirit to the Lord. So if you withhold yourself from loving the person, and releasing what you have to the person, nothing will happen, so if I was to go [blows three times] and just blow, nothing's happening because I'm deliberately choosing to withhold me.

But if I begin to think how wonderful Josie is, and how God loves her, how God's heart is filling me with that love [blows once deeply] and something happened that time that was different. Now what happened that time that was different was there was a flow of the spirit. There was just a flow from within my spirit, or we could do this another way - just take your hand again, just look up. Now I get her to look to the Lord, not to me, takes the pressure off me. Then I look to the Lord who's the source, so we're both looking to the Lord. We'd expect something to happen, so the Bible says: have the faith of God, and if you'll speak to the mountain, be removed and cast into the sea and not doubt - notice this - not doubt what you say will come to pass, then you'll have what you say. So notice it says: you speak, so the power of God can be released by speaking, so if we're going to minister in healing and deliverance, we will have to speak.

So power flows when I am connected to God and I hear what He's saying or doing, then I speak, see? POWER - and she gets touched by the power of God. Oh! See? So we'll just give you one more blast. [Laughter] You ready this time? This time - Holy Ghost. Now Holy Ghost, I just ask that you would come upon her, and just make her drunk, [laughter] just fill her with your presence until she can't stand. Fill her Lord until she's drunk. Let the joy of the Lord - drunk, drunk, drunk in the Holy Ghost. Now notice she's starting to get that feel about her, that she looks like she's drunk? [Blows once deeply] Fill her with joy Lord, fill her with joy, joy Holy Ghost, Holy Ghost, fill her, fill her, fill her Lord, fill her with joy, fill her with joy. Let the joy just rise like [laughter] a mighty river. [Lots of laughter! (female participant)] Give her more Lord. [Laughter] See?

Now this is exciting. We are ministers of the spirit. You have something to give. Whatever God has given to you, you can give to someone else. Think about that - so the more you can receive from God, the more you have to give. If you experience His love, you can release His love. If you experience His joy, you can release His joy. We need to engage God regularly so we have something to overflow, to give. We're not trying to make things happen. We're taking what we have, so I've taken a long time to gain these things. It's taken me time and effort to work on my mind, and deal with fears and things, but you have something to give because of that. Isn't that exciting? Isn't that great fun? Would you like to try that on one another later on this afternoon? [Laughs] Well you see, why not? We're only going to practice. We're just going to practice. We're just going to experiment and explore, what happens in our life, trying to work with God.

Now what happens when you work with God He's always willing to work with you. What happens is you become aware of blocks and barriers and things in you that you need to address in your journey with Him. We don't have to have it all now, it's a journey with God, so on the journey we're learning stuff. On the journey you find there are blocks, and so you work to remove the blocks. Is that good? Okay then, praise the Lord. Peter, why don't we pray with you then, while you're just here? Why don't you just come and stand here, just take your hand, just look up with your other hand to the Lord. Holy Ghost, come on him too, let him get drunk in the spirit. [Laughs] Drunk, drunk, drunk, drunk, DRUNK in the Holy Ghost. [Laughs] [Blows once deeply] Fill him with joy Lord, fill him Lord. Let your presence - now you notice I've avoided touching him. We're just calling on the spirit of God to come, just decreeing it. You've got to learn to exercise your faith, not try to make things happen. See if I step out of faith, then I'll try and make something happen, but if I don't step out of faith, if I just stay in the place - I believe God is full of joy, [laughs] God is full of joy! [Laughs] And I see that joy - HOLY GHOST come on him now mightily! He's starting to feel the spirit of God come on him.

So I ask him to connect with God, and reach out expecting, and I myself reach out expecting and make God my focus. It's quite surprising what can happen, you know? It is quite surprising what will happen. You might like to try it. Would you like to try it? [Mm-hm.] You'd like to try it, well come on then. We need two others - you'll do, come on, one, there's another one there. Why don't you come on over here too? Come on, that's right. Okay, so we'll just put you in three. Come up on the stage. Everyone can sit down, and this is something you may like to try a little later. Okay, so there we go. Come on, all up on the stage now, okay, there we are, isn't that wonderful? Three beautiful girls, and thank you for being part of all of this. Now remember that, for the anointing of the spirit to flow, the anointing flows from within the person's spirit, through their soul and body, out to touch a person. So if your soul is in turmoil, and blocks and argues, there's no flow from your spirit. Bible says out of your belly flows, so your soul, your mind and thoughts have got to cooperate. I've got to choose to set my heart to believe, and to resist the distractions. If I do that then the spirit of God can flow quite easy. He wants to do it.

Okay then, so what we're going to get you - we're going to get you to pray and minister, and we'll get you to come around here, you can stand in the middle this time. You ready? Everyone will have a chance. Stand here, put your hands up, that's ready to receive okay? And you can be the catcher - oh no, you've got a catcher over there. Oh okay, we've got a catcher, we can pay for both of them then. All ready? Okay then, so ask if you can practice on them. [Can I practice on you?] Absolutely, isn't that fantastic. Alright then, okay then just put your hand up here, just lightly there, so we're not going to push. I'll just stand with you to help you, so we're just - God is as close as I am to you. He's even closer, because He's inside you, see? So if you can just close your eyes, now begin to pray in tongues [Prays in tongues] and focus your thoughts that God is inside me. All that power, the power of God, Mighty God is inside me - and then on the count of three, I want you just to release that, just you'll blow on her, ready? One, two, three [Blows once deeply] like that, see what happens. Ooh, look at that, okay. Ooh, wasn't that good? You ready? Okay, pray in tongues, let your mind and heart rest no the fact that God is inside me, the spirit of God is with me. [Prays in tongues] Are we ready now? You're going to release from inside. You're going to give your heart to her. You're going to release the life of God that's in you to her, ready? One, two, three - there we go. There we go. She's been touched by the Lord, that's right, that's right. One more time? Ready? One, two, three [Blows once deeply] Holy Ghost, touch her. There we are. She's been touched by God, see her?

You can sense the anointing is all over it, here it is see? [Woosh] there we go - a bit of a delay there. She was trying hard of course, and trying hard tends to block things off. [Laughs] Okay then, we'll get you to get the other girl to pray for you, how about that? Come on up here and she can pray. Come on then, come on up here. What did you feel when she ministered to you? You felt very relaxed, okay, very good. Would you like to try, like to practice? Ask if you can practice on her. [Can I practice on you?] Yay! That's it, okay, put your hands up ready to receive. Okay, put your left hand just on her shoulder there, just lightly, just touch her there, that's right, okay. Just step in a bit closer, that's right. I want you just to close your eyes and begin to pray in tongues, become conscious God is with me. [Prays in tongues] The spirit of God is with me, Mighty God fills me, great God who created who created heaven and earth is filling my inner life. Thank You Lord. On the count of three, you're going to release what's inside you to her - one, two, three [Blows once deeply] there you go, there you go. Look at her getting touched by God. Whoop, whoop, whoop, she's staggering. [Laughs] Thank You Lord.

There you go, looks like you can hardly stand up. [Laughs] Okay, what did you sense, what did you feel? Something forth from you? [Forth, yeah.] That's right. Was that a new experience? Ha, you have something to give. See most people are waiting for God to do it, rather than we have something, we're connected to God and He works with us, and we'll release what we have. As you do that you'll become more aware how important it is to develop your spirit man, develop your inner life, deal with issues in your mind and emotions, so you have more to give to people. Fantastic, thank you very much. That was good. Let's give them a clap shall we. [Applause]

Okay, let's open our notes. We'll just do our last run before lunch, and we want to look at words of knowledge, words of knowledge. Number 16, word of knowledge, so word of knowledge is a gift of the spirit. A word of knowledge is a manifesting of God. This is what a word of knowledge is. It's just a little piece of information. It's not that you know everything. If you have a word of knowledge, you don't know everything, you only know a little bit, so a word of knowledge, it just comes as an impression, a thought, it comes as a mental picture, a still voice, and you become aware of something about a person, you had no natural way of working it out. So it is given to you, it's a revelation. You don't work it out, so you don't look at the person, and try and figure this thing out. You listen, and God just shares the secret with you. Oh really? I didn't know that - so it's like a thought that comes to you, so it's not accumulated knowledge. It's actually revealed knowledge; God reveals something to you.

So what is the purpose of the gift? There's a whole range of purposes, but when you have a word of knowledge, it helps you see what in a person's life, God is wanting to work on, so for example in counselling words of knowledge are just so important, because you'll just get something about a person, and it's related to their past or their current situation. It's like their whole life starts to open up, and you have access to minister into them, so a word of knowledge can uncover some details about a person's situation, and it enables you to minister and help them very, very clearly. It's just such a huge asset to get words of knowledge, because you know things that you couldn't have known naturally, and the person is so surprised, and it opens the way to minister to them, help them, and so on. Words of knowledge are just wonderful. There's a few Bible examples listed there. Elijah, the king, the enemy of Israel kept planning these plans to invade Israel, and every time he got there he would find that the Israeli army was there already. In the end the king got very angry. He said who's selling me out? Who's telling our secrets? They said no one's telling your secrets, but God is telling the prophet. Get this - he said: well let's go get the prophet then. Hello! If God's telling secrets about army battles, He's going to tell the prophet about what your plans are too, so it didn't work out very well at all.

So in 1 Samuel 9, Verses 15 to 20, Samuel received about 16 pieces of information about Saul, what he was doing, where was going, his father, his donkeys, what God had planned for him. It's one of the most accurate words of knowledge in the Bible. There are about 16 specific facts that God gave him, he could not possibly have known. It's extraordinary. John 4:18, remember the woman with the marriage failure, and she's just there talking to him, and he said go and get your husband. She said oh, I haven't got a husband. He said yes, you've been married five times, and you're living with a man right now. That is a word of knowledge. Words of knowledge can really - they actually scare people. I remember the first time I was in a meeting where words - I had no idea what words of knowledge were. All I knew was that man there was calling out secrets of people in the congregation, and I was overcome with horrendous fear. I remember - now this is how smart I was in those days - I remember hiding behind someone bigger than me, just going down in the seat [laughter] so that he couldn't look at me, because I thought if he looked at me, he would be able to see what was going on in my life, or where I was at. It didn't occur to me actually God was telling him, and he could say there's a guy over there hiding behind that guy there [laughter] Haaa! [Laughs]

I remember one of the most outstanding words of knowledge I heard of, was with Frank Houston, and they'd been having trouble in their church with someone breaking into their church and stealing sound equipment, and quite a bit of sound equipment had gone. Frank's a Holy Ghost man, and he was overseas and he rang back the church, he's ringing in the middle of a service, he's talking to his son Brian. He said Brian, God's been speaking to me. I've just been to place a of prayer and he said if you look down the back there you'll see right down to the back on the right side - you looking right the back side? He said now go three rows forward on the right side there. Now he says a guy two in who's got long white hair, is he there? He said yes. He said that's the man who's been taking stuff from the church. The guy leapt and ran, he literally ran away, but he had been the thief. He was the one seen. He'd come into the church meeting to case out what was there, then later on come and steal stuff and so eventually he was caught and returned the things. Isn't that extraordinary? Scary isn't it aye?

So the supernatural realm, when it operates well, is scary. It scares, because everyone has this illusion that you're secret, and you can cover everything from everyone else. When you suddenly realise, from God's perspective, it's all open, so He can see it all, and He can tell someone, that's a little scary isn't it aye? It's just because you haven't had that experience. I remember we were in Nigeria, and I had another one of the most accurate prophetic words of knowledge. There was a whole row of people lined up there, and the prophet had this first lady there, and she was pregnant. He stood in front of her for a little while looking at her, didn't say a word, but he was listening to God. He said to her: the child you're carrying is not your husbands. She was shocked of course, and he said then, actually when you got married, you didn't realise that your husband had a low sperm count, and so when you couldn't conceive, you went to the witch doctor to get a potion for your husband, but he deceived you, and gave you a potion that would turn your heart from your husband, and bring you to him. This child is the witch doctor's child - and she just broke down, and wept and wept and wept, because it was true. It was all true, so she repented, she was forgiven, and God touched her. Then she had the baby quite soon afterwards, because the baby was well overdue, there was a problem.

So these are the sorts of things that words of knowledge can do. Words of knowledge are stunning, because they actually open up people's lives, in a way nothing else can. When you know something about someone, and no one but God would have known, they don't know about - they don't see you. They just actually know God is really opening up their life. It's a dramatic, dramatic - I love it. Words of knowledge are great, so words of knowledge are great in areas of counselling, when you can't sort out the root of a problem, and then you just get a word of knowledge. I had someone come up to me, and they were describing a certain problem, and I just had the word 'occult' come to mind. I said have you been involved in the occult? We talked and interacted; yes, there was heavy involvement with the occult, and there was heavy involvement in the background with it as well. I said well this is the root cause of your problem, why you're having this particular struggle, so that was able to be ministered to. So how about that?

Ananias received words of knowledge about Paul. Remember, we read that Verse in Acts, Chapter 9, Verses 10 to 16, and God told Ananias go there, and go to that place, this street, that house, this man, and he's blind, and he's been praying. I want you to lay hands on him, he'll be filled with the spirit, and he'll be healed, and I've got a message for him. So there it is, the prophetic word, the whole area of words of knowledge, all flowing in together. Isn't it wonderful? Now this is in the Bible. Start to look for it, where Jesus did words of knowledge, for example: He's going into town, there's a man up a tree. How did He know his name was Zacchaeus? It's a strange town, strange people, there's a guy up a tree. Whoa! Who's that? He said: Zacchaeus, come on down, I'm going to your place for tea. How did He know his name was Zacchaeus? Word of knowledge, so words of knowledge can even get names of people, dates, events, specific things that have happened. God knows everything about your life. Now that means it's a good incentive to get your life right.

I remember when we went to this prophet, I remember thinking oh, I was in the terror of the Lord, I think dear Lord, I don't want to have him say all my secrets out in front of everyone, got to make sure my life is right before God! So the fear of God comes in that kind of situation. One of the meetings we were in there, I remember there was a whole group of us from the west had gone to this country, and there was one man there, the guy said you're a businessman aren't you? He said that's right. He said you're a leader in your church aren't you? He said that's correct. He said no one knows that on your last trip, you were involved with a prostitute over in this country, and he specified the country. He was just shocked - but it was true, absolutely true, and so he repented right on the spot, and got his life right.

So we tend to think that no one sees what we do, and no one knows what we do, but God sees it all, and when the words of knowledge start to flow, it brings to the light pieces of information, not to shame or hurt someone, but rather to actually help the person. So I would probably have done it a little bit differently than that, but in this particular situation, the guy came into a meeting where this was happening, and he came in with a sin hidden in his heart, so it was outed in the meeting. Scary, so my first introduction to Pentecostal meetings was scary meetings. They were scary meetings alright. I was scared anyway. [Laughter] So when the supernatural operates, you hear people use the term it 'freaked me out' you know, because they can't understand how this sort of knowledge would happen, but it's words of knowledge, words or a piece of information.

So how does a word of knowledge come to you? Well it may come to you just as a picture. You just get a picture just come. You may just sort of see something. It may come just as a spontaneous thought, you just have a thought turn up in your mind, and just suddenly you have this thought. It may come as you feel, or you have an impression inside you, about someone or something, so words of knowledge are wonderful when they come, but they come as a picture, come as a thought, they might come just as something that just - and very, very little, very, very small. So when you get a word of knowledge, it helps if you ask for details, just enquire for a little more, so instead of it just being general, it becomes more specific. Then we find that we can start to - the more specific it is, the more risk you take, but the more specific it is, the greater the release and the blessing for the person concerned.

So words of knowledge, so mostly it comes as a very little impression. You have to ask God to give you words of knowledge, and when you get the word of knowledge, you'll still actually go through the wrestling; man, I wonder how to say that, and how can I share that? Now most of the words of knowledge you'll get will be of quite a gentle nature, a simple nature. The ones I've described were people operating in a prophet office, and so it was a different level altogether. So for example, Peter operating in an apostolic office, and a man comes up to give, you know, Ananias. He said did you sell the property? We did. Is all the money from the property? It is. He said how come you and your wife have conspired in your heart to lie, not to men, but to the Holy Ghost, while you sold the property and had the money it was yours to choose what to do, but you have tried to lie to the Holy Ghost? With that he fell down dead. Isn't that interesting? His wife came in, the same thing. How did Peter know that? He knew it by word of knowledge.

Peter was not worried about the amount of money. That was not the issue. The issue was hypocrisy. The issue was: it was his property. If he wanted to sell it, he could sell it. If he wanted to give it, he could give as much or as little as he liked, but he gave pretending it was ALL that he'd sold. In other words he was trying to create an impression or an illusion of a generosity that wasn't there. He was trying to lie, and he said you're lying to the Holy Ghost ,and so it had huge consequences for him. So so many times in the Bible there are examples of words of knowledge. Anyone who flowed prophetically moved in a mixture of prophecy, word of knowledge, right through the Bible. I'll give you an example of this operating with Peter, when Simon the sorcerer got converted, got baptised, and then he saw that when they laid hands on people, that power came. He wanted that power, and Peter looked at him and said: I see that you are in the gall of bitterness, and the bondage of inequity. He said underneath, driving that request, is bitterness, and there's a whole crookedness in your life around the area, of wanting power so you look good in front of people, so he was able to, with a word of knowledge, go right to the very root issue that was there, and help the man face and see what his motive was for doing things. So that's actually like a - it's revelation knowledge, and it could be described as a word of knowledge, or it could be described as discerning of spirits, picking the motivation of the man's heart.

It's a very powerful thing. Words of knowledge are great. One of my daughters served as a - what do they call it? A responsible person, or responsible adult, RA, in a hostel, and she had responsibility for the whole of the second floor. She had to look after all the students, make sure that there's no one in the rooms, and that kind of deal. She would lie down, and the Holy Ghost would speak to her, if there was a guy had come onto her floor, and had gone into one of the rooms. He would just speak to her and tell her, and she'd go down, knock on the door, ask to come in and so you've got a young man in the room, and they would be shocked. How could she possibly know? But God told her, so she just took it, and acted on it, and it opened up, and the whole thing came out in the open. It's exciting isn't it? [Laughter]

You think you could hide from God - it's a bit scary isn't it? But this is normal in the Bible, that the supernatural realm would operate. It's a normal kind of thing, so it could operate around a whole lot of areas, around causes of problems in people's lives, circumstances, family situations, and so on and so forth. God can open up these things by revelation, can reveal, so when you're working with people, it's a great help if God gives you words of knowledge, and prophetic words for them, because you start to see things you couldn't see before, and it helps bring God to the person. It's a wonderful gift, great gift and it comes very gently. It comes very gently. It's just like the slightest, least impression, so in a group like this, there are bound to be many, many needs and so we could reach out and say well Lord, is there someone here who has a need? Suppose if we just, for example, we look at the area of healing. We're going to look at how could I move in words of knowledge around the area of healing?

So I'll just show you a simple way of approaching it. There's many different ways of approaching it, then we'll just step out and see what God does. Alright, so the first thing is we look at - now suppose, how am I going to get a word of knowledge? A word of knowledge will come as just an impression, a thought, a picture or some kind of thing and be very gentle, very light. So if I was to begin to just picture the outline of a person's body, and I would just ask the question, I wonder is that a man or a woman? Now when you ask God things, ask always, is it this or that, this or that? You'll feel drawn to one or the other - oh, I think it's this, see? So ask the Lord; Lord, is there someone here that you want to minister to, and is it a man or is it a woman? A man or a woman? Which way they were drawn, I sense a woman. Alright then Lord, well where would she be? Would she be on the right side of this room, or on the left side of this room, where would she be? Is it the right side, or the left side?

Now just listen for the gentlest impression, gentlest impression see, so is it a man or woman? Is it on the right side, or on the left side - it's on the right side. Alright then, so therefore, we know it's probably in this area. So I need to know, what is the area? So if I just look at a person's body, and start to look just at the head, and is there any part of the body I'm drawn to? So I'll just look at the head, maybe the ears, the eyes, I just begin to just slowly, just mentally, just walk down through her body. Is there any place that I'm drawn to, any place that stands out, any place I feel oh, there could be a problem there? So what I sense is this: I sense that someone has a lower back problem, a woman on the right side of this room. Is there any woman here, around this area here, that's got a back problem, in the lower back there's pain, and we will just pray for you right now and you're healed. Who's that? And there's another woman here, and you've got a problem in your hip, in this right hip. Who's that's got pain in the joint, it's actually in both your hips? There's a pain in the joint. Who's the person who has that problem? Who's the one has the back problem? Can you just come? I'll pray with you, the back problem. You probably think - there it is, look at that. Woman, right side, back problem.

Okay, God bless you. So how long have you had the problem? [About eight years.] About eight years? What happened eight years ago? [I'm not sure if it was anything, just deteriorated]. It just deteriorated? [Yeah.] Did the doctor tell you what the problem is? [Yeah, I go to the chiropractor every week.] Every week you go to the chiro - you've been going for nearly eight years or something have you? [On and off, yeah.] On and off for a long time. Are you in pain today? [Not right this minute but yeah, hard to sit in this seat.] Yes, of course it is, okay, so is there something you couldn't do, or would be painful to do? [Not in this situation, but like if I was doing something really active, like picking up kids at work, like picking up...] Right, so picking up things creates some difficulties, yeah, right, okay, like that. Okay then, so because the reason I'm asking that is to try and identify where the problem lies, how long it's been there, and then what it's painful to do, because I was going to get you to do something that would be difficult to do, see?

Okay, but if you can't think of anything that's okay, don't worry about that. Can I just have your hand then? Thank you, and can we just pray with you right now? So look to Jesus. He's the source of healing. He is the healer. Now we know that because of word of knowledge, God does want to heal her. This is a long-standing problem that requires expensive treatments with a chiropractor. It'd be great if God healed her, so now we need to pray. So we've got a word of knowledge on the healing situation, now we need to get to believe God for a miracle of healing, so you believe for the word of knowledge, then you believe for the miracle of healing, two things, okay. So I need to believe for healing, so I need to start to pray in the spirit, and look to the source. If I focus on the need for her to be healed, I'll feel stressed I've got to do something, but if I look at Jesus, the healer, then I can become aware, and filled with awareness, there's nothing too difficult for Him, and I can then, at the right time, just release healing.

We ready? So I just begin to thank You Lord. I thank You Lord - I'm just speaking out loud now okay - I thank You Lord, You are the healer. There's nothing too difficult for You. You're the Lord, our healer. I just love You. Thank You Lord that you desire to heal this young lady right now, right now I thank You for Your power touching her. In the name of the Lord, Jesus Christ, I speak into the spirit of infirmity, I command You release her spine, release her back right now. I break all witchcraft that's come around your life, to hold you back. I speak and break all generational witchcraft. I speak and command that spirit of infirmity, loose her right now, in Jesus' Mighty name. Now Lord, we just pray for Your healing power to just flow into her, and restore her completely, in Jesus' name.

Now you notice as I began to pray, I started first of all to focus on the fact there could be infirmity, and I started to not just pray for healing, but consider the possibility there could be a spirit. Then as I began to pray into that area, I began to realise there's occult, and there's witchcraft, there's something has been around her life, got on her spine, and attached to her, so when I rebuked it, you notice the power flow was immediate. How are you feeling? ,[Laughs] You feel a bit of a shock wasn't it aye? [Yeah.] There we go. Did you get surprised how suddenly... [Yeah.] What did you feel? What did you experience? [Just like release I think, I don't know...] You felt release? [...sorry, I can't pinpoint it.] Yeah and when you fell over what happened, just suddenly couldn't stand anymore or what? [I don't even know, I wasn't really...] You were over before you knew it? [Yeah.] Wow, that's great. Okay, how are you feeling? Just move around, just see how you feel now. Okay, look for a chance to lift someone. You feel different? Okay, come on, let's give the Lord a great clap now. [Applause] Praise the Lord. Isn't that wonderful isn't it?

See, now you notice we are moving from the simple, you know, just ask someone about something, to listening for inspired thought. We're coming up to starting to get inspired thoughts, words of knowledge and starting to look then at being able to minister to needs in people's lives. You see, it's just a slow journey, but it all works on the same thing, getting something from God, so remember what I did was, well Lord, is it that side or that side? Oh, maybe that side. That's all I got. Is it a man or a woman? Man or woman? I think maybe it's a woman. That's all I got. Then I began to look at the outline of a body, and suddenly I could see - I saw almost like there's like a glow, or attention was drawn, right to the lower back, so then I've just got to step out, actually there's a woman here on this side, and you have a problem in your lower spine. Now if there's no response, I'd have to then get more information, so the person then, it has to be me - there's only one person could be like that. See?

Right, now who was the other lady that's got problems in her hip joints? Might as well pray for you too. There's someone who's got problems with hips, I'd like to pray for you. God bless, come on then. I did feel it was on the other side this time too so that's good. There we go, so there we are. Again, just a slight draw, different side. Okay, now tell me a little bit about the problem you've had. [I had a fall] You've had a fall? Right. [I fell over and I hurt my shoulder and all that, but sort of later on... but the last three and a half weeks I've had this...] Right, lower back, right. [Yeah.] Right across the back? [Yeah.] Yeah, right across there. Okay, so she had a fall and injured her shoulder, and she was prayed for and the shoulder was healed, but since then she's had this pain right across the back, and so - stiffness inside, okay, so it's painful to bend or anything like that? [Well it's very...] Yeah, it's stiff? [Yeah.] Okay. [It catches me.] Catches you, alright then. You believe Jesus could heal you? [Too right.] Too right! Good on you, that's the spirit.

Well look up to Him, He's the healer, not me. You look to Him, and focus on Him. God, I just thank You that You're a great God. Thank You Jesus, You're the healer - so again I just centre my attention on the Lord, and should I be praying against an infirmity, or just praying for healing? So I'm reaching out for the healing power of God to flow. If I focus on the source, that God is the great healer. I thank You Lord for Your mighty healing power. In Jesus' name, I command this infirmity to loose your spine right now. Father, let Your mighty healing power flow. Let the POWER of God just come right through her body, in Jesus' name. Lord, fill every part of her body, just restore completely this spine, this back, in Jesus' Mighty name. Thank You Lord. Thank You Lord. Thank You Lord. Why don't you just begin to move your back, just see how you are, see how it feels. [unclear] What's that? [unclear] Okay, has it improved at all? Is there any shift or change? [Not at the moment.] Not at the moment. Well we'll pray again - never quit after the first time. [No.] See, Jesus prayed for a man and said: do you see? He said no, I see men like trees, and so He said look up, and He prayed again another time. Okay, so we'll pray again one more time, so just look up to the Lord.

We thank You, You're a mighty God, a healing God. Now it's quite important that you don't get pressured to perform, quite important you just keep your eyes - it's God who heals, so it's His healing power we need. So as you're reaching out now, you're asking is there anything that would block, anything that would hinder? Lord, I thank You, the mighty God who heals. Let Your anointing just flow right now, just speak into the spine, command every part of your spine to come into divine order. I command this infirmity, to release your spine in Jesus' name. Father, let Your power flow, TOUCH her Holy Ghost right now, in Jesus' Mighty name. Fill her, fill her, LOOSE her now in Jesus' name. Thank You Lord. Whoa! Feel the power of God now. Okay, now just begin to move around now. Okay, now what I want you to do, is I want you just to begin to move and walk towards me, begin to move like this. Just do the best you can. In other words, instead of focussing on what hasn't happened, just begin to take steps of faith, okay? Thank You Lord, thank You Lord, thank You Lord. Okay, thank You Lord.

Okay, now just begin to move around more - stretch. Sometimes miracles are immediate, and the change is immediate. Many times they're like a seed, you get a little bit of a shift, and then as the person just stretches and exercises faith, thanks God, then it frees up completely. So you never know which it's going to be, and you have to consider both are possible. Most of us just want it all to happen at once. I've found many times nothing happens, overnight they're healed or sometimes they get a little improvement, so I ask the question - this is the question I'd ask; has there been any change? Did it get worse? If it got worse, I know it's a spirit. If it gets better, a little bit better, I know the healing has started, and we persevere in the praying.

I remember praying for one lady, a severe back problem, and I prayed for her, and it was in a group of Pastors. I prayed for her, and she got worse. She started to actually physically be in pain, and you could see the gasp of disapproval from all these Pastors. You have ruined her! You've hurt this poor lady by your praying. Now she hadn't fallen over, or anything like that, but they just thought I'd hurt her. Now it just shows the level of understanding. I said better or worse? Oh, a lot worse. I said okay, that's good, we know what the problem is. It's a demonic spirit, and it's now manifesting, and resisting the healing. I'll pray again, you will be healed - and she walked away completely free. But see, people don't understand that. Yes? Okay, right. Okay now let's just move around a little bit, move around a little bit, okay. That's looking a little bit freer isn't it? [It's a little bit freer.] It's a little bit freer isn't it? We'll just keep thanking God, and you see - yeah, that's right and just keep moving now, keep moving and enjoying your freedom.

See, most people focus on what didn't happen, rather than what did happen. Focus on what did happen, and thank God, and let it grow in your life, rather than focusing on what didn't happen. When I was trained, I trained in physics and science and maths, so my whole orientation was what didn't happen, so I couldn't move in these kinds of things at all, until I changed and said, well what has happened? Has anything happened? If there was a little improvement, something has started. Thank God, and keep moving, and believe God for the full healing to take place, okay? Praise the Lord. Let's give the Lord a clap [applause] then we'll have a break for lunch.

Father, we just thank You for this time. We thank You for everyone learning so much, in such a short space of time. Thank You Lord for miracles of healing, deliverance. We love You. We're just so glad You do these things, and we want to see and experience more. Father, we pray blessing upon every person here, during this lunch break. When we come back this afternoon, we want to see more miracles, more things happening, in Jesus' name. Amen.

4. Discerning of Sprits (4 of 5)

https://vimeo.com/45951460
http://youtu.be/1iuOs5Q9sh4

So in this session we're going to start, I'm going to do some teaching in discerning of spirits, and then we're going to do some activations for a little while just to get you busy. So if you open up your notes there in Section 17, you'll see the section on discerning of spirits. I'll just read to you a scripture passage, then we'll go into explaining it. This is out of Book of Acts, Chapter 16, Verse 16 and Luke is writing. He's writing about his adventures with Paul: and it came to pass, when we went to prayer, a certain young woman who was possessed with a spirit of divination met us, and brought her masters much gain by fortune-telling. The same followed Paul and us and cried out, saying these men are servants of the Most High God, they show us the way of salvation. And she did this many days, but Paul, being grieved, turned and said to the spirit: I command you in the name of Jesus Christ, come out of her. And he came out that very hour.

So this is an interesting story in the New Testament, of Paul is going to a prayer meeting, and as he goes to a prayer meeting, the place that they were in was the centre of occult activities. It was a centre of spiritism, divination, that kind of thing, and so what happens is there's a young woman there. Notice her message; her message is: these are the servants of the Most High God. Is that correct? Yes, it was. They're showing us the way of salvation. Is that correct? Yes, it was. What she was saying was correct, but the motivating power behind it was a demonic spirit, because she herself was involved in divination. It said: there's a young woman, who was possessed with a spirit of divination, met us. The word possessed is a very bad translation because it actually means literally to have a spirit, not to be totally controlled. You use the word possessed, you think totally controlled. She's not totally controlled. She had a familiar spirit, because she was involved in fortune-telling.

It says she had a spirit of divination. The word divination is the word python, literally she had a python spirit wrapped around her, speaking into her ear, talking into her. It was invisible to the natural eye, but it was very real in the spirit world, so constantly, because of her involvement in divination, in the occult, she had this spirit familiar to her, attached to her, joined to her, would talk to her and give information about people. So people would come, they'd pay money to have their fortune told, and the spirit, because of that access to the spirit realm and spiritual network, spirit internet, it could share facts about people that would stun them. Then as a result of that, they would open up their heart to receive direction, and their lives would come into agreement with the spirit and into bondage.

Now when you look at it, the woman is saying all the right things, but Paul discerns that behind it there's a spirit operating, and he discerned exactly what it was. Luke said it's a spirit of a python, and it brought the masters - so she was a servant girl - a lot of money because of her fortune-telling. So the whole of that area was given over to fortune-telling, was given over to divination, given over to the demonic realm, and this girl came with a spirit. Now Paul, it says an interesting thing. It said Paul - although she followed us and cried out so and so, she did this many days - so Paul didn't address it immediately, but he became irritated by it. It says Paul being grieved, or feeling oppressed. The exact meaning of that word I'll just get for you. Let me just find it here - the exact word there means literally to toil, or to struggle to break through, or to feel worried or pressured, or to feel grief. Isn't that interesting?

So when a spirit is operating against us, then you can feel all kinds of feelings or sensations, like difficulty breaking through, there's no freedom or flow. You can feel turmoil around you, you can feel perhaps stressed trying to achieve what you're trying to achieve, or you may even feel grief. Those are the kinds of meanings associated with that word, and so he was experiencing the sensations, what she said was okay, but what was behind it, at the root of it, was demonic, and eventually when the Holy Ghost led him, he turned around, spoke and directly commanded the spirit: come out of her. Immediately the woman, or over the next hour, she was delivered of that spirit, and of course if you read on, you find then that there was a massive reaction, and Paul was then put into jail and beaten up. But there was again further miracles took place.

So this is a region full of demonic activity, and this is the gift of discerning of spirits operating. He discerned, or looked right through and found what was at the cause, or what was the source of the problem, so discerning of spirits, this is what it is; it is knowledge God gives you, so it's a revelation God gives you. God reveals something to you. What does He reveal? He reveals what spirit is operating right behind some activity or action. It's a supernatural gift of revelation. It means to see right through to what is the root, or what is behind this matter, so the gift of discerning of spirits gives you information, or insight, or revelation about three areas; one, the activity of the Holy Spirit. We need to discern the work of the Holy Spirit. Jesus consistently discerned what the Holy Spirit was doing, and did it, so one aspect of discerning of spirits is the realm of being able to see right through what the Holy Spirit is doing.

Another aspect of it is to be able to identify demonic activity. When there are spirits in a place, spirits in a person, or spirit behind someone's actions, we need to be able to discern, or see what is operating there, otherwise we come under the influence of it. Many times, on some of the big moves of God, they lacked experience in discerning of spirits, and a lot of things they said were the Holy Spirit, were actually demonic manifestations. I can remember being in a meeting one time, and they were just saying: this is all just a Holy Spirit working and so on, and I looked at the person who was next to me, or just in front of me. I could see clearly there was a spirit operating, so I just quietly went up and just commanded the spirit to go. The person dropped to the ground, it was all over, and she was set free. I found it impossible to just focus while there's all this demonic stuff just going on around me, so that sort of dealt to that.

So you have to understand one of the things it's not; it's not natural discernment. It's not working things out. You know some people train in body language, so they can work out things from body language, look at the person, figure them out, you know? It's not natural. It's not, you've developed some skill at being able to work out some things going on in people. It's actually, revelation just comes to you, God just speaks and reveals it to you, and so that's how you know. So He can reveal the activity, or nature, or name of spirits that are in a person, so this morning when I was praying, you notice I spoke against a spirit of infirmity. Now you notice that the moment I stood against that spirit of infirmity, there was quite a quick reaction or response, so that tells me that it was exactly what the problem was. There was a spirit was causing the pain in the person's body, for example I had a young man - I was speaking in City Harvest and I had a word of knowledge, it was a young man with a shoulder condition.

He had pain in his shoulders, so the young guy came up, and as he began to speak to me, interact with me, I felt the Lord say he has a major root of bitterness against his father. So I asked him how do you get on with your father? He said I love my dad, so it seemed like his initial response contradicted what God had shown me. I said to him well, isn't it true that your father travels a lot, and is not there for you, and actually you've got quite a lot of feelings about that? He said that's right. I said: the Lord shows me that you've been quite angry, and actually become resentful and bitter that your dad has not been available for you when you needed him, and he said that's true. I said: well the Lord's shown me that the reason you have this pain in your shoulder, it's actually a spirit of infirmity, and it's come because of the unforgiveness in your heart towards your father - now you see, so some of that was word of knowledge, and some of that is discerning of spirits. The cause of the sickness is a demonic spirit - that's discerning of spirit. The nature of the problem, the issue with his father, that's word of knowledge, see?

So I asked him if he's willing to forgive his father, which he was. I led him in a simple prayer, forgave his father, then as soon as I commanded the spirit to come out of him, it manifested quite strongly, he fell on the ground. He got up after that, and he then testified. He said actually, I didn't just have pain in my shoulder, I had pain everywhere, all over my body I've had these pains. The doctor has told me my back is stiffening, and by the age of 40 I would not be able to bend or move or twist at all, but he said I now am completely free. So the spirit of infirmity had created pains in his body, and they were associated with an issue in his life of unforgiveness with someone.

So you see how gifts work together, and we'll get onto the word of wisdom shortly - so the gift of word of knowledge, and discerning of spirits, they work very closely together. One gives you some information you couldn't have known, the other gives you discernment to see right through to the problem. So discerning of spirits is not natural figuring things out by studying a person's body or body language and so on. It's not a natural gift, it's supernatural, where God just reveals to you: that's what the problem is. So again, with all of these gifts, we need to learn how to listen and receive from God. Another thing that it is not, so it's not natural, but there's another thing it's not. It's not judging. I want to show you another scripture in Matthew, Chapter 7 - it's not mentioned in there, I don't think, but in Matthew, Chapter 7 and the first few verses. Discerning of spirits is not the same as judging, in the worst sense of judging. Let's read a few verses.

In Verse 1, judge not, that you be not judged. For with the same judgement you judge, you will be judged; and whatever measure you measure to others, it will be measured back to you again. So why do you look at the small speck that's in your brother's eye, and you do not consider the beam is in your own eye? How will you say to your brother: let me pull out the speck from your eye, and behold, there's a beam in your own? Hypocrite! First cast the beam out of your own eye, then you'll see clearly to cast the speck out of your brother's eye. Don't give that which is holy to dogs, neither cast your pearls before swine, lest they trample them under their feet, and turn again and render you.

Right then, now let me just go into that scripture. Jesus is speaking about a principle that's very important. He's talking about a principle of judging. This word judge means literally, to make a decision against someone, because of what you see, or think you see, or whatever, and virtually to pass a sentence on them. You are guilty according to the way I've judged you, therefore you need to pay the price. So He's talking about having a judgemental attitude, and what He's saying is that if you judge others, you unlock against yourself a spirit of judgement. The very thing you've judged will come back to you. Okay, let me just give you an example of that. I had to pray for a woman one time last year in Taiwan, and they sent her in for ministry. I asked what the problem is, and she said well, I've got this young man interested in marrying me. I said okay, so what's the deal? She said well, we were going out before, and then our relationship broke up, and I got involved with someone else, had a baby to him, and now I've got the baby, now this guy's come back, and he wants to marry me, so what do you think?

Now people only give you the sanitised version. It makes them look really good, you know? So I said is he Christian? No, he's not a Christian. I said well, alarm bells go off for her straight away, and I say, what about this other guy? She said well, he really would like to marry me too, he's the father of the child. I said what do you feel in your heart? No, not for that person. I said well, now tell me then, why did your relationship break up? She said well, while I was going out with him, he was unfaithful to me, he had other girls on the side. So I said well, is there any evidence that that has changed in his life? Is there any reason why he would be different - and he hasn't become a Christian, he hasn't changed in his heart. You're in for more of the same, and so why would you want to marry him? She said, I really feel he's right for me.

I said tell me about your father - so why would I ask about the father, when it's an issue of marriage? Because the Lord dropped in there's an issue with her dad - so she said oh, well I don't talk to my dad. I said why is that? She said well mum and dad broke up. They divorced when I was in early teens. I said really? Do you have any contact with him? No, no, almost no contact whatsoever, and I said is that right? I said tell me what was the reason that the marriage broke up, and she said very simply, he was unfaithful to my mother. I said how many times? Three times he was unfaithful to my mother. I said isn't this extraordinary. You've got a conflict in your heart with your dad, and you have judged him. Now it's replaying in your life again. You actually - the judgement you gave out about him, now it's being replayed back in your life again. Do you not see the connection that what you're struggling with currently, actually is an overflow of what's been going on in your path? She couldn't see it. I said I don't think I can help you then, because you're going to go down that route, and play this thing right out until you've actually experienced all the consequences of what you've got in your heart towards your father.

Now you understand she had judged her father, and found him lacking, and now unlocked against herself a real cycle of issues that would then go through the rest of her life, so that's what judging is about. Discerning has more to do with being an observer than a judge, for example, a judge will stand up, or a judge will usually be seated in an elevated position. You go into a court, the judge is in the high position, so when the Bible talks about judging, it's speaking about elevating yourself up, as though you know everything and why people do things, and then passing a judgement on someone against them. You've found them guilty, see? And now you've condemned them. Right, now this is different to discerning. Discerning, you're not coming from the high ground of pride, and being above everyone else. You're coming down from, you're actually a human being yourself, understanding that people do have issues and make mistakes, and you're looking as an observer, to see what God says about the situation. So God shows you the root of this is a spirit, the root of this is bitterness, the root of this is this. It's informational. It's not judgemental. It's to inform you of the nature of the problem, not step up on the high ground and look down, and find the person guilty and condemn them. That's the difference.

Now many people think that Christians shouldn't judge, but the Bible says the spiritual man judges all things. Notice what Jesus just said in those verses. Notice He said: don't give what's holy to dogs, neither cast your pearls before swine, lest they trample them under their feet and turn on you. Clearly He's saying you need to know what to share, and who to share it with, because some people, if you share it with them, it's like casting something out before pigs. They'll trample it underfoot and turn on you. He's not being judgemental. He's just saying that you have to look at people, and look at situations, and be understanding of where they're at, and how they receive things. He said: you don't give everything you have to everyone, so the Bible's very clear. A spiritual man judges all things, but that means he looks right through to what the real issue is and identifies it, not as one sitting up high looking down, condemning, but as a fellow traveller, looking and observing and seeing that something is like this. You getting the idea?

Okay then, so for example - and the more you have examples the easier it is to see it, so discerning then is to be able to look through, and see what is behind this matter. I know what they're all saying, or I know what I can see, but what lies behind it - that's the driving factor? We need discernment, because in the world, and in the church, people have all kinds of agendas, and it shouldn't be that way, but that's how people are. People have usually hidden agendas, and the agendas are not so obvious, but if you are discerning of spirits, you can pick what lies behind it, so there are a number of Bible examples of that. We shared with one of you in the last session, and that was found in Acts, Chapter 8, where Peter discerned the motives of Simon the sorcerer, so everyone was coming up and saying: we want the power of God, we want the power of God, we want the power of God. He came up and said listen, I'll give you some money, just give me the power of God. He was able to look in and say no, you have got an issue. He said underneath this desire for the power of God, is a deep rooted bitterness and a crookedness, that makes you seek power so you can promote yourself. You've got a deep rooted issue of insecurity in your life.

Peter discerned it. He saw right to the root of it, and confronted the man about it. Getting the idea? So discernment enables you to see what is really there. As you'll see shortly, we'll need a word of wisdom to know what to do with it, so in Luke, Chapter 13 - I'll just find another example in Luke, Chapter 13, Verse 10. Jesus was teaching in the synagogue on the Sabbath, and behold there was a woman who had a spirit of infirmity 18 years, was bowed down and could not lift herself up. Jesus saw her, called her to Him, and said to her: woman, be loosed of your infirmity. He laid hands on her, and immediately she was made straight, and glorified God. Now Jesus is in a synagogue, a place of prayer and there's a woman who has an incredibly serious back problem. She's bent and crippled right over. Now to everyone who looked, it's a back problem, and she has a back problem, that's true. But He saw the root source is a demonic spirit. There's a spirit attached to her spine, and when she was delivered, immediately she was set free.

I had a situation in Fiji. I was invited by one of the members of our church to go up with him to his property up in Yasawa, which is beautiful, a most beautiful area of Fiji but it's very remote. It's right at the outer end of the Fiji area, and right up in the outer islands, so in order to get there we had to catch a boat, and then we had to kind of catch a little boat ashore, all of that kind of thing. Then we were invited to a meeting for me to speak, at a meeting in the village, so to get there we waded out into the surf, got into a boat, travelled around through the reefs and landed on another beach. Someone met us with a lamp, and we went in, and we were in a building. I was the first white man to speak there apparently - and there was a gathering of people there. The men had fled the place. They heard I was coming and they fled, and there was a problem with spiritism and witchcraft going on in that area, so I went into the meeting.

At the end of the meeting there was a lady came up, and she - when I say came up, she crawled up. She crawled herself up, and she came up there, and I could see that she was in trouble from her waist down, that she actually could not walk. She had come with two crutches, she was unable to walk, and so I looked at her and I asked some questions, first of all: how long have you been like this? She said 10 years. Then the Lord just dropped into my heart exactly what the problem was. So how did I get it? I got one, discerning of spirits and two, word of knowledge. The first word of knowledge was, it had to do with her husband. The second was discerning it was actually a spirit of infirmity, associated with the occult, so I asked her the question then - and this is how you can bring out revelation, just ask questions - I said: what happened 10 years ago? I said did someone near you, close to you die? She said my husband died. I said: is it not true that he was involved in the occult and witchcraft? She said yes.

Now this was very significant, because this is a religious community, everyone's supposedly Christians, but actually many of them were not, and many of them were practicing witchcraft, and this was why the guy had got me to come over, because the conditions he described, I could tell were witchcraft operating. Everyone was denying it, including the local Minister. This brought it right out into the light, so now the woman's saying yes, my husband was involved in witchcraft, he was involved in spiritism. I said the Lord shows me, because the two of you will become one through marriage, that when he died, that spirit has come into you. You have a spirit of infirmity, associated with your husband and the witchcraft, so now everyone's absolutely stunned. So I broke the curse, I broke the soul ties to her husband, I broke the curses that had been upon her through her husband's activities, commanded the spirit of infirmity to go, helped her to her feet and she stood up, and she walked without crutches, she walked home.

So you see again that the discerning of spirits helps you know what the issue is, and you get a revelation, you get it from God. Getting the idea? So we've seen a number, a number, so the gift of discerning of spirits enables you one, to discern the activity of the Holy Spirit; two, to discern what the motives of people are; three, to discern the activity of demonic spirits and identify what they are. Now it would help if I just shared a little bit about your senses and how they work. We touched on it before. You have natural senses and you have spiritual senses, so your natural senses - after a little while you gain a memory bank of experiences, so you smell food, [sniffs] ooh, curry, Sargin's in the building. [Laughter] So you identify with a physical sensation, you have a memory you attach to it, and you identify it like that. So after a little while you can pick up lots of things. You can recognise voices. If someone rings up and they don't tell you who they are, oh, I know that voice, I recognise that voice.

So we attach associations to the experiences we have naturally. Now spiritually the same thing happens. You are a spirit being, and do have spiritual senses, and you do pick up stuff. People often call it a sixth sense, but it's actually your spirit man, for example, how many of you have had some decision you had to make, but you felt this terrible uneasiness, and lack of peace about that? How many have known that experience like that? Okay, very good, and of course if you went against that and did it, you ended up in trouble. We won't ask about that. [Laughter] You put that down to wisdom, okay, so that's one thing. How many of you have met a person - most of the women have met a person, and that person, a male, was incredibly creepy? There's something about them - don't go near me, I feel defiled just being near you, okay. So how many women would identify that experience? Quite a lot of women, okay.

So probably the second thought that came into your mind was, I shouldn't think like that, but actually you are right. What's happening is, you're discerning an unclean spirit or intention around the person, and you are feeling the impressions of it, and you're identifying it as a yuck, I don't like this, I don't trust that man, I'll stay away. Understand? That's actually discernment. Your spirit is sensing things. You've got to learn how to recognise what it is, and how to work with it, and I'll show you what to do in a moment. Okay, and men have a similar kind of thing. You may find yourself in situations, or have you ever been into a house for example, and you go in there to meet some couple, and as you go in there everyone's being polite and nice, but you can feel like the whole atmosphere is full of tension, as though there's been a big row or something go on there. How many - now let me ask you this then. How on earth did you feel tension? What part of you felt that? Your spirit felt it.

So all of us have a human spirit, and all of us can sense things, but we can develop that so we become sharper at it, and become more used to dealing with it. Getting the idea? Okay then, so you have ability then to sense things spiritually, and when we're born again of course, that whole - it's brought to a different realm altogether. We now have the Holy Spirit with us. He can actually identify for us, what the things are that we're dealing with, so here's a thing. Remember in almost all of the moving in the spirit, what you get seems to be a thought, or impression, or picture comes into your mind. It's not strong necessarily, or very big. You could easily sweep it aside if you didn't stop and focus on it, so the way to deal with it is simply this, is - I think there's a couple of practical things. Number one, I think we need to ask the Lord to help us to deal with having a judgemental attitude. You can never discern properly if you have a judging attitude.

You notice what Jesus said in Matthew 7? He said: if you judge, you'll be judged. The measure you give to others is how it'll come back to you. Then He said an interesting thing. He said: why do you say, I want to get the speck out of your eye, when you've got a big beam in your own? Notice then what He said. In other words He's saying - I'll put it to you a different way; if you had a little speck in your eye, you wouldn't ask someone to help you dig it out, who had this huge log covering most of their vision. You'd say, no way do you get near my eye, you can't see clearly, you'll mess this up. You'll damage me and hurt me, see? Now so what Jesus then said was, take the beam out of your own eye - speaking of judgement - and then you'll see clearly. So putting it another way, He's saying if you have a judgement in your heart against any person, or you hold judgements about certain matters, it will affect how you see and interpret what's in front of you in life. So in the journey of growing in the things of the spirit, we need to deal with bitterness and judgements and unforgivenesses in our heart, because it will colour how we see people, it'll colour how we interpret life, it will affect our ability to discern. We will tend to judge rather than discern, and think we're completely right and justified. That make sense to you? Very, very important.

So if I was to allow the Lord to help me deal with any judging attitude in my heart, against myself or against people, and to begin to meditate on the love of God, and His great love for me, and grow in that love, I will see clearly, because when you love people, you see clearly. When you have judgement in your heart, you can't see clearly, and you mess it up every time, so this is an important thing. I need to cultivate purity of heart in my motives towards people, or I can't see very clearly, so that's a very, very important thing. I'll just stop from that point, and then just move on to, so how can you work in this area? I'll give you an example of it.

A person - I used this illustration recently because I've had this experience. There's two people standing in the entrance of a church, and one of them has got a deep rejection in his life, or a judgement that there's something wrong with me, people don't like me. He learnt that years ago. The other one hasn't got that at all, he's quite free. Suppose the Pastor walks in and he's very, very busy, preoccupied and he walks past and both say hello Pastor, and he just doesn't hear. He didn't hear it, he was preoccupied, so there's no willing rejection of them. He just didn't hear, and carried on. Now each of them has had an experience, an identical experience. Each of them will interpret it. Now the one who's got the rejection and judgement in his heart will pass judgement on what it means. He'll say: this means he doesn't like me, and he'll get angry, won't enjoy the service at all. He'll be angry all through the service - Pastor doesn't like me, and it'll stir up all his anger over this, but the judgement was in his own heart. The other person looks and says: oh, he can't have noticed me, he must have been busy, I'll catch up with him later.

Two people, same experience, but responded completely different. One just observed it, and worked out a different strategy. The other judged it, and ended up in turmoil. Getting the idea? So if you've got judgements in your heart, it'll filter all discernment, so discernment - practice ridding your heart of judgements about people, and learn to be an observer. To be an observer, you ask the question: I wonder what this means, rather than: this means that. See? You ask the question, what does this mean? What am I feeling? What am I sensing? What does this mean? You let God help you see His perspective on it. Jesus said: I don't judge as the world judges. He said I judge righteously. I don't judge what I see, I judge by what my Father says to me, so He judged things on what He heard from God.

So how can I develop the area of discerning of spirits? Very, very simply. One, I need to deal with the issue of judging in my heart that will cloud my ability to sense; two, I can develop my sensitivity through fasting. Fasting and prayer helps me develop sensitivity to the Holy Spirit, and then what you need to do is, learn how to identify what you feel when you're in different situations, identify impressions you have when you're talking with someone, when you are meeting someone, when you come into a meeting, when you come into a room. When you go to different places, look for chances to identify what your first impression is. The first impression is usually the one that impacts you as you engage something, then you just move out of that, and start to reason everything out, and interact with it differently. But when you're a spiritual person which you are, you tend to be more sensitive, so you can feel things or sense things quite easily, and so try to, when you sense something, ask this question: what do I sense? What impression do I have? What am I feeling? Try to just get a name for it. Don't dismiss it. Just enquire, Holy Spirit, what is that? Then the next question; what do you want me to do with that? What does this mean?

If you judge, it must mean this, you've then lost your discernment. If you just say Lord, what does this mean, and how do you want me to deal with this, you'll start to then develop a lifestyle of being able to discern things, so there's heaps of places that you can pick it up. One of the places to pick it up, is when you meet people. When you meet people, just come with an open heart and shake their hand and look them right in the eyes, and just let them interact with you. As they interact with you, you'll have an impression come. Try to identify what the impression is. Listen for the things the Holy Spirit drops in your heart. You walk into someone's house, what impression do you get? What does the atmosphere feel like? You walk into a church meeting, what does it feel like? What does the atmosphere feel like? When everyone's worshipping, or things are happening, what does it feel like? What does it sense, is there? Develop, practice discerning, or exercising your senses, to listen and identify impressions you have about situations, and then act as an observer, not a judge; oh, that's interesting, I'm feeling this. I wonder how I should respond? I wonder what God wants me to do? So you don't move into judging mode, you stay in discerning/working with the Holy Spirit mode.

Now notice Paul went for several days before he turned around to the woman and rebuked the spirit. In other words, he waited until he had actual wisdom from God what he should do. You notice this, if he had stopped and reacted on the first day, he'd have been in jail straight away, and had no chance to do any ministry at all, so he didn't immediately address what he could see was the problem, until he felt the Holy Spirit show him: this is what you need to do, do it today. A lot of people can't handle that. They pick something up, they want to deal with it straight away. That isn't always how God works, because dealing with it straight away can create more problems than what - you may solve one, but you've actually created something bigger, and different. So if Paul for example, had turned and rebuked the spirit that same day, all those days that he was able to preach and minister would have been cut out and cancelled short like that, so he knew there was a spirit, but waited until the right time, and then turned and dealt with it, and that triggered off a reaction in the whole city towards him. Shortly after he exited the city.

So we need to know and be able to discern what God is saying, or what God is wanting us to learn, and we need to be able to identify those sensations and impressions we have, so all you do is just identify, what did you feel?. You're on a phone to someone - we used to teach this when people were doing phone ministry to people. After you get off the phone, just quieten down, and just worship the Lord, and just sense - what are you feeling in your spirit? I'll give you an example. I had someone that I spoke to, and they were incredibly angry, and they were angry with me. I thought that's interesting, I wonder why they're angry with me, so we checked it out, and this is what had happened. They had been talking with someone else who had an unresolved offence, and was angry at me and after being with them, they came away angry at me as well. So what had happened was, they had not discerned this person has an offence, and the biblical way of dealing with the offence is to put it right with the person. They came under the influence of the spirit of anger and bitterness over the person. It affected them, and they were then operating with that thing around their life - so I always ask people, after you've been in an interaction, how did you feel? What did you sense? What are you sensing in your spirit? Just practice doing it, try to identify the sensations, identify the feelings.

Then we need wisdom from God, what to do, so in the next session we will look at the word of wisdom, and where to go with that, and how to respond to that, but I'll get you now to just do some interaction, we're going to do activations. I think you need to do something now, otherwise you'll fall asleep. [Laughter.] Okay then, so we've got heaps of things that we could do, but I'm going to give you one that's an interesting one, and this one will challenge you a bit, so you'll need a pen and paper to do this one, because you're going to write something. You'll need a bit of space. If you need a bit of space, you can move your chair out, and this is what we're going to do. This activation is called inspired writing, so you've had an inspired picture, an inspired thought, inspired prayer. This is inspired writing, so if you haven't a piece of paper, write it on the cover at the back of the manual will be fine.

I want you to write up this question, and you're going to listen, to let God speak to you about you, okay, so here's the question you write up: Lord, how do You see me? Lord, how do You see me? Write it down exactly as I said it, Lord, how do You see me? This is your prayer or question to the Lord, and what we're going to do is we're just going to pray for a little while. We're going to do this just like you are ministering to someone, except you're just coming into a place where you're listening to let God speak to yourself. If you can get into a flow of this, this will be one of the greatest assets to you over the course of your life, to help you hear from God, and develop hearing from God. It's called journaling, and journaling's got a number of aspects, but this aspect of journaling, one aspect of journaling, is just writing your thoughts and feelings, experiences. This aspect is journaling what God is saying to you, so you ask the question; God, or Lord, how do You see me?

Now, I know how some of you see yourselves, and you may not see yourself too good. You come to all kinds of conclusions about yourself. Wouldn't it be good if you stopped listening to all of that junk and instead, Lord, how do You see me? You might find it a little hard to take how He sees you, because it's very loving, and very kind, and it's not like others who you may have experienced, so He can be incredibly kind and loving. So what I want you to do is we're going to do very simply like we did the others. We would say hey, can I practice on you? Well this is just a practice. You're practising on yourself, okay then and a very positive response, yes, this is going to be great. Then we're just going to pray in tongues for a little bit, and I want you just to pray in tongues, and then begin to focus, just begin to think about the Lord, think about His goodness to you. Then you may start to get Him, just some thought come to mind, start to write.

Now don't try and work out what you're going to write next - aah, ooh, you're a loser. [Laughter] Don't work it out you know? You may get terrible things if you try and work it out, and you certainly won't hear God on that, so what you do is just relax, listening to Him until you sort of start to get a thought or an idea, then start to write. Now just relax as you write, and just let it flow, let it flow out of your writing, flow and flow and flow. If you find the flow stops just rest again; thank You Lord. Lord, just speak to me, give me more Lord. Just stay focussed on Him, and then just continue writing, begin to write again. What will happen is, write from the flow that comes from your spirit, don't try and figure this out with your head. If you try and figure it out with your head you'll be completely limited, you won't have revelation. God actually wants to speak to you.

Now it's like prophesying over yourself virtually, and here's the interesting thing. When you learn how to do this, you can do this any day you like, all the rest of your life. You can ask the Lord questions, and begin to journal what He has to say to you. For some it may be lots of things to say, some it may be just a few lines. Hey, we're just practising. Ready? Okay then - and some may have a blank paper, that's okay too. If you find you have a blank that's interesting - I have a blank. I wonder why I can speak to others about what God sees about them. I'm finding it hard to speak to myself. What's going on here? Why is there that block? Can you see, it's like instead of being a judge, you just be the observer, and the listener, and the one who shares what you're observing and hearing. It's a very, very important positioning in your heart to take, where you don't become a judge anymore in life. You become an observer; oh, that's interesting, I wonder what that means? Lord, how would You have me respond?

So this one, Lord, how do You see me? How do You see me Lord? How do You see me? Lord, I just reach out to you now - so come on, let's just begin to pray in tongues, and then we'll give you just a few minutes to write. If you're looking at this on the Internet you could sit down with a piece of paper, and you could do this too. Write down the question: Lord, how do You see me? Just begin to pray, pray in tongues, just worship God for a little while, and then as a thought comes to you, begin to write. You're writing a letter to yourself, like you're writing from God to you. You're putting words to what God's saying. Let's do it together shall we? Thank You Lord. Lord, release a spirit of revelation right now. [Prays in tongues] Thank You Lord. Thank You Lord. Lord, begin to speak to individuals here, reveal the tremendous, amazing love, the wonderful heart that You have for each of us. Let it just flow out of their hearts onto paper. Thank You Lord. We just bind every distracting influence, everything that would hinder us, stop us and we just release that life and vitality now in Jesus' name. Thank You Lord.

As soon as you feel free and start to get an idea, just begin to write. You're not trying to work it, you're just writing out of the flow of what's in your heart like you're listening to someone dictate to you, and you're writing it. You're actually writing it to yourself. It's this flow of the spirit, coming up from within. If you get stuck, just pray in tongues, relax and re-focus on the Lord again. [5mins]

Alright then, how are we doing? I see a lot of people are writing, and all got to different levels. Let me just ask for a little bit of feedback. How many had a flow of writing, you had some thoughts come to you, that came from the Lord? You obviously felt a flow of things start to come? Alright then. Did anyone get stuck, you just went blank? No one got completely stuck. Did some find they just had a little bit, but there wasn't much flow in it? Some had that. There would be always some like that, and sometimes that can reflect we're not good writers, we're better talkers and we talk better than we write. But again, relax and let the flow come. How many of you found that what God spoke to you was very personal, actually was extremely specific for you? How many found that? Wow, that's great! How many were quite encouraged by what God said? Oh, that's really good too. Well this is very, very good.

How many of you, God told you how much He loved you? [Laughs] He often starts with that, and talks with that. How many of you, did God give you some kind of direction, or insight to what you need to be doing at this time in your life?

Isn't that good? Wow, that's great isn't it? That's helpful isn't it? So it's quite good for you to come to the Lord, and to learn how to journal daily with Him, and keep a track record of what God is speaking to you, because you can go back and look at it again. If you have a journal, and you're keeping a journal that God is talking to you, it still helps if you've got someone else who you can run your thoughts around, and run your thoughts with before you make any major decisions, just so you've got the wisdom. The Bible says: in the wisdom of many counsellors there's safety, so this is a great way - it also has limits on it, and so it's helpful if we stay having counsel about any major decision.

So there's many questions you could start to ask the Lord now, so if we just asked you, how does He see you, and He would talk about the goodness and the good things He sees in you, the possibilities in you. You could ask about, how He sees your church. You could ask about various aspects, and then wait on the Lord, just let Him talk with you about life, and about things. Isn't that wonderful? Isn't that great? Thank You Lord. How many people were quite surprised by what God shared with them, gave you a bit of a surprise? Oh, that's interesting. What was it surprised you? [What was it that surprised me? I just get that He talked about seeing me as I am now and just how precious I am to Him, about how He has a greater plan and...] Wow. [...and just yeah, He actually showed me I'm like a precious stone, you know, like inside the rock...] Right. [...rocks on the outside, but He sees the raw, unfinished product but that He's got such greater plans that will take me out of that...] Wow. [...clarity will increase.] Wow, so it's very specific and it's... [...precious as I am.] ...even as you are you're precious. That's... [And He's got the plan] ...wonderful, so God assured He had a plan. She's precious as she is, but that plan will bring enlargement and greatness. It's wonderful, don't you love that? Such a wonderful thing. So you're in a good space now to be able to minister to someone else.

So what we'll do now is get you to break into pairs, and what I'd like you to do is to bring a word of encouragement. Now we're not going to prophesy, that would be too spiritual for us. [Laughter] What we'll just do is, we'll bring an inspired word for someone, so again we'll get with someone that - preferably someone you have not prayed with before, someone that's different and remember, ask permission; can I practice on you? Get a good, positive response, then we pray in tongues, pray in the spirit for a little bit, then listen and then share something that you feel God shows them that would encourage them. You've just done it for yourself, now do it for the other person. So you're looking for a thought, and an idea. Remember, pray, relax and focus on the source, listening, just waiting and just let thoughts just come. Something drops into your mind, focus on it until it comes a little clearer, then start to share; well I just sensed this as I was praying for you. Keep it simple and easy and light. Okay? Let's see how we do. Find someone and let's have a practice. If you're watching this on the Internet, why don't you find someone to practice on, especially someone you don't know so well?

Okay, let's just come back, close up what you're doing. Let's get some feedback on how it's going. How many of you were really touched by what the person shared with you, it was very appropriate for you? Wow, that's wonderful, great. How many sort of felt God as they shared with you - oh my, that's God speaking to me? How many felt that? Very good, wonderful. Okay then, anyone got blocks in this? How many struggled to get something? Okay, we've all moved quite a long way now, that's fantastic. How many of you, it still just feels like it's you doing it? You kind of think this so much, seems like me, I don't sort of feel much of God in it? How many found that? Actually that's quite normal. To tell the truth, some of the best ministries I've had for people, I didn't feel a thing, but I have learnt to just relax, and understand I am a spirit being, God is in me, and if I will yield, He will speak through me. Whether I feel anything much, or experience anything, is irrelevant. It's not about me, it's for the other person. I'm just the servant, to bring about the work.

Once you get that idea we're just here to serve people, it's not about your feelings or experiences at all. It's actually what God does in their life. It's about them, and God, and of course as you do it, you just grow so immensely. Amen, okay, so you've found that's been a good challenge for you? Okay then. Would you like to stretch out a little further, and try a little something harder? Little bit harder? NO! Please don't make it any harder. [Laughter] Okay, alright then, well this is - I just need someone to help me, just need a volunteer really, someone that can help me? Okay, you're going to help me? Alright then, so just come on up here. Now this is what I want us to do this time. We're going to get you to do two things. The first thing I want you to do is, see if you can get a word of knowledge about the person, in other words a little piece of information, that we wouldn't have known naturally.

Now I do know Caroline, so I've got to then dismiss from my mind everything I know about her. I have to just literally push aside, and listen to my heart, not listen to my mind. If I go anywhere towards what I know, then I won't hear my spirit at all. I've got to just push aside anything I may know about her, and then actually just identify what I'm feeling in my spirit. Alright then, and I want to show you just simply how you can. Remember, we shared with you for getting words of knowledge about the body? Just begin to think about a person's body, and you may just find is the right side, the left side? Is it, you know and just go through the parts of the body, and you may feel drawn to a part, just only the slightest draw - that can be what a word of knowledge is, just a slightest little impression. So what we're going to do is, we're going to look for an area where the person is facing a struggle, asking this question; Lord, is there any area of this person's life where they're facing a struggle? Okay, and we'll show you just how to do that in just a moment.

Then the second part will be now Lord, how do You want to speak to them, to encourage them? Okay, so first is the word of knowledge, the second's the prophetic. The word of knowledge: is there an area where there is a struggle going on? Second part, is there something God wants to say, to help the person in that part of their life? So if God identifies the struggle, He certainly will want to do something to help them, and there could be many ways they could be helped, but at this point, the level of help we'll give is, we'll look for a word of comfort and inspiration, encouragement for them, okay? That keeps it quite an even level. We're not trying to prophesy. We're actually just - see if we can find out a little piece of information. Now remember, when we asked you in the second activation of this series, go to someone and ask them a question, find out something about them? So now we're going to ask the Lord the questions, so you've already done it for yourself: Lord, how do You see me? You know you can ask God a question and He will answer, so now we've got to, in love, say Lord, is there any area this person's struggling? There may well be there's none, and if there's none, then there's none. Don't make one up. [Laughter] Don't put on them, your struggle. [Laughter]

Is there a struggle? And if there is a struggle, see if you can frame what it might be, and then lay out then,, just we need to look to God for a word for the person, okay? Alright then, so just come and stand in front of me there. So if I have to pray and minister to a person, there's a number of ways - you can just say well God, just show me, and just wait for something to happen. That's one way, or you can use your imagination a little bit, and just reach in to different areas. Now for most people in their life, there's not a lot of areas that they would have a struggle. If you think about it, if I was to just say, look back through Caroline to her family background; she could have a struggle with her father or mother or in the family, so if I was just to mentally just look, has there been a struggle there? Yes or no? No, I don't feel anything. Okay, alright then, well that's alright then.

So if she's a married person, then I might look is there someone on the right, the person standing next to them, is there a struggle there? No. Alright, that's okay. Alright, are there children? I look down because there's offspring, so is there some issue there that there's a trouble? No. Alright then, so what other areas are left? Well is there trouble in her body? Look at her - is there an area of sickness or struggle going on? No. Alright then, so then we look then what other areas are there? Well, is it work related, or is it finance related, relationship related, or ministry? It's not so many areas, we've covered most areas of the person's life now. So if I just mentally just stop and look, and while I'm listening, I'm just mentally going around is there any one of those I'm drawn to? Then I may just find a draw to one of them, so I'll just stop for a moment and if I feel a draw there, then there's something going on there, that I need to be able to get a word from God for, okay?

So it's not such a hard thing, so if I just - can I practice on you? Great stuff, and so bearing in mind I've got to dismiss anything I might know, and now just begin to look into the Lord. So Holy Spirit, You just know everything about Caroline. You know Lord where her life is at this point and Lord, You can just reveal things that You want to help her, and encourage her. So Lord, I'm just asking You, well just show me where there's any area of struggle, so I'll just start to mentally now do what I'm going to do, just go looking in each area, mentally reaching in to see if God will show me something, so I reach in the background. I don't feel God quickening. There could be an issue or something, but God's not wanting to do that today, so I don't have to worry. I'm not trying to make something happen. I'm just looking and enquiring, I'm just an observer, listening for God, see? So I could reach in there, is there anything there? No, reaching in then, marriage, no, there's nothing there. Reaching then to any children? No, there's nothing there, so then what other areas?

Oh, and I just become conscious of her hand, and I'm thinking finance. Now I could look around all the other areas, but I might just stop there. So I'll just stop, thank You Lord. I sense that's a struggle area, so I could say Lord, what is the struggle, and what do You want to say, to help her in this area? There could be other areas of struggle, so we can pray for two or three people, and you may pick up - people pick up all kinds of different things, but this is not about knowing a problem. It's about loving a person. It's not about being nosey. It's about finding a way to bring God to them in their struggle, because when you have a struggle, you get preoccupied with it, it overwhelms you, it gets out of perspective, and you feel alone. So if you identify a struggle a person has, even if you don't go into all the details of it, and you bring something from God, it can bring tremendous comfort. Alright then, so Father, I just thank You.

What I sensed was, there's a struggle around finance, as though there's not enough. It seems like there's never been enough, and it's been quite a difficult situation for you to manage, because in your heart you don't feel there's enough for you. God wants you to know that He is your source and supply, that you can trust in Him. Have you ever gone without? Have you ever gone in lack or need? Have you ever suffered? The Lord says, I've always been there to provide for you, and I know the pressure and difficulty you're feeling right now, but the Lord says, I will help you. I will give you victory in this area that's been a struggle for you. I will help you come from the place of struggle into the place of rest, and the place of abundance. The Lord says: in Me, there is always more than enough. Right, now I'm going to go a little further, because I feel God wants to help her, wants to minister to her.

So you notice we've just touched an area. I didn't go and expose all kinds of details or anything, but there's enough has come for me to be aware, God wants to comfort and help her in the midst of the struggle. Now you notice what I said, with struggles there's also a lot of emotion and pain in it, but with this particular struggle, I feel a spirit has come against her to continually tell her there's not enough. There's something has rested on her, so even in good times, and when there was enough, there's never been enough. See, it doesn't matter how wealthy you are, if there's a spirit sits on you, and your heart believes there's not enough, there's not enough, because you can't see there's enough. You just can't see it. You're in torment all the time, and there's a wrestling goes on, so what God's given you, you can't enjoy, because of the torment. So I've found that people enter into peace, not because of how much they have, but because they find contentment in their heart, and learn to live within the framework God has given them. Godliness and contentment's tremendous gain.

Let me just pray. Thank You Lord, so this has come over you a long time ago. This came over you when you were a young girl. It came over you in the midst of turmoil. It's come around your life through your mother. God wants to help you today, wants to break the belief there's not enough for me. He wants you to see that He's a God of abundance, and will help you in every situation. Father, in the name of the Lord Jesus Christ, I break the ungodly belief that there's not enough for me. I break the ungodly belief of financial failure and poverty. I come against fear, and the spirit of poverty, loose right now, in Jesus' name. Let your presence and peace just come over her life. Thank You Lord. There it is, God just touching you now, just bringing rest around your life, in Jesus' Mighty name. Thank You Lord. [Laughs] Holy Ghost. Just stay there and just enjoy Him.

Now, did you notice, all I did was just start to just look, waiting, listening on God to give me something. If He doesn't give anything, that's okay. I'm not going to nose. It's just I have a heart to love the person and help them, and so because of that, we're willing to just look, and reach into God for something for the person. Now sometimes God can just drop it in, and you didn't even do any of that, but I'm trying to provide for you an approach that you can grow in this gift area. You understand that actively pursuing is always a vital part of it, and so I just look, the background, the parents, spouse, children, finance, work, relationships, ministry, is there any of those areas? And that pretty well covers everything, so in the midst of looking like that, God can just cause you to be drawn to something, feel a struggle around a relationship. I wonder what the struggle is, or what the relationship is? You don't have to get all the details, but if you can get a little bit of detail, then now you've opened up the person, and what does God want to do to help them? Amen.

Bless you. How was that for you? [Can I just share something?] Sure. [I don't know whether it's connected, but when you said about finance, but I felt all the time I've been a Christian, I don't know whether it's connected with what you've said...] Yes. [...that [unclear 01.07.54] other people that it's like you feel sometimes your need is so deep and so great and the whole thing is so big in your life...] Yes. [...that there's not enough of God.] [Laughter] [I don't know whether that's connected...] Yeah, they are connected, yes. [...with that too?] Yeah. [Because He's sort of brought me to a place recently of being - well I thought I'd been okay with what I've got and...] Right. [...that probably there's areas of need for discipline...] Right, yes. [...in my finances too.] Yes, of course. [So that's - I don't know whether that's relevant.] Mm, I didn't say anything about that area. [Laughter] [No, well actually I haven't been - like He's sort of told me to stay away from shops...] Yeah. [...and actually I feel I've been - the spirit of materialism has almost sort of been broken...] Yeah. [...in my life because of that...] Yeah, right, that's great. [...because I've been obedient, but - so yeah.] Right, so this is obviously what's shared is in line with what God is speaking to you about this area in your life right now. [Oh definitely.] Yeah, that is why... [Not to be impulsive and...] No, great. [But I failed yesterday.] [Laughter] And hence today! [Laughter] Well thank you for your honesty. Let's give her a clap and just appreciate her. [Applause]

Remember, the ministry of the spirit is always gentle and loving, so when Paul is writing about the gifts of the spirit in Romans 12 and Romans 14, in the middle of it he stops and he said: you have to be loving. Of all things be loving, or this is very empty, and doesn't represent what Christ is like. So the power of ministry is wonderful, but we have to be loving of people, honouring of people, valuing of people in the flow of the ministry, so we don't do things that would embarrass them. You can word things in ways that are not embarrassing. I could just say well, you know, do you have a struggle, or is there a difficulty in your life in this area? Is there something going on, and just put it in the form of a question, or if God spoke to you more clearly, you may just put it, I feel this. So God has got to show you, and we'll talk about that when we get to words of wisdom - so why don't you all have a try, and have a practice aye, how about that? Oh, that's a very excited response isn't it aye?

So what we'll do for this one here, what we're going to do is this. We'd like you just in this time, instead of all of you just going at your own pace and let it free run, I'd like us just to do it as a step by step, so what I'll do is, I'll encourage you where to look, otherwise you just get then you can't remember everything, and where to go. So what I'll do is, we're just going to do it step by step, and I'll guide you, and all I want you to do is just be open to the Lord, and if you feel a draw around something, just identify it, and that's it. That's all you need, that's my one. There may be others, but you won't worry about those. The one you feel that, that's the draw on, or that's the, you know, I feel something draws me other that one, that's the one, you just hold in your mind, and then we'll ask the Lord for what to say, okay? Alright then, so get in pairs, especially with someone you don't know.

Okay, let's get in pairs. You can come out the front here, over the sides. Okay, alright, now I want you just to do this. If you're watching this on the internet, you can just follow it through step by step, just leave the volume on, and the picture on, and you can walk through it step by step, then later on, turn it all off, and just try it without me guiding you in it. For this session, we're going to just guide you step by step, okay, so the first thing is of course, what we've done, smile and look at the person, can I practice on you? Give a very positive response. Okay, alright then. Now you may know a little bit about the person. Please just push aside all you know, because if you look in that area of what you know, you'll just have turmoil. You've got to be listening for God. You're listening for the impression of the Holy Spirit, so let's just begin to pray quietly and just worship God just for a little moment there, just begin to worship the Lord. [Prays in tongues]

Thank You Lord. We thank You Lord. We love You Lord. We thank You, You know everything about this person. You love them deeply, and You're so willing to help them, right where they are right now. Okay, now just go quiet. I want you to look with me, there's the person standing in front of you. Look like you were looking behind them, and in the background behind them are their parents, the father, the mother. Is there a problem there between the parents, or with a father, with a mother? Do you sense something there? Alright then, now just look to the left of that person. Maybe there's a spouse. Maybe there's an issue in a relationship. Is there a difficulty or a challenge there? Yes or no? Do you feel a draw there? What is that problem? Then look like you're looking down at their children. Is there a problem in family, a challenge, something that's creating difficulty? Now look over to the right of the person, their workplace, what they do. Is there a challenge they're experiencing?

Just look at the person again. Is there a problem in their body? Is there some struggle that they're having internally? Is there a difficulty in a relationship? Then look upward; are they having a struggle in their walk with God? Perhaps you've felt something there - I'll just go back through them again, and as I go through them, if you feel a draw on one of these, just stop and enquire what is the struggle Lord? What do You want to say to them, to share with them? Is it a problem in their background with their father or their mother, their family? Is there a problem with a spouse? Is there a problem in the family? Is there a struggle in some relationship? Is there a struggle at work, financially? Is there a struggle in their ministry? Is there a struggle inside themselves? What is the struggle?

Now Lord, give me something to encourage them, so just begin very simply, well I just felt an impression that there's a struggle going on in this part of your life. Maybe it's this. Just be quite gentle and easily entreated over it and then share what God has given you, share what God is saying to encourage the person. Let's just do it and see what God does. Okay, first one begin to share. [Background conversation] Okay, change over so the other one's shared. [Background conversation] Okay, let's close our sharing, and let's get some feedback how it went. [Background conversation]

Alright then, okay, just sit down for a moment, let's just see how people got on. How many people had this experience, they identified exactly an area of struggle that you had. How many had that experience, the person identified very clearly? That was very good. How many of you found it was a struggle to get that one? [Laughs] Because it's a bit more specific, you're reaching into an area. That's okay. Okay, how many of you were deeply touched by what was shared with you, it really helped you? Well that's wonderful. Come on, give yourselves a clap then, very, very good. [Applause] [Laughs] Well done, well done. Okay, so you can see that you approach it where focus is on Jesus, and we are listening and observing and seeking to find something. That's the spirit that you work in. It's one of enquiry, and observing, and then sharing what God is giving you. It's not over the top, or way out there, it's quite a gentle flow of the spirit. Everyone can practice these things.

I'm going to share with you - we'll have a coffee break shortly. I want to share with you a little bit on the word of wisdom, and then we'll have a break for afternoon tea, so you've done very, very well. So the word of wisdom, that's Section 15 in your notes. Wisdom is a great gift. Wisdom is knowing what to do. Wisdom is knowing what to do, and when to do it, and how to do it. [Laughs] Wisdom is knowing what to do, when to do it, how to do it, so we face many challenges in life, and in ministry, when you're working to minister to someone, if God gives you a word of knowledge, you need wisdom to know what to do with it. If God gives you prophecy, you need wisdom to know what to do with it; God gives you discernment, you need wisdom to know what to do with it, so wisdom is a very important gift to get, and to get a word of wisdom does not make you a wise person. You are wise for five minutes, that's it. [Laughter] I'm sorry - and it doesn't stick, because five minutes later you can be very foolish [laughter] so the word of wisdom does not make you a wise person.

It does not make you a spiritual person. It means someone smarter than you, shared with you, something very smart. [Laughter] That's really what it is, that's all it is. Someone who is very wise, shared with you, something that was surprisingly wise and appropriate, so the word of wisdom is just a revelation from the Lord, what to do in a certain situation, when to do it, and how to do it. Remember I shared with you a story about buying a gift for my grandmother? Only God could have known what to get, and what would do the trick. Only He knew, so listening to Him, I was able to get wisdom, and get an outcome that far surpassed anything I could naturally do, so we need words of wisdom.

So one is given the word of wisdom through the spirit. It's the first one mentioned in the list of the gifts of the spirit, is the word of wisdom. It is a great gift to pursue. God, give me wisdom to know what to do. In James 1 it says: if any man lacks wisdom, let him ask of God who gives freely to all men, but let him ask in faith, not doubting, for he that doubts is like the waves, just tossed this way and that way. So if you're going to ask God for wisdom, expect Him to give it to you. Then you've got to step out, that what He's given to you, is the right thing to do, and the right way to do it, and the right time to do it. Okay then, so that's the word of wisdom. So wisdom works on how to do - it shows you what God wants you to do, how He wants you to go about doing, how to resolve a situation. Sometimes problems you know, are really messy. Sometimes you try, and you can't seem to fix it. You've got to ask God for a word of wisdom; God, what do You want me to do? Then be happy to trust that that's actually the right thing to do, and leave it at that.

Sometimes we can be in so much turmoil ourselves, we just want to get everything right so we feel better, and God will just say no, I want you just to leave it be for the moment. I'll work on it myself, and then I'll show you when you need to step and do something. So I've found some situations I haven't known what to do, and haven't been able to do it, and actually attempts to do it have made it worse. I've just left it to the Lord, and said God, show me what to do, and when to do it, then He'll suddenly just now, move now, act now, speak now, this is the time to say something. When that happens don't miss it. Don't miss that moment. That's the important moment - so how to pray for a person. Someone tells there are problems, you think oh my goodness, what do I do? Lord, I need wisdom what to do. Show me how to pray, because what they ask for, may not be what you really need to be praying about. That's the dilemma. People come, and if you tell them what's your need, or what is your problem, they'll spill you with so much stuff. They already have lost their way, and they're trying to get you to also lose your way, by telling you all the problems. [Laughter]

What you really need is - I've learnt now when people come for prayer, say: don't tell me all your problems, just what is it you're believing God for? What do you need from God? That forces people out of, I'm full of problems, to looking for solutions, so for example, if you go to McDonalds and line up at McDonalds and they say what do you want, you just stand there saying oh, I don't know, you know, whatever you feel to give me. It's sort of nonsense isn't it really, so - and suppose you go to McDonalds and stand in line up there, and they say what do you want, and you begin to talk about how hungry you are, and how long it is since you've had your last meal, and you start to - you know, they're going to get bored with all that, so just tell me what you need, you know? So when you come to an altar call, or someone's come up for prayer, and you ask: what do you want, and they say oh, whatever God wants for me.

I say, well He wants lots of things for you, but if you don't know them specifically, you probably won't get any of them. People don't like that answer, but it's actually very true. It sounds very spiritual, oh whatever God wants. Actually, if we know what God wants for us, we can ask specifically, and believe to receive it. If we have that kind of attitude, whatever He wants to give, it's passivity and full of unbelief. It'll produce nothing. You've got to realise that, so that's why Jesus many times in the Gospels asked people, what do you want? The blind man comes up. Now hello, what's up with Jesus? You know, there's a blind man, and He said: what do you want? Hello! [Laughter] I know, I can't see. [Laughter] But can you get the idea? But Jesus was wanting him to verbalise what He was looking for, so many times Jesus asked the person: what do you want, so He made them express their need, or their faith. He made them give voice to what they were wanting from Him, so when you're ministering to people, it's helpful if they tell you what they want, what they're believing God for, or looking to God to do.

You may not have all the answers, but at least you're focussed on the solution, not on all the problems. Having said that, there are some counselling issues that people need help to pull their problem apart, and find out what it's rooted in, and sort that out. Without knowing that, you can't deal with it, but it just helps if you can keep people in a faith mode. So the word of wisdom is, what do we do? In 2 Samuel 5:22 to 25 David was anointed king, and immediately he was anointed king, the Philistines rose up to go out to battle, and they wanted to kill him. His immediate response was this; he put on his armour, put on his sword, got the army together, went out to fight. Then when he slowed down a bit, he said Lord, do You want me to fight? [Laughter] Should I go into this battle - two questions: Lord - now notice they're simple, and they both actually have a yes/no answer. Lord, should I fight this battle? Yes or no? God says yes. The second question, will I win the battle? Yes.

So he said: then how do You want me to do it, and He showed him how to do it. That is a word of wisdom - what to do, when to do it. Next time he comes back, they come back again, he defeats them, routes them out, gets rid of their idols, they come back a little while later, back into a new battle. So now the tendency is to think like this: oh, the Philistines, I know how to deal with them. I've already one victory. I'll do it this way, leaning on your experience, rather than leaning on the Holy Spirit. He was not like that. He went God, what do you want me to do? God said don't do it the same way, this is how you do it this way. You wait, go around behind the trees and ambush them from behind, when I set it up for you - so that is a word of wisdom, what to do, when to do it, how to do it. You'll find many situations in marriage, family, ministry, work, you don't know what to do, you need a word of wisdom - what to do, when to do it and how to do it.

Noah got a word of wisdom. God showed him to build an ark. God revealed what's about to come, gave him a prophetic word: there's going to be rain. What's rain, Lord? They hadn't any rain. He said okay, let me put it to you this way, there'll be no ground to stand on. [Laughs] The whole place is going to be covered in water. He said well, what do I do? Build an ark, so He showed him what to do, gave him the pattern and how to do it. That's wisdom, wisdom from God. Think about this. Jesus was out with a group of the religious leaders. They brought a woman caught in adultery, she's caught in the very act. Now she's caught in the act - where's the man? They caught them in the act, I mean if they're caught in the act, there's got to be two of them. Where's the guy? So there's a hypocrisy here, where they're judging the woman, and they're trying to set Jesus up, so they bring in the woman to Jesus, and say Jesus, Moses Law said she's been caught in adultery, we caught her in the act, there's no doubt about the crime. Moses Law said she should be stoned to death, what do you say?

Now it was a set up from the beginning because if He said - or Moses Law said, stone her to death, then they say whoa, what kind of loving creature's this? Man, He's hard. We don't even do that. You know, we let them off from time to time too, so they'd do that. If He said oh, let them off, they'd say oh well, He's against Moses' Law. Moses' Law is very clear this is what needs to happen, hear Jesus against the law, He's eroding the law. We need to put Him away and kill Him. You see the trap? Religious spirits will always try to set up this or that, right or wrong, yes or no. God has got 100 ways through it, and so when you're trapped in a right and wrong, yes or no, Jesus never, never went either way. He found a different way through it - word of wisdom. So Jesus, in this case, didn't even answer them. He just carried on writing in the sand, and while He's writing in the sand He's thinking Father, what do You want Me to say? What do I say? A word of wisdom drops in. He said okay guys, yeah, you're right. That's what the law says. Whoever's got no sin, cast the first stone, and He just carried on writing. Now He stunned them, because now they're trapped.

Sure, that's what the law says - stone her, okay. If you've got no sin, you go and throw the stone. Really, no sin? [Laughter] They walk away. Their own conscience convicted them. They knew what they were up to, and there's no way - if they came out and did that, someone would expose them. There's no way they're going to go - so they set up the trap, and He snapped them, then He turned to the woman. He said: where are your accusers? I don't see anyone. He said I don't accuse you either, go your way, don't sin any more - so He didn't minimise the issue of sin. It's just He didn't judge it. Son of man's not come to judge, come to save, so He didn't judge her. He just said: this is destructive in your life, don't do this, you know? You need to change your lifestyle, change what you do, don't sin anymore.

So that's a word of wisdom, so there are many situations we need a word of wisdom, and so let me give a few practical things just on the word of wisdom. The first one is, don't be impulsive in making decisions. Don't be impulsive in making decisions. Impulsiveness inevitably ends up with a disaster or some kind of problem. The second thing is don't act under pressure of people or circumstances. Don't react because people are pressuring you, or circumstances are pressuring you. Saul did that in 1 Samuel 13, it cost him his whole leadership, because he so blew it by responding to pressure. So ask the Lord for wisdom. Lord, what should I do? Or we talked to you about experiencing things of the kingdom, how you need to have the attitude of a child; Father, what do I do? I don't know what to do. Help me to know what to do. Give me an insight how I should respond, and what should I do, and when should I do it - so we just have a simple thing.

You may just suddenly see a picture of what you need to do. It can drop in like a picture, drop in as a thought, drop in as an idea, and you suddenly - you don't know how you know, you just know exactly what you need to do. When you know what to do peace comes. The problem isn't solved, but you are at peace because now you have wisdom, you know what to do. So a word of wisdom is an important gift to seek after, because in every situation where you're ministering, you have needs or whatever, it gives you direction from the Holy

Spirit what to do. It comes as a picture, an impression, a thought, inspired idea, and you might just be reading and suddenly something leaps out and you've got it - a word of wisdom from God, just exactly what to do. You might even be listening to someone speak ,and they're speaking on one thing, and in the middle of it you just hear, I know exactly what to do.

You might even be having a shower, and in the middle of the shower, [whoop] I know exactly what to do. You might just be lying down resting, as you're going to sleep. More often it happens when you wake up. You go to bed asking the Lord what to do, wake up, oh, I know what to do, because your spirit stayed working through the night. So that's all it is, it's just what to do, when to do it, and how to do it, and it comes as a picture, an impression, and it makes a huge difference. The biggest issue is, we tend to react to circumstances and people rather than waiting and leaning on God for wisdom what to do. Here's a simple, typical example. Jesus had a very close friend called Lazarus - John, Chapter 11 - and Lazarus was sick. They said your friend is dying. He did nothing. They said excuse me Jesus, your friend is dying. Did you hear the word DYING? And nothing. Then a third time, you know, Jesus, he is nearly dead - so there's pressure. In other words, the implication is, you're his friend, some kind of friend you are. You could heal him, and you won't. So you see the pressure that brings?

But Jesus refused to respond, and then He got a freedom - He saw what the Father was doing. This is not going to end with death, it's going to end with glory. There's a resurrection coming, so when He got there, already the family were offended, because they expected Him to come straight away. This is their friend Jesus, and He didn't help. What is that about! But He had a word of wisdom, and He was able to bring a much greater miracle into that situation, a resurrection. So pressures of people and circumstances can lean you into having to operate in the flesh, rather than just lean into God and say, I can wait until God speaks to me what to do. It's so important to really desire of all things seek wisdom, wisdom, knowing the right thing to do, the right time. This is one of the biggest and best gifts to have. Solomon, when he was given an opportunity for everything, riches and whatever, he said I have one thing. Give me a heart that hears, and wisdom to know what to do. God said boy, you asked an important - that was a great request. I'll give you that and I'm going to give you everything else that you didn't ask for as well, because if you have a hearing heart and wisdom you can handle all the other things.

5. Faith, Miracles, and Healing (5 of 5)
https://vimeo.com/45886661
http://youtu.be/pcCg6HFjdWQ

We've talked about the gifts of the spirit being for everyone, the flow of the spirit, hearing the voice of God, how God speaks to you, how the gifts all work out of hearing God. It's not so religious or so outrageous; it's just actually quite simple and very natural. Then we saw then how to get words of knowledge, we saw how to get prophetic words, how to actually pick up a thought, pick up an idea and begin to move. Then you have to then learn how to minister to people as well, so we'll give you a few practical's on that, but I might just pray for a few minutes just to get warmed up, and then we'll look at the area of healing, then faith and miracles, then just some practical's in ministering to people, and pray with you.

Now whatever you get, you've got just the seeds of it. Everything that you grow into your future, you have to grow by diligently working with God in this area, so you can just have a one-off seminar - get some experience, see God work, have Him work through you and then go no further; or you can make a decision that I want to grow in these things. All of us have to make growth in this area, a pursuit. It just does not happen. It's a pursuit to stay alive in the spirit; it's a pursuit to deal with issues in your life. It's a pursuit to keep stretching out looking for opportunities, and letting God work with you. It takes courage and effort to put yourself out into the risk zone. It's easier to be comfortable and not do it, but it's so exciting when you do. [Laughs] It's so exciting when you do.

It's God's plan in this hour that the church be filled with power, and it go out in the community, and that most of your ministry's done outside the church walls, so we've provided an easy and safe setting, and I've tried to break the teaching down so you could see it easily, then begin to just have a chance to practice. All of you have really broken through beyond where you started, and some have discovered you've got some internal blocks. How many found that you started to notice internal blocks in your life? Okay, that's alright to have those. That just is where you are, in your stage of your journey. Let me just help you, by describing the internal blocks. Most of those internal blocks have to do with yourself. They have to do with fear, they have to do with what you believe about yourself, about God, and about circumstances of life.

So when there's a block, it means you're not connecting with your heart, so you say: I don't know why I'm not connecting with my heart - because your heart has been trained to shut off when it's in certain conditions or situations. All of us, the Bible tells us very clearly in Proverbs 4:23, keep your heart with all diligence, for out of your heart flows the issues of your life. So your life, what you live out, actually comes out of not all that you think - it comes out of the issues that are in your heart, and those issues you learn over the course of your life, so some of the things that are blocks in the heart are what I'd call generational curses and generational spirits. They're generational in origin. You were born into life with them, and you can be delivered of those blocks. Unless you're delivered of those blocks, of the inequity, and the spirits around it, you tend to repeat the patterns of your parents, although you fight against it all the way, and don't want to be that way.

A second area that is a cause of problems, are where we actually have bondages in the heart, where there's been painful situations, trauma or abusive or hurtful situations, betrayal in relationships, and as a consequence of that, you have defended yourself by building walls and barriers in the heart. It could be inner vows, death wishes, it could be control, it could be statements that you've spoken into yourself, that now build a wall around your heart to keep you safe, and that's what now you're dealing with, because you're trying to access your heart. So when you were young you defended yourself, because you had no other way of coping. Now you're older, you've got Jesus to defend you and to help you, but now you find you can't break out, because you've got these things inside you, so this is the journey of walking with the Lord, and we run various things in the church to help with that. Pastor Sargin and his wife Jessie run a course for healing the heart, prayers that heal the heart. From time to time we run a deliverance course and a restoration course with Pastor Lyn. It helps open these areas up, so whenever you see something advertised, enroll and get into it, so that you can address opening up your heart, and growing in freedom of heart.

Another thing that happens in life is, we come to believe certain things. Whether they're right or wrong is not the point at this moment. If you believe it, then it's true for you, so if you believe that no one likes you, that everyone is against you, if you believe I'm not good enough, if you believe I'll always fail, then that's actually what you'll begin to experience in life. It's like a negative expectancy pulls things into your life, so if you, for example, had in your heart these firmly rooted beliefs that have been there for years: I'm not good enough; I'm a failure, or I fail; I never get anything right; or people will laugh at me if I make a mistake; if you've got those beliefs in your heart, then the moment you're put in a situation like this, where you're in front of someone and vulnerable and you're wanting to reach into your heart to get something, all of that stuff bubbles up, comes up and creates turmoil around you.

So if you've had turmoils, the turmoils are like I'd call flows of energy, destructive energy. That's the best way to describe it - that frustrate you moving to do what you really want to do. Now the first thing is, just face that that's what it is, and explore it - that's where I'm at right now. Don't condemn yourself - that's just where I happen to be. If a person's got a broken leg and they're hobbling along, you don't mock them, ridicule them, or push them, because they're hobbling along, they're just hobbling along. They're doing the best they can you know, it's hard to walk along you know, got a broken leg. So if you, in that sense, have got a broken leg in your soul, your emotions or somewhere, and you're hobbling along, that's just where you happen to be right now - but it doesn't mean you have to stay there. You could engage the journey with God, of resolving those conflicts and shifting your belief systems. This would then change and bring freedom and you're no longer hobbling along, you're a lot freer on the inside.

The ministry of Jesus, if you notice it, He said in Luke 4:18: I've come to preach the gospel to the poor. I come to reconcile people, and build relationship with the Father, second thing, to heal the broken-hearted. In other words, He came to restore intimacy, and the capacity to be intimate, which is damaged in life's relationships, when we have trauma. Thirdly, He's come to proclaim deliverance to the captives, or deliverance to set you free of the things that restrict you from intimacy, connection, relationship and connection specifically with God; fourthly, to open the eyes of the blind, or literally, to put vision in your life, so that you can see what you're called to do, and escape from the prison of having no dreams, visions or future; called to lift off us the crushing loads of guilt and blame and burdens, all this stuff that we've carried like junk that stop us going forward. That's the ministry of Jesus, to bring us into the destiny He has for us.

So wherever you are right now for you is okay. It's okay - but don't stay there. Determine to grow, so if there are blocks that come to the surface during these times of these opportunities to do activations, take note of what they were, and what you think they've originated in, and start to pray into them that God would bring them to the surface, help you see them, and then explore getting some help, whether it be counseling or a course, or something that will help shift the blocks. They're only there if you let them stay there. It probably wasn't really - you know, it just happened that that's where you are. There were some choices you've made, but you know when someone's hurt, and they've got no one to turn to, they just do what they can to save themselves. Now you're an adult, you don't need to save yourself. You can let Jesus save you, by opening that part of your life, surrendering control, and letting Him helps you in the inner journey. Unfortunately, many people won't do it, because there's pain in it, it's uncomfortable. But you've got to see the other side of it is the victory. The other side of it is a changed life. The other side of it is flowing with the Holy Ghost. It is worth it to get your future back again.

So if you're operating at this level, you could operate at that level. What would it take to shift you up there? What would you have to grow in? What would need to shift in your life? That's what you're going to work on. Now for me, I was challenged by a message someone spoke one day, Pastor Clark Taylor, and he said: if you knew that there was one issue in your life that was hindering your life, wouldn't it be worthwhile investing, even if it was six months, in dealing with that issue, knowing that all the rest of your life, you would live life at a different level? I thought that's me! So I went home, and I recognized that what I was wrestling with was rejection, and fear of rejection, self pity and unbelief. These things were sitting around my life, and they were spirits pushing on me, working in brokenness in my heart, so I made a decision that I'm going to fight this thing. I got into prayer and fasting, and every day decreed victory over these spirits, every day declared to the spirit world that I was broken out of this thing, it had no power any more, I'm free of it. Then I would spend the rest of the time releasing forgiveness where I felt I needed to, blessing people that had hurt me, then most of the rest of the time in meditating that God is with me.

I meditated Psalm 23, in the presence of God being with me. I took time to picture it, imagine it, and imagine what it would feel like to have Jesus, my friend. I would picture it - it felt ridiculous. It felt unreal, because my heart was saying: you haven't got any friends; you're alone; nobody likes you. My heart was lying all the time, and I had to reject the lie and meditate in the truth, until it began, eventually, one day the truth become real in my heart. The day it became real, I suddenly felt the spirit world around me change. No longer were those things pressing on me, and I was just overwhelmed with the reality of the love of God. I then practiced daily for a while after that, just remaining and coming into His presence to enjoy Him, because what I got by revelation I can give to you, so what I got then, I've carried all over the world. It was worth the couple of months, it was worth it to carry something that could change lives.

It may take you longer. It doesn't really matter how long, but it is your life, and your journey. Why not just decide whatever blocks your heart, you'll address it. Meditation and fixing, learning how to train your mind to fix on the presence of God so you become conscious of Him, so now I can just stop at a moment's notice, even just driving the car, and just stop at the lights just for a moment, just go down into my spirit, become aware that God is with me, and His presence starts to come. I didn't used to be able to do that. I used to feel in the middle of a party with alcohol and drink I'd suddenly have this overwhelming I'm alone. It's an unreal thing, like you're there in the middle of it, but you're not there, and not connected at all, but now I can feel the presence of God, so that means you've got something to bring to people. You are a minister of the spirit. It is worthwhile doing that, not just being filled with information, but letting the heart be transformed, so we have reality of God. Wouldn't that be great? Just think if you could do that.

So I've given you keys, and tried to make the teaching simple, but the real journey is outside here, what you do. The real journey is the journey of resolving things in your heart, so you begin to become more conscious of God, and then able to bring what you have to other people. It's well worth it, well worth it. I mean wouldn't it be worth it just to be able to pray and things happen? Isn't that great? Ooh yes, it's well worth it alright, see so I can have a confidence that if I just go - look, for example I'll just show you. I wonder if I could just pray with you? That's right, just come, that's right, this one here come, yeah, just come, yeah, that's fine. I'll pray with you later if you like? I saw you - why don't you come too? Come too, come on, come too. No, both of you come. Alright, just come and stand up here, that's right, okay then, wonderful, thank you. Can I practice on you? See, good, I'm still practicing see, and great to have people, happy people, ready to let me practice on them, isn't that good. Now what I want to do is, I want to just talk to you, just for a moment, about just this power of meditation to change the spiritual realm that you live, and flow in.

So all I want you to do is, very, very simple, you don't have to do anything at all. You just have to relax, and close your eyes, and I want you just to become aware what you feel of the presence of God, okay? So just close your eyes now, and I'm holding your hand so we're connected to one another, and what I'm going to do now is, I'm just going to begin to meditate in the 23rd Psalm, so how do you do that? Well first of all I memorized it, so it's no strain trying to remember, because if your head's trying to remember, your heart just can't engage at all. Your head's too busy, so I've learnt the 23rd Psalm, so I then make it very personal. The Lord is my shepherd, I shall not want. You all know that bit, but what perhaps you don't know is, this is the greatest king of Israel, is saying how he's made God Almighty his personal friend, so if you were to pray it slightly differently, and to pray it and let your whole imagination enter into the experience, so let me show you how you'd do it.

So the Lord, Almighty God, who made all heaven and earth, is my personal friend and companion, and so if He's my friend and companion, how would He look? Well, He would be smiling at me, because He's my friend. If I meditate as much as I can, and try to see the smile that Jesus would have, the joy that's on His countenance, the wonderful happiness He has at seeing me. He's so glad to see me, His eyes absolutely no condemnation, no judgment whatsoever, full of love and fire, absolutely wonderful. His countenance, full of life, and His hands reaching out, He's so glad to see me. This is my friend that I love, and He loves me - so I reach out and I just imagine, thank You Lord, You're my friend, You're with me. I have everything I need. I receive your love into my life right now. There it is, it's the presence of God just starting to touch me right now, see? Now she's getting the overflow. I'm not actually ministering, but as soon as I started to connect with Him through meditation, now she's starting to feel the overflow of it right now, see?

So meditation, when coupled with faith, links you into the spirit world, and the reality of God. It's one of the great things in the Bible, it's a great truth. If you're too busy, you can't do this. If you hurry, you can't do this, and if you've got lots of clutter in your head, it's not easy to do it either. You've got to de-clutter, slow down and reflect, so television and internet get you busy. You've got to find a way to find space to just slow down, and just for a few moments allow yourself to dwell in the presence of God, and become conscious of Him. Like to come - now, so she will have felt the presence of God. That's good, praise the Lord, okay. It'd be good for you too, wouldn't it aye? [Laughs] So just close your eyes, and so I'm not trying to make too much happen. At the moment all I'm trying to do is just encounter the presence of God, so I just again thank You Lord, You're my shepherd.

I went through every line of that verse. Sometimes I prayed the whole thing, then I'd go back and pray one verse, two verse, three verse, meditate on one verse, then another verse, try to meditate on any of the verses, until I could feel the reality of it see? So thank You Lord, You're my shepherd and friend. I love that. Often I'd never get past that, just that first oh, He's my friend, and He's there with me! I begin to see Him, and feel His presence, and then thank You Lord, my cup runs over. Oh the joy, of just full of the presence of God. Thank You Lord for Your wonderful presence just flooding me right now. I just begin to enjoy it, so I learnt to just stand by the bed, and just fall on the bed and yield and see, just - no bed here now, so I'll just stand on my feet. I just learnt to receive from God, and so what would happen is, you start to feel His presence. Thank You Lord, just touch her now Lord. [Releases one long breath] Let your presence flow all over her life right now. There we are, and you're starting to sense something there, the presence of God is on you just like that.

So learn to yield rather than wrestle, so I practiced just yielding to God, yielding to His presence. I'd just put the bed behind me and just stand there and just yield, and I'd be childlike, and just let myself fall [like whoa!] at the presence of God. Then I'd lie there and enjoy Him, and get up again and do it again, and again, and again, until it was easy to just open up and oh, thank You Lord. There's His presence and POWER of God just come over her life right now. Don't you feel the touch of God? You start to experience like a peace comes around you see? What else did you feel? Calm, isn't that great. It's good isn't it aye? Praise the Lord. What did you sense and experience? Yeah. Yeah, huge love, so as I was meditating, meditation opens up the spirit world, or your connectedness to God, and there's an overflow of life through you, and around you. It's great to understand that, isn't it aye? Otherwise you're going to be a performer, trying to perform, rather than a relater, have a relationship, and abiding, and receiving, and being able to give things to people. Isn't that good?

Okay then, well I'll just show you how I did something here. We'll just take a look on this gift of faith, and let me share on that, and then I'll get back. I'm going to minister to some, and just pray for a few people shortly, because I want to just put together these areas of moving in the spirit, words of knowledge, prophecy, discerning, and I'll just put it altogether for you, and start to pray for a few people, and explain which gifts are operating as they're operating, okay? So we'll do that shortly. So we'll just have a quick look here, and I won't take too long on this one. I want to look at faith, gift of faith, the gift of faith. Okay, there it is, 18, alright then. So a gift of faith - now a gift of faith is not the same as walking by faith. It's not the same as your daily faith life. It is not the same as getting saved, although when you are saved, you receive a gift at that point to believe, so in a sense, getting saved is a gift of faith at that point. You got faith, and you believed immediately that you're saved, okay.

So what the gift of faith is; it's not a fruit of the spirit, and it's not just daily walking trusting God. A gift of faith is an ability to believe at a moment in time, you know something is going to happen, you absolutely know it. You say: how do you know it? I don't know how you know it, you just know inside what God is going to do, and that it will happen. You have an assurance it's going to take place, absolute assurance it'll take place, and so when you have that deep assurance, then you absolutely know something's going to happen. I want to tell you one, this is a classic one for me, and then we'll give you a few examples about it, but the best thing is if I just share a personal story, and you'll see how it can operate. I go to Taiwan and minister up there reasonably regularly, and they set up various meetings, and the Chinese have got their own way of doing stuff you see, so anyway I went up there into this particular meeting, and as I came out, I stepped straight into the meeting out of the lift, into this room where there's meeting, and then right in front of me there's a wheelchair, and a guy sitting in the wheelchair like this. I think oh no, a wheelchair! I know we'll have a great meeting - this is all what went through my mind - have a great meeting, and then at the end nothing's going to happen over this wheelchair.

I was just a bit put out, and so anyway I went over to my seat, and as soon as I got to my seat and began to worship the Lord, He said you've got a bad attitude. [Laughter] I rebuke the devil! [Laughter] No, that was you! He said you've got a bad attitude, and I just went quiet and listened, so while everyone's worshipping, I'm listening. He said your attitude is wrong to this man. It's filled with disappointments, where you've prayed and nothing happened. He said: I want you to meditate on this man being healed, really. So while everyone else is worshipping, I was just in my mind seeing the wheelchair, and seeing the man stand up, seeing the wheelchair, seeing the man stand up, seeing the wheelchair, seeing the man stand up. I was looking, just imagine, just praying, just an attitude of worship, not struggling or striving, meditating, watching, and suddenly oh! It's going to happen, I know it!

So before I was imaging it, and then suddenly there was a point where faith came. I thought oh, he's going to get healed. I was so excited - a bit nervous too, because I didn't know what to do you see, whether to go over and pray for him straight away, or whether - I just think I better warm up first you see, so [laughter] pray for the easy ones. [Laughs] So anyway, we sort of shared, and then I began to move in the spirit, began to pray for various people, and some different people got healed. The Pastor came up to me, he said: well what are you going to do now? I said: see that guy in the wheelchair; I'm going to grab his hands, and pull him out of the wheelchair! He said [inhales sharply] you're freaking me out, you can't do that. I said: you watch! [Laughter] So anyway we prayed for a few more people, and then we got there, and by the time we got there to this guy in the wheelchair, there was a second wheelchair there. I don't know where that one came from. [Laughter]

There was a lady in a wheelchair, so she's sitting in the wheelchair. I thought no, he's going last. I felt in my heart this is where I'm going to go, finish the meeting on that, so anyway I prayed for the lady in the wheelchair. She'd been in the wheelchair for three years, she'd had tremendous pain, a whole number of things happening in her life, and she hadn't walked for three years. Normally the muscles all shrivel and everything goes. Even if you get them on their feet, they don't easily walk, so I prayed for her, helped her out of the wheelchair, and she stood up and blow me down, she began to walk a few steps. I thought whoa, look at that! This is great. I'm feeling very encouraged now, ready to get this guy. So I went over to the guy, and I asked him the question: how long have you been here? Ten years, and he'd been having operations on his back, and he's just sick of the operations, he's had enough, and he's just - there's no more operations, there's no more hope.

So I said to him: wow, so I just knelt down and just prayed, said thank You Lord for healing this man. There was no big prayer, no great issue, no nothing. I said: now can I help you to your feet? I took his hand, helped him. He stood up just next to the wheelchair, and then I'm thinking I'll just help him walk, you know, don't want him to fall over [laughs] so I'll help him walk. He made me let go of his hand, and then he began to just walk like this [laughter] right across the room. I'm terrified he's going to fall over and hurt himself [laughter] and he walked across the room and back again, and he's totally healed! Now what amazed me was this - the caregivers immediately wanted him back into the wheelchair. Now notice this. He hadn't walked for 10 years, but they want him back in the wheelchair, because that's where their paradigm is, still locked in, that he's crippled. They could not quickly catch up he's now walking, and I didn't feel a thing. I absolutely didn't feel a thing when that happened, not one little feel, not an ounce of God, not an ounce of emotion, nothing. It's just, it just happened, so that was a gift of faith.

You just know. Now does that mean everyone I pray for? No, I knew that guy, that day, that time, would come out, and I could act boldly in that situation. Later, he came up in the altar call, gave his heart to the Lord. They were still trying to get him into the wheelchair, so now I've learnt that if they get out of the wheelchair, fold up the wheelchair as quickly as you can, get them walking - same with walking sticks. So again, that's how faith just came. It says faith comes by hearing the word of God, so as I meditated, I heard from God in that sense. Faith rose. Now I'm not saying that I can turn that on or off for any situation. All I'm saying is, that it is a gift, comes in a moment of time, and some people operate in it so much, and so frequently, it's like around their life, the gift of faith, and many miracles happen around their life, and around their ministry.

I know one particular person who's a friend of mine up in Malaysia, tremendous miracles he has happen everywhere he goes, just stunning gift of faith. There's a resident gift lives in his life, and he just operates in a whole faith dimension. It's very inspiring. There's a gift of faith comes just in a moment, and then you can grow in that whole dimension, until you actually seem to have a residing gift, or mantel of faith over your life. It is astounding when that happens, to see these things, so I've seen that happen a couple of times. I had one, a lady that was totally deaf, and born deaf. I prayed for her, nothing happened, and then I felt something in me rise up. I cannot describe it, it had to be faith. I just refused to give up. I prayed not once, I prayed four times. On the fourth time, her ears popped, and she could hear. Imagine if I just quit, and had given up after the first time, she'd still be deaf.

What about the other guy in the wheelchair? Imagine if I'd allowed myself to stay in that cranky, unbelieving attitude. He would still be in the wheelchair. People need someone to break through on their behalf. Why not you? Now you don't necessarily quickly get to that. You grow your faith level by level, so don't matter how many times you pray and nothing seems to happen. Just keep meditating in the word of God, expecting God to work in your life, and believing that you'll break through, and come into different dimensions. Amen. Praise the Lord. Why don't we get you to step out in faith for something in a moment aye? Would that be good? Step out in faith and pray for someone, that'd be really, really good. Then we'll just look at the gift of healings and working in miracles, then just some practical keys, so why don't we just get you to do something with one another, how about that?

So I tell you what, this'll be quite a good thing to do, and this is, we'll get you now into groups of about four or five, and this is what I want you to do. I want you to put one person in the middle, and the others all get some word of encouragement for them, so instead of it being one to one, you maybe have at least three people ministering to one person, no more than three, so no bigger groups than four, or it just takes too long to do it. So you get one person in the middle, and then you all pray, then one by one, you share a word of encouragement for them, to bless them, encourage them, and help them. How about that, can we do that? Okay, let's do that.

Okay, let's be seated, I want to get on with the next session, and then we want to just minister and pray for you. Let's be seated, and this time look at Section 19, Gifts of Healings. In 1 Corinthians 12, Verse 7, the Bible talks about: to another is given gifts of Healings, by the same spirit. Notice He used the word 'gifts' of Healings, and so a gift of healing is a gift given to you, at a time where you just have faith for someone to be healed. Now what I have noticed happens, is that when a person has a gift of healing, there is always a result take place, so we can pray by faith, or if we get a gift, God gives a gift at a moment of time - you can call it faith, call it a gift of healing - the person gets a breakthrough straight away at that time. So notice it says: gifts of healing, not gift, so what I have observed is, some people get very good in praying for backs. They'll just get freedom every time they pray for a back. They've got faith for backs, they've got like a gift of healing around their life. Some have got it for ears; some will have it for other areas, so people can develop and focus in a particular area of healing.

Some are very good in getting deaf ears opened, some are very good at getting backs and joints healed and freed, and you get them to pray, they get 90 to 100 per cent success rate. They've got a gift around their life of healing, that's faith for that area. I was reading just concerning Todd Bentley and some of his ministry, and he teaches on how you grow from level to level in this area, and he had a point where I think one of his family members, his mother was deaf. He began to contend in prayer for breakthroughs with deaf people, and he prayed for hundreds and hundreds of people, nothing happened. He just began to contend, and eventually got a breakthrough. Once he got one, it just kept growing, until now wherever he goes, he will pray for the deaf, and get something like 80, 90 per cent of people with deaf ears will open up, so that's a gift of faith, or a gift of healing in that area. So we're all on a journey, so don't compare with someone else, just settle in your heart how God wants to work with you, and start to believe to grow in that area. So let's just give a couple of examples of it.

In Mark, Chapter 16, and we read here at the Great Commission. We're commissioned to go into the world, which is full of sickness and demonic oppression, and it says we're to preach the Gospel about how people can come to Christ, come to God, come to know the Lord, and walk in His kingdom, but it says - notice this - it says in Verse 17, these signs shall follow them that believe. In My name, they'll cast out devils, so if you can believe for it, when you pray, demons will come out of people. You have to believe it'll happen, not doubt, or wonder whether it'll happen. It says in the last one, they shall lay hands on the sick, and they shall recover. They will lay hands on the sick, and they shall recover, and that means gradually, or progressively, come to a state of wholeness. So when we think of praying for healing, we tend to think of it all being instantaneous. That was kind of like a mentality I had, probably seen it in one of the movies or something, I had this idea you pray, there's this immediate miracle, everything's just exactly back to normal. I realized actually in real life, God does not seem to operate that way. He operates in different ways around the healing area.

So for a gift of healing, at a moment of time, you just know in your heart when I pray something's going to happen. That's a gift of healing. The rest of the time, we just pray by faith. In other words, we follow the scripture: you lay hands on the sick and they shall recover, so sometimes you get a miracle, the healing is immediate. The transformation takes place immediately, like if deaf ears open it is immediate, they hear or they don't hear, but it can come in a couple of stages, where they hear a little, then it comes complete, and they hear the whole. Same with the eyes; the eyes are either not seeing, or seeing, and if they're not seeing, you pray and they start to see a little, then pray again, and believe for it to be progressive. So I have noticed that sometimes, the majority of times I've prayed, I've had to persevere in prayer, and believe that this would work, and then they break through, and they get the miracle. Sometimes I've seen cataracts healed, just gone. People couldn't see, and then suddenly they see, but it took praying a couple of times to push through the barrier and resistance that was there, same with hearing of ears.

I began to grow faith for walking sticks, for people on walking sticks to be healed. Initially I just hated praying for people with walking sticks. I'd want to run the other way, because I never got any results. [Laughs] I just didn't like that, but I made a decision I'd persevere, and believe God I could get breakthroughs, and so I started. So now most of the time when I'm in Asia, if I've got any evangelism meetings, I will look for people with walking sticks when they come in. I'll look for them, and I'll ask for them to come up, and give it a go. I had one meeting, I had about 45 people get off their walking sticks and walk, but that - faith is grown for that area. I found sometimes I'm getting better results in some areas than I've done before, but you can grow in this area, so notice what it says: They'll lay hands on the sick, so God called 'laying hands' is to identify with a person, so we lay hands on the sick person and pray for them. They may get a miracle immediately. It may be progressive, and they recover over a day, two days, three days, four days, so you need to take into account you may not see anything immediately happen. It doesn't mean it hasn't happened.

I found when I first started to pray, it used to so put me off, because I'd pray and nothing would happen, I'd feel discouraged, and not even enquire later on whether anything happened. I've found since then, you can't believe the number of people I've prayed for them on Sunday and Monday they were well, that when they walked away they weren't well. It didn't seem like it anyway, but actually something had been imparted to them, and it began to manifest. The healing gift manifested, so instead of thinking of it cut and dry, yes it happened or not, learn to just persist in prayer, and sow in prayer, and believe in prayer. A gift of healing, you just know it, and when it comes the person's going to be healed straight away - but the rest of the time, we pray by faith. So here's a few simple things. The first one is, it's helpful to lay hands on the person, lay hands, identify, connect with the person, and let the Holy Spirit show you where to lay hands.

He may show you to lay hands on the head, may get you to put your hand on the part that's - if it's appropriate - on the part that's sick or not well, or He'll put your hand on top of a person's hand, whatever seems appropriate. The second thing you need to consider is, maybe you need to cast out a spirit of infirmity. If you have a look in the Gospel of Luke, Chapter 13 and Verse 10, Jesus is teaching in the synagogue on the Sabbath, and there's was a woman had a spirit of infirmity for 18 years, and was bowed down and could not lift herself up. She had a back condition that was caused by a spirit. It was a demonic spirit that caused the problem. Medicines could not fix it. It required deliverance, so if there's a spirit of infirmity, praying for the sick person won't set them free. You have to cast the evil spirit out. You've got to speak to the spirit, and command it to go, so you notice when the girl was standing there, I spoke to the spirit, commanded it to go, and as soon as it left her, she just fell over straight away, and then there's a change in her condition in her back.

So when you're praying in this area for people who are sick, think in two dimensions; think one, it could be a spirit that needs to be cast out; two, it could be just a weakness in the system, a virus in the system, a degeneration in the system, or it could be some kind of thing that needs healing to take place. If it's degenerative, it needs a creative miracle for God to restore. If it's just something damaged or broken or whatever, it needs God to heal, so keep thinking in terms of: one, I may need to cast a spirit out; two, I may need to pray and release God's healing power into their life. A third thing you need to learn to do, is to command, to speak to things, like they are living. In our western culture, we're not used to doing that, but if you look in Acts, Chapter 3, Peter and John went up to the temple - Verse 1 - about the ninth hour, and a certain man, lame from his mother's womb, was carried, whom they laid daily at the gate of the temple called Beautiful, to ask alms. He saw Peter and John going into the temple, and asked for alms. Peter fixed his eyes on him. He must have got a gift of faith for the healing, must have got a gift of healing then, because he knew something was going to happen, so notice what he did.

Silver and gold have I none, but what I have - so what did he have? The gift of healing - such as I have I give you. Now notice how he did it. In the name of Jesus Christ of Nazareth, rise up and walk. That's not namby-pamby stuff. You've got to learn to speak with authority. These things resist. They resist wellness; they resist health, so learn to speak firmly - not loudly. Shouting doesn't do it - with authority from your spirit, fully believing what you say would happen. Notice how he's prayed: In the name of Jesus Christ, rise up and walk. See? So he didn't even go talking about the curse, or the spirit, or whatever it was, just said rise and walk. Now notice what else he did. He took him by his right hand, and he helped him up. Now notice this, when the miracle happened, immediately his feet and ankle bones received strength. When did they receive strength? When he got on his feet, see?

So if he had stayed on the ground, he would not have walked. He had to be helped up onto his feet, and when he got him onto his feet, that's when the miracle happened, so it doesn't always happen immediately when you pray. Sometimes you've got to take an action of faith, that precipitates the miracle happening. If you study Jesus' miracles, many times miracles happen when the person did something, or when He did something, so for example, remember he told the guy - the blind guy to put a mud pack on his eyes, and said walk through the town and go to this pool, and wash and you'll come back seeing. So the guy walked from when Jesus spoke to him to the pool, and he was blind all the way, until he washed his eyes. When he washed his eyes, he could see, so Jesus required a faith action of him. The lepers, He said: go show yourself to the priest. Now they were still lepers when they walked away from Him, but as they walked, they were healed, so when they did what was physically impossible, when they did what they could do, God did the rest.

There's another guy standing there, and he's got a crippled hand, and Jesus is getting him to stand up in the synagogue - not very nice to make a handicapped man stand up in front of everyone, but he gets him to stand up. He says: now stretch out your hand. Now that's physically impossible, but when he began to stretch, suddenly the power of God came. Now it's helpful for you to understand, sometimes you've got to get people to do things, so I had one person for example, a lady had a shoulder, and her shoulder was a lot of pain, so I prayed for her. I said any improvement? She said just a little. I said: well then, why don't you move your hand. She said: oh, it's a pain, it's hurting, it's hurting, it's - oh, it's gone! [Laughter] So it was as she ignored the pain, and took the faith action, that's when the healing power began to flow, and she got free, and got the miracle. If she hadn't taken a faith action, nothing would happen, so many times when you pray, don't just think God will do it all. Often you need to get the person to give some feedback to you, what's happened, and then get them to take a faith action. So if I pray for someone and there's no immediate result, I will pray again, and try to get them to do something they haven't done before, and it's often in that that you get the breakthrough.

Now one caution, one word of caution: do not encourage a person, or tell them to stop taking medication. You're not a doctor, you're not a prescriber of medication, and therefore, you're not authorized to tell them not to take it. Not taking medication has legal consequences, and physical consequences potentially, so what is important is we understand, if a doctor has prescribed medicine, let the person go show themselves to the doctor, and let the doctor release them from the medicine, or let them take responsibility. Don't you go diagnosing someone doesn't need medicine anymore, okay then? So don't encourage them to no longer see a doctor, if they're going to a doctor, just pray for them. Don't be something you're not - you're not a doctor, so our role is to pray for people. We just pray for them, and see how they are, and check them out afterwards, and just encourage them then to continue to thank God for what's happened to them - so that is the gift of healing.

So the 'gift of healing' is different to 'praying by faith for healing'. We pray by faith for healing, we just believe, according to the word of God, that if we pray for the person, they can be healed. Are some people not healed? Yes, sometimes unforgiveness will block their healing, sometimes unbelief will block their healing, sometimes there can be control or occult powers will block their healing. You've got to ask the Lord to show you, what blocks the healing. When you get a gift of healing, you just know the person's going to be healed, and when you pray, it does happen, and it happens pretty well straight away. The rest of time, pray, check the person out, break the power of a spirit over their life, and encourage them to take an action that they haven't taken before - so there's ministry of the healing gift again.

Now gifts of healing are wonderful. Pray for gifts of healing - there are so many sick people. They go to chiropractors and doctors, and it costs them thousands of dollars, and here one prayer could set that person free. What a great thing, if you could begin to flow in gifts of healing - in your workplace, wherever you are. People can be stunned in the community, they just get a healing in the workplace; get a healing wherever you happen to see them. They get so shifted, it's quite astonishing the effect it has on their life. Wouldn't that be great? Now related to gifts of healing are the working of miracles. We won't spend a lot of time related to that area, but a miracle involves the breaking of a natural, or it means that the natural laws are overridden by the realm of the spirit. God brings a superior power into play, so there are heaps of miracles in the Bible where God has invaded the natural realm, and a miracle took place.

I'll give you some examples of Peter walking on the water. You can't walk on water. You all know you can't walk on water, so what kept him up? The power of God! Now I guess, how did he know? I guess he never knew he could walk on the water, until he stepped out of the boat, and got his foot in the water, and who knows how far down it went before it was solid? You don't know. There's been examples of people doing this in Indonesia during revival, crossing rivers that you couldn't cross, and the people came after them, went in the river and they were swept away it was that deep. So there are many examples - the feeding of the 5000. You notice that what Jesus did was He took the bread, He blessed it, and He spoke over the bread. He spoke words over the bread; He looked up to heaven to the source, spoke words over the bread, then broke it, and gave it to the disciples. Now at that point, it still hasn't multiplied. It was when they distributed it, it began to multiply, so they give out a piece, and there's another piece taken its place, and so on, and so forth.

We heard from Heidi Baker in Mozambique, and they had a huge number of people to feed, a large number of people to feed, and they looked at the food they had, and it wasn't enough, so they just began to pray over it. Well, they fed everyone, and had food left over. No one knows how they did it. So I've heard a whole number of stories like that, in modern times, of the food just being multiplied. How did it happen? They asked God what to do, just prayed over it and distributed it out, and God did the rest. It was a miracle, a working miracle, so some aspects of miracles are overriding natural laws. Another aspect of miracles is deliverance. Deliverance is the working of miracles, because in deliverance, God displaces a demonic power by the working of miracles, so deliverance is also a working of miracles. There are many examples of these in the Bible. How do we move in it? I think you've got to desire miracles, you've got to hunger for them, and pray for them, reach out to God for them, and I've noticed that most of the miracles take place where there are needs that are being met, by people serving people. I've noticed that's where most miracles take place.

Most common miracles are not necessarily in a church meeting, they're actually out where people are doing something, to help someone. It's in those environments that God works the greatest miracles. It's where the unsaved are. I've looked at the meetings I've taken overseas in Asia, because I've seen heaps of miracles, heaps of healing, heaps of deliverance, and I noticed that the best miracles, the best miracles, were with people who were unsaved. Time and time again, I'd have a word of knowledge on people that were unsaved - I didn't know whether they were saved or unsaved, they're just Chinese people to me. But they'd come up and we'd pray for them to get healed, and then later on they're in the altar call to get saved. The miracle power opened their hearts to get saved. They saw the reality of the power of God, so it's fantastic.

How many enjoyed that, liked that? Is it good fun? We should pray for a few people shouldn't we aye, should reach out and pray for a few people? Alright then, so what I'll do now, is just start to pray and minister to some. Then what I want to do is to lay hands and pray, and just release an empowerment in your lives, and I want you to go out, and just give it a go. Never give up, just practice. Ask God to give you words. Ask God to bring people into your heart life that are ready to receive something, and then give it a go. What have you got to lose? Learn on the way. Don't wait until you've got your head full of theory, just learn on the way. If someone's sick, offer to pray for them, and there's a few practical things in offering to pray for them. We've given you some of those, we'll get to that in just a moment.

So what I'll do then is, I'll just show you what I mean. I'll just put some of the gifts together, and just begin to flow with the Holy Spirit, and I'll identify the different gifts as we're flowing, then you'll see how they just operate. Now most of us, are not going to be in a meeting, doing something in a meeting, so for most people, it's as you interact with people, and they identify a need; you step up and say: I'd just love to pray for you, or you may just sense something about a person. Go over and relationally interact with them, and then share with them what you feel God showing you, and do it in a non-religious way, so it's very, very simple, and someone can easily receive it. So for most people, it's quite a simple sort of process - and expect that as you're doing, God will give you things. Now clearly, no one wants to step into that unless you've had time with the Lord, and are building a personal relationship with Him, but if you are, then let's go for it.

So what you could do simply in your personal preparation, is go through the Gospels reading the stories of Jesus, and healing, and meditate on those stories of people healing, meditate, see it, thank You Lord, when I lay hands on the sick, they shall recover. I thank You Lord, when I lay hands on blind eyes, they open. Begin to picture it, and see it, and hold it, that this is what's true in your life, even before it happens. Don't wait to see it, and then I'll believe it. Believe for it to be seen in your life in ministry, see? So thank You Lord, that when I pray, that deaf ears will open. I thank You Lord, that as I minister to people, Your presence touches them powerfully. Today Lord I surrender my hands, I yield all the works of my hands today Lord. My hands are blessed. All I put my hands to Lord, are blessed. Lord, when I lay hands on people, the power of God will touch them.

Start to decree and declare over your life, the things you're believing God to do. We talked about removing some of the blocks in your heart, but arise expectantly day by day. Today Lord, bring someone into my life who is in need of prayer or help, and show him to me in a way I can see it. Then enjoy looking out for people. Give it a go, you know, and if nothing works, or nothing happens, well you've got nothing to lose, just - well, you were giving it a go, and it's in the giving it a go, you grow. I've never seen anyone, get anywhere, by just filling up on books, information and meetings. It's actually, at the end, you've just got to get down and pray for someone, and see what will happen. You might be surprised what happens, and there's an element where, you don't know until you're engaging with them, what God will do, so for example if I was just to pick this girl out here - would you like to come up? Yes, that's right, why not, come up here, that's it.

Now you see what you've got to do is - I've got no idea. I'm just going to just take an opportunity to just, reach out, and just see what God will do - so can you tell me your name? [Wooty] Wooty, that's a great name, great. I'm so glad you came. Have you been enjoying yourself? That's awesome, that's great. Okay now, the moment I started to interact with her like that, then immediately I got a word from the Lord. I'm expecting it you see? I don't want it to be something that's very hard, and very difficult. I want it to be something that's very, very easy, so I just interact with her like that, and just try to make it as relaxed as possible, and I really am glad that you've come, and you've been enjoying it, but this is what I felt. I just felt the Lord show me, that you struggle with fear, that you've got real desire in your life to actually do a whole number of things, but often fear will lock you back, as though I'm afraid to step out, or afraid - and so now I'm going to reach out to see, I wonder where that fear's come from, see?

So what I'll do is - what I feel the fear has come, it's from people around - it's from around family, it's like, it's tried to push you down into a box, that that's where you belong, and would you be younger in the family? Yeah [laughs], you're pushed down, like the young one in the family, and so it's like there's an order, and you're at the bottom, or way down here. That is right? See, words of knowledge. Now can you see it's sort of natural? It just flows naturally, I'm just talking with her, see, and so what I'm seeing is this, is that God's wanting you to - you're not in a box any longer, and you're not subject to that any longer. You can actually rise up. You have got a wonderful gift in your life, and so I wonder what the gift is. See? Well, I see - what I feel is, I feel you're a very creative person, you've got a very soft spirit, you love to worship God, and you're very creative on the inside. In fact actually, you have been restricted so long, but you long to break out, you've got lots inside you to come out, and the thing that's been holding you back, is just the words that were spoken, that have put you down, and the fear of doing anything to break out of where you feel you're assigned to be - and God will help you with that today.

He wants you to know, you're not what they say you are, you're who He says you are. He says you're a mighty woman of faith. He says you've got a ministry to touch many,

many people, you've got a heart for young people, you've got a heart to reach out and help them, and God says that you have got greatness inside you. You are not the youngest in His eyes, you're not the least in His eyes. He sees you as great, because you've got a real desire to love people, a capacity to work with people, and you're in training for this, aye? [Laughs] Can you see it's quite natural? I can see you're already being touched, because you know I could not have known any of these things. I don't think I've met you before today. [No.] So how could I read her mail like that? So what you're experiencing then, it's something like, first of all you're a bit frightened - is that right? That's because the spirit knows I'm onto it, because I'm about to pray for that spirit in a moment. [Laughter] So that fear you were feeling, actually was the spirit being afraid. That's why you suddenly felt the fear, see? And like it gripped you suddenly. That's because the demon knew I'm onto it, he knew what's going to happen, and so you suddenly feel his fear. It's not your fear, it's his fear. He's the one afraid. You've got nothing to be afraid of.

God loves you. I love you. The people here love you. There's nothing to be afraid of, see? But the fear you're feeling, is actually not your fear, it's the demonic fear, but it's gripped your life for years. It's been like a part of your life, see, and you don't have to live that way anymore, okay? You don't have to. Today's change day for you. You're not going to go back into that box, go back into that way, alright then, so we want to pray for you now. Alright then? Okay.

So your heart's been touched, that's right. That's great. We need tissues. [Laughter] Okay then, can I take your hand? Just come forward a little bit now. Alright, I want you to close your eyes. Just close your eyes. Now this is - I'm not going to do this in front of everyone, but there's some specific people who've deeply hurt you. I want you just in your heart, to picture them, and then release forgiveness. Lord, I just forgive them. I forgive them for what they said, I forgive them for what they did, I forgive them for how they've treated me. I forgive them for boxing me in, like they did. Just let it go.

God sees your heart. He knows why that's there, and not forgiving will block the deliverance you see? [Mm.] So now I thank You Lord, You love her. Thank You Lord that Your presence is coming on her life right now, in the name of the Lord Jesus Christ, I break abusive words spoken over your life. I take authority over word curses spoken over you. I break them in Jesus' name. I come against words of death, I come against words of hatred, I come against words of despising, I break their power over your life today, in Jesus' name. You spirit of fear, you tormenting spirit, loose her in Jesus' name. Right now, let her go, let her go, let her go, NOW in Jesus' name. Thank You Lord. Thank You Lord. Thank You Lord, thank You.

Father, I just pray peace into her now. Father, I thank You for the anointing of the Holy Spirit flowing right now. I break the generational curses of hatred, and abusive women, I break them in Jesus' name. I release you from the grip of those things. I break the negative words spoken over you. Spirit of death, I command you: loose her, in Jesus' name. I break all agreements wanting to die, loose her in Jesus' name. Now Lord, let Your peace just come around her now. I just call forth creativity, life, freedom, in Jesus' Mighty name. Father, bring her complete peace.

Now you notice then, the gifts of words of knowledge, then prophetic flow mingled in, and then discerning of spirits, what actual spirits were there, that need to be broken off her life, and then ministry. See how it all just flows together, just like that? I got her to interact with us, so you can see one, how natural the flow is. It's not a forced or difficult or hard thing, it's just remaining relaxed, and just interacting, and listening to the flow from your heart. You can see as she talked and interacted back, you could see how deeply she's been touched by, suddenly, God knows me, He knows my difficult journey and my struggles, and He cares about me, He wants to help me. This is a most wonderful experience, absolutely blessed experience. Praise the Lord. How are you doing now? How are you feeling now? [I feel really good.] You feel really good, isn't that fantastic?

Now when we prayed to command that fear to go what happened, what did you sense? [unclear] Something came out of you? [Yeah.] You felt something leave you, and go out of you. You won't feel the same again. You'll feel quite different. [Not heavy.] No, not heavy, no. It's gone, it's gone, [Thank you.] [Applause.]

So now, so you see we taught you just foundations of this. All you've got to do is grow in it, and who knows what you could do. There's no limits! There are no limits really, with what you could do, because God has got an area of people for you, to be with, and interact with, that I'll never meet, so He wants to work through you to touch them, and not in a church meeting, but outside, wherever you are. Isn't that exciting possibility that God would use you in such ways? Isn't that great? So praise the Lord. There's someone here who has trouble at night times, and its a woman and you wake up with severe nightmares, you have these tormenting nightmares, you wake up and they're quite a trouble for you. They occur quite regularly, they disturb you at night, and you wake up and you're quite frightened. Who's the woman that has that problem; if you could just come right now we'll pray for you? Woman, young woman, you've had this problem for quite some time and God wants to set you free. Who's the woman that has these nightmares, you wake up and these tormenting thoughts and dreams - I'd love to pray for you right now. Who's that person? If you think that's you, just come quickly, come quickly. God bless you, there you are there [Thank you.] Come on up, that's okay. It doesn't matter if you're the only one comes up, I'm still happy to pray for you, praise the lord. [Laughs]

Okay. You're special today, God bless. God loves you. You're special to me, we've been able to practice... [laughter] And you're special to God, He loves you, and today's your day. You know, He's been wanting so much just to have some change, why would it not be you? Why not you? [unclear] Exactly, why not you and you begin thinking that way, instead of why me, rather why not me, aye? Praise the

Lord, okay, and you've had this for quite some time. Now, okay, so since you were a child? [A child.] Since you were a child, okay then, and about age six, somewhere around about that? [Oh, probably four.] Four? Quite young, okay, and you'd wake up at night quite afraid? [Yeah.] Okay... [Definitely.] ...you'd feel the presence of something around you? [Absolutely.] Okay, when's the last time that happened? [Probably last night.] Last night, okay. [It's constant.] It's constant torment? [Yeah.] Okay, alright then, so what I'm going to do is, I'm just going to help you - tonight isn't all the ministry you need, but we can just help you with this part of it, okay? Alright then, so now there's clearly occult background in your family? [Yes.] Whereabouts is it located, parents or grandparents? [Great grandfather.] Great grandfather, what was he? [I think he was a warlock.] Oh, he was a warlock, oh that's... [Or something like...] ...a big deal. [Yeah.] That's a big deal, yeah. [He was seriously into...] He was seriously into it... [...satanic...] ...satanic stuff, okay then.

Because he was seriously into those kinds of things, he would have committed his family, for generations, to occult powers, and the spirit world would recognize that, and it would lay claim to every one of the descendants, and particularly the girls. So unusual things would happen to all the girls in the family, they're unexplainable it seems, and you'd end up thinking why me, why has it always been, why is this stuff happening? [Mm-hm.] That be right? Okay and that's because of a curse running down through the family. Now Jesus died for our curses, and so what we need to do, is reach out to Him. We become accursed, so that the blessing of Abraham would come on us, so here are two things that we need to get you to do. We need to get you to follow me in a prayer, just to confess Christ and what He's done, okay and secondly, to release forgiveness to your ancestors that have opened the door for this problem. You need to forgive. Hello, we've got a problem. [Laughter]

[I've tried before...] Okay, you've tried before? [Yeah.] It's hard, it's hard, okay. Why not believe today, that you can let it go? I'll just help you with that in a moment, then we need to renounce, or speak off your life, speak words, to break that curse, in other words get hold of your life again. We're going to put the cross of Christ between you and your background, you've got a new start in life, okay? [Okay.] So forgiving, is not a favour you do someone else. Forgiving is for you, to move forward. It's releasing the debt that they owe, so when you look back - you did this, you hurt me, you've messed my life up. You know you've got to let it go, and say hey, that's not my business, that's God's business. I'm just releasing it, so I can walk on. [Yeah.] So unforgiveness will lock you to your past. It just keeps you frozen in time, and you can't move on, so that's why it's so important. [Yeah.] Not only that, God forgives us so much. Has God forgiven you much? [Big time.] Big time! [Laughter] Well that's called grace. We don't deserve it, but He gives it, and so to stay in grace, we release forgiveness to others, not because they deserve it, by the way... [Yeah.] ...but just because that's what we do. If we want to stay in grace, we let grace go to others.

So letting go, is letting go... [Yeah.] ...okay? We're alright, now I needed to do this, because it's no use me ministering, without your understanding a little bit about the part she has to play. See I can't just fix all her problems. What I need to do, is lead her to the One who does, and there may sometimes be a part she has to play. Notice I talked about letting forgiveness go in the heart. It was quite important to do that, so from a heart level, she let go, then she's free to get out of that stuff, and the spirit left straight away, so something will happen this time. So I may get the names of certain spirits and things to break, it'll be discerning of spirits, and operating in revelation knowledge to do that, okay? So we're on the way now.

How are you feeling? You look like you're getting agitated? [Yeah.] Okay, tell me what you're feeling. [Pretty exposed.] You're pretty exposed? [Yeah.] Close your eyes and turn everyone off, and focus, just let your heart reach out with love to give. This is a very vulnerable position to be in, especially in front of everyone like that. I just appreciate your honesty, but anyway it's over in a few minutes aye, and that's the great thing. I just thank you for just being willing to just respond, and being so open. It really is of God do that, and we can all learn, and we all witness, so you may be watching - what I'd like you to do is to be praying, praying quietly in tongues, and lets all join together. She's part of our family, the family of God, and when one suffers, all suffer, so let your heart flow with compassion. We don't know all she's faced, and gone through, but what we're looking for, is God to bring release, is that right? Okay, so just close your eyes, just make everyone vanish for a moment, there's just you and me and the Lord here.

Thank You Lord. I want you to just follow me in this prayer. Father, I come to You in Jesus' name. I confess Jesus Christ is my savior and Lord. I am redeemed by the blood of Jesus from every curse. I belong to You Jesus. I renounce now every generational curse, every generational agreement with evil spirits, for all my family members, I renounce it. I put the cross of Christ between me and that curse, and I break it. I release forgiveness for family members who opened the door to spirits by their actions. I forgive them. I let them go, and I turn to You Lord Jesus, and I ask You to set me free. Thank You Lord. It's going to be real easy now. In the name of the Lord Jesus Christ, I break all agreements formed by your great grandfather with evil spirits. I break the curses that came through his life, and his actions. I break the agreements he made with evil spirits. I break the power of agreements made through blood on altars. I break all blood covenants that he formed with evil spirits. I break written agreements he made in blood, that enabled family members, generation after generation, to be afflicted by evil spirits. I cancel the right of all evil spirits from your grandfather, to enter, or to remain in your life, in the name of the Lord Jesus Christ.

Now I just speak now, in the name of the Lord Jesus I command this tormenting spirit, that's tormented you since a young age, of four, with nightmares and dreams, I speak to you now and all related spirits, spirits of torment, I command you now GO in Jesus' name right now, release her now in

Jesus' name. Thank You Lord, thank You Lord. Just rest there, that's right. Father, in the name of the Lord Jesus, we just pray for your healing anointing and flow of your blessing upon her now, in Jesus' name. I just take authority and break every ungodly belief that you had, there's something wrong with me. I break your agreement with that lie right now in Jesus' name. I break every desire, every death wish you've spoken over your life, just wanting to die, I break it in Jesus' name. Now Lord, I just ask for Your loving presence to come around her life. Thank You Lord, You love her. Fill her, in Jesus' name. There you go, how about that? [Applause.]

You feel awesome aye? [Yeah.] Isn't that great? You'll enjoy some happy nights now aye? [Yeah] A peaceful night, instead of being tormented, isn't that fantastic? Thank you for coming back - we had someone else who was tormented, but he didn't come back. [Laughter] So I want to thank you for your courage in coming tonight. Let's just give her a great clap. [Applause.]

Someone else here, you've twisted your right shoulder, and you're in pain in your right shoulder. Who's that person? This one, yeah, here we go, come on, come now. Okay, so how long ago did you do this? [...in January.] Right, so all since January you've had problems with that shoulder? [Yeah, I've been trying to cast it out myself] [Laughter] Okay, well that's - today God knows about that, so what is it, it looks like it's stiff, you can't move it or raise it? [Very sharp pain.] Very sharp pain in your shoulder. It just came on you suddenly? [Yeah, suddenly.] No reason at all? [Yeah I feel like it's just not going away, so I was praying that you would call me today.] [Laughter] Well there you go. See what happens? When there's hunger and desire that's when these kinds of things happen, okay, right. [The pain is terrible.] The pain is so terrible, so since January she's been in tremendous pain in her shoulder, she's been asking the Lord to help and came in pain today, believing God to do something.

When did you come back from Malaysia? [In January.] Isn't that interesting? [Yeah.] Okay, so what I'm... [I have this in

February]. So I'm just looking to how to pray, so here's the options. One is we just pray for healing, one is we pray into the realm of the spirit, that there may be a spirit causing the affliction, and I've noticed that she has been trying to cast it out herself, so it's almost like, in her heart, she's aware there's a spirit there. [Yes.] See? Okay, now so then the question is, if she's been doing that, and hasn't had any result, I wonder why that is so. I kind of ask questions. I don't just quickly, just jump in. You just start to ask questions, and how long were you over in Malaysia for? [Four months.] And you were sharing about Jesus for lost people? [Yes.] Were they all happy about you sharing Jesus? [Yes, really.] Yeah? That's good. okay. [A lot of restoration.] A lot of restoration? That's good, okay. Was there anyone that was unhappy with you doing that? [Not really, although when I went back, there was a spiritual warfare, but then that - I mean my sister, she really know Christ, came to Christ...] Oh good. [Yeah.] Listen, just give me your hand then. Thank You Lord. Father, I just thank You that you're a God that reveals, and that there's nothing too difficult for You. In the name of the Lord Jesus Christ, I take authority over witchcraft. I come against every word curse spoken against you. I come against every spirit of witchcraft assigned against you. In the name of the Lord Jesus Christ, I break that spirit of witchcraft off your life. Infirmity, I command you to let her go now, loose her now in Jesus' name, loose her now, loose that shoulder in Jesus' name. We just break your power, and command healing to flow in the joint, and the nerves, we command this shoulder to be released now, in Jesus' name. Thank You Lord. Whoa! [unclear] Okay, so it's leaving your shoulder? [Yeah.] Do you feel better now? Okay then, just begin to move around, just see how it feels. [It feels better.] It feels better? I can see you doing things you couldn't do before. Isn't that wonderful? [So stiff!] See it was very stiff, it was visibly stiff, and the pain - how's the pain? [Yeah, it's better.] It's better now? [Yeah.] Isn't that wonderful? Lets pray for her one more time. Thank You Lord. Just look up to the Lord. Holy Ghost, just come upon her, fill her Holy Spirit right now, in Jesus' name, wow! User her in healing.

Now - so what, how do we pray? So I listened. Don't jump into conclusions; just stay long enough to listen. Listening is the big deal, then act boldly on what you see. So I listened, and I felt that feeling, and that's why I was asking the questions, I just felt someone actually was very upset with her, and had cursed her, so that's why I broke that witchcraft curse, and spoke against the spirit of infirmity, then immediately she just freed up, just like that. Isn't that wonderful aye? Oh, how glorious is our God.

Well, we're just running out of time now. How many other people here are sick today, anyone here sick? Why don't you just stand where you are, if you're sick in your body, got a sickness that needs healing? Why don't you just stand right where you are, because the table's going to gather around you, and pray for you. That'll be great, won't it? You'll have a chance to do something, to pray for a sick person. Okay, we've got a very sick table down there have we, three people? [Laughter] Okay, move around, and go to one of the other tables, and let some people there pray. Gather around the ones who have got a sickness. When they come to you, tell what the problem is, what you're believing God for, and the team will pray for you, and lets just see what God does. Afterwards try doing something you...

Alright then, okay, let's just be seated. We'll just finish up, tidy up now. Wonderful. Well, I wonder if we had some healings here? I'd like to just identify if anyone got healed through prayer? One, two, three, four - great, what happened to you? You can bend right down? Awesome, wonderful! [Applause.] Okay, someone else have a healing they'd like to just testify to? Yes, what happened? Right shoulder, it loosened up? Boy, she got up quick, didn't she, ahead of you aye? [Laughter] You could have said it was right shoulder as well. What happened to you? Your shoulder got healed, and freed up. Show us what you can do. [unclear] Yeah. [unclear] Yeah. [unclear] Yeah, great. Alright, okay, wow. [unclear] Wow, so praise the Lord, God's touched you today. Wonderful. Come on, let's give Him a clap. [Applause.] Amen. Alright then, praise the Lord.

Why don't we just pray? I'd love to just pray for people, just to get an impartation, just so you can go away fired up, so why don't you come up, just make rows here, we'll quickly pray for you. Front row stand here; second row, eyes open, catching. [Laughter] Okay, and where's - Pastor Lyn, would you like to come up and help us with praying for people? Joy, like to come up, and help with praying? If you can get away from there, you can come up and help pray. That'll leave Horowai with the cameras. Okay, just lift your hands up. You know what it is you've come for, you're wanting God to touch you. Just close your eyes, lift your hands up. Now, we won't pray for you if there's no one behind you to catch you, I don't want you to fall over. There's no one there, that's right. Okay, are we ready? Okay, let's begin to pray in tongues, just pray in the spirit now.

Thank You Lord for Your goodness, thank You for Your presence, thank You for Your power. Thank You Lord. Holy Ghost come, thank You Lord, thank You Lord. [Prays in tongues] Father, we just pray release, increase, of the flowing of the gifts of the spirit. We pray an impartation of faith, that from this day forward, each one would be empowered in a new way, to bring Your presence to others. Holy Spirit, come mightily, come powerfully in Jesus' name. Power of God, just touch her right now, in Jesus' name. Thank You Lord. We'll just speak to these ears, we'll just command them right now, OPEN in Jesus' name, release her right now. Thank You Lord.

Printed in Great Britain
by Amazon